Palgrave Macmillan Studies in Banking and Financial Institutions

Series Editor: **Professor Philip Molyneux**

The Palgrave Macmillan Studies in Banking and Financial Institutions are international in orientation and include studies of banking within particular countries or regions, and studies of particular themes such as Corporate Banking, Risk Management, Mergers and Acquisitions, etc. The books' focus is on research and practice, and they include up-to-date and innovative studies on contemporary topics in banking that will have global impact and influence.

Titles include:

Yener Altunbaş, Blaise Gadanecz and Alper Kara
SYNDICATED LOANS
A Hybrid of Relationship Lending and Publicly Traded Debt

Yener Altunbaş, Alper Kara and Öslem Olgu
TURKISH BANKING
Banking under Political Instability and Chronic High Inflation

Elena Beccalli
IT AND EUROPEAN BANK PERFORMANCE

Paola Bongini, Stefano Chiarlone and Giovanni Ferri *(editors)*
EMERGING BANKING SYSTEMS

Vittorio Boscia, Alessandro Carretta and Paola Schwizer
COOPERATIVE BANKING: INNOVATIONS AND DEVELOPMENTS
COOPERATIVE BANKING IN EUROPE: CASE STUDIES

Roberto Bottiglia, Elisabetta Gualandri and Gian Nereo Mazzocco *(editors)*
CONSOLIDATION IN THE EUROPEAN FINANCIAL INDUSTRY

Alessandro Carretta, Franco Fiordelisi and Gianluca Mattarocci *(editors)*
NEW DRIVERS OF PERFORMANCE IN A CHANGING FINANCIAL WORLD

Dimitris N. Chorafas
CAPITALISM WITHOUT CAPITAL

Dimitris N. Chorafas
FINANCIAL BOOM AND GLOOM
The Credit and Banking Crisis of 2007–2009 and Beyond

Violaine Cousin
BANKING IN CHINA

Vincenzo D'Apice and Giovanni Ferri
FINANCIAL INSTABILITY
Toolkit for Interpreting Boom and Bust Cycles

Peter Falush and Robert L. Carter OBE
THE BRITISH INSURANCE INDUSTRY SINCE 1900
The Era of Transformation

Franco Fiordelisi
MERGERS AND ACQUISITIONS IN EUROPEAN BANKING

Franco Fiordelisi, Philip Molyneux and Daniele Previati *(editors)*
NEW ISSUES IN FINANCIAL AND CREDIT MARKETS

Franco Fiordelisi, Philip Molyneux and Daniele Previati *(editors)*
NEW ISSUES IN FINANCIAL INSTITUTIONS MANAGEMENT

Franco Fiordelisi and Philip Molyneux
SHAREHOLDER VALUE IN BANKING

Hans Genberg and Cho-Hoi Hui
THE BANKING CENTRE IN HONG KONG
Competition, Efficiency, Performance and Risk

Carlo Gola and Alessandro Roselli
THE UK BANKING SYSTEM AND ITS REGULATORY AND SUPERVISORY FRAMEWORK

Elisabetta Gualandri and Valeria Venturelli *(editors)*
BRIDGING THE EQUITY GAP FOR INNOVATIVE SMEs

Kim Hawtrey
AFFORDABLE HOUSING FINANCE

Otto Hieronymi *(editor)*
GLOBALIZATION AND THE REFORM OF THE INTERNATIONAL BANKING AND MONETARY SYSTEM

Munawar Iqbal and Philip Molyneux
THIRTY YEARS OF ISLAMIC BANKING
History, Performance and Prospects

Sven Janssen
BRITISH AND GERMAN BANKING STRATEGIES

Kimio Kase and Tanguy Jacopin
CEOs AS LEADERS AND STRATEGY DESIGNERS
Explaining the Success of Spanish Banks

Alexandros-Andreas Kyrtsis *(editor)*
FINANCIAL MARKETS AND ORGANIZATIONAL TECHNOLOGIES
System Architectures, Practices and Risks in the Era of Deregulation

M. Mansoor Khan and M. Ishaq Bhatti
DEVELOPMENTS IN ISLAMIC BANKING
The Case of Pakistan

Mario La Torre and Gianfranco A. Vento
MICROFINANCE

Philip Molyneux and Eleuterio Vallelado *(editors)*
FRONTIERS OF BANKS IN A GLOBAL WORLD

Simon Mouatt and Carl Adams *(editors)*
CORPORATE AND SOCIAL TRANSFORMATION OF MONEY AND BANKING
Breaking the Serfdom

Anastasia Nesvetailova
FRAGILE FINANCE
Debt, Speculation and Crisis in the Age of Global Credit

Anders Ögren *(editor)*
THE SWEDISH FINANCIAL REVOLUTION

Dominique Rambure and Alec Nacamuli
PAYMENT SYSTEMS
From the Salt Mines to the Board Room

Catherine Schenk *(editor)*
HONG KONG SAR's MONETARY AND EXCHANGE RATE CHALLENGES
Historical Perspectives

Noël K. Tshiani
BUILDING CREDIBLE CENTRAL BANKS
Policy Lessons for Emerging Economies

The full list of titles available is on the website:
www.palgrave.com/finance/sbfi.asp

Palgrave Macmillan Studies in Banking and Financial Institutions
Series Standing Order ISBN 978-1-4039-4872-4

You can receive future titles in this series as they are published by placing a standing order. Please contact your bookseller or, in case of difficulty, write to us at the address below with your name and address, the title of the series and the ISBN quoted above.

Customer Services Department, Macmillan Distribution Ltd, Houndmills, Basingstoke, Hampshire RG21 6XS, England

---

Corporate and Social Transformation of Money and Banking

Breaking the Serfdom

Edited By

Simon Mouatt
Senior Lecturer in Economics, Southampton Solent University, UK

Carl Adams
Principal Lecturer, School of Computing, University of Portsmouth, UK

palgrave
macmillan

First published 2011 by
PALGRAVE MACMILLAN

Palgrave Macmillan in the UK is an imprint of Macmillan Publishers Limited, registered in England, company number 785998, of Houndmills, Basingstoke, Hampshire RG21 6XS.

Palgrave Macmillan in the US is a division of St Martin's Press LLC, 175 Fifth Avenue, New York, NY 10010.

Palgrave Macmillan is the global academic imprint of the above companies and has companies and representatives throughout the world.

Palgrave® and Macmillan® are registered trademarks in the United States, the United Kingdom, Europe and other countries

ISBN 978-0-230-27594-2 hardback

This book is printed on paper suitable for recycling and made from fully managed and sustained forest sources. Logging, pulping and manufacturing processes are expected to conform to the environmental regulations of the country of origin.

A catalogue record for this book is available from the British Library.

Library of Congress Cataloging-in-Publication Data
Corporate and social transformation of money and banking : breaking the serfdom / edited by Simon Mouatt, Carl Adams.
p. cm.
ISBN 978-0-230-27594-2 (hardback)
1. Money. 2. Banks and banking. 3. Finance. 4. International finance. I. Mouatt, Simon. II. Adams, Carl, 1958–

HG221.C74165 2010
332.1–dc22 2010027539

10 9 8 7 6 5 4 3 2 1
20 19 18 17 16 15 14 13 12 11

Printed and bound in Great Britain by
CPI Antony Rowe, Chippenham and Eastbourne

Contents

Acknowledgements

With special thanks to Catherine and Melanie, and further thanks to Emily Fowler, James Fowler, Oliver Snow, Christopher Snow, Alexander Mouatt, Daisy Mouatt, Heather Adams, George Adams, Wesley Adams and Chloe Watson.

List of Tables and Figures

Tables

Figures

List of Abbreviations

3D-Set	Visa 3-D Secure
4G	4th Generation
AAA	Triple A Credit Rating
ARPA	Advanced Research Projects Agency
ARPANET	Advanced Research Projects Agency Network
ATM	Automated Teller Machine
B2B	Business-to-Business
B3g	Beyond 3G
BACS	Bankers Automated Clearing Service
BIS Basle	Bank for International Settlements
BPM	Business Process Management
C2B	Consumer-to-Business
C3	Commercial Credit Circuit
CBC	Corporate Barter Council
ECB	European Central Bank
ERM	European Exchange Rate Mechanism
FRBK	Federal Reserve Bank of Kansas City
FSA	Financial Services Association
ICTs	Information and Communication Technologies
IMF	International Monetary Fund
IPR	International Property Rights
IR1/IR	Industrial Revolution
IR2	Information Revolution
IRS	Internal Revenue Service
IRTA	International Reciprocal Trade Association
LDCs	Less-Developed Countries
LETS	Local Exchange Trading System
LIBOR	London Inter-Bank Overnight Lending Rate.
LSE	London Stock Exchange
LTFRP	Long-run Tendency for Falling Rate of Profit
MB	Monetary Base
MBs	Megabyte/Second
MELT	Monetary Expression of Labour Time.
m-payments	Mobile Payments
NAFTA	North American Free Trade Association
NII	National Information Infrastructure

OPEC	Organization of Petroleum Exporting Countries
PERT	Program Evaluation and Review Technique
PSPs	Payment Service Providers
SDSS	Sloan Digital Sky Survey
SET	Secure Electronic Transaction
STRO	Social Trade Organization
TEQ	Tradable Energy Quota
Terra TRC	Terra Trade Reference Currency
TSSI	Temporal Single System Interpretation
UCAF	Universal Cardholder Authentication Field (Mastercard)
U-PFI/C	User-Pay-for-Information/Content
U-PFS	User-Pay-for-Search
Wac Ac	Wonderful Aging Club, Active Club
WIR	Wirtschaftsring-Genossenschaft (Swiss Economic Circle)
WW2	World War 2

Notes on Contributors

Carl Adams is Principal Lecturer and Research Degrees Co-ordinator in the School of Computing at the University of Portsmouth, UK. His research focuses on mobile information systems, innovation cycles, open-global sourcing and the impact of new technology on society.

Peter Challen is a Sloan Fellow of the London Business School and was the Senior Chaplain of the South London Industrial Mission between 1967 and 1999. He now campaigns for monetary reform, and earth jurisprudence, and chairs the Christian Council for Monetary Justice.

Bernard Lietaer, whilst at the Belgian Central Bank, worked for the European Union in helping to establish the European Currency Unit (ECU), during the operation of the Exchange Rate Mechanism (ERM), and was President of the Belgium Electronic Payment System. He has taught in Colorado at Naropa University, has 25 years of currency system research and is generally recognized as an authority on alternative and complementary currencies (having been influenced by the work of Silvio Gesell). He currently resides in Belgium and is a research fellow at Berkeley University (Centre for Sustainable Resources) in California, USA.

Simon Mouatt is Senior Lecturer in Economics at Southampton Solent University, UK. His research focuses on the notion of the erosion of state (financial) sovereignty, and general transformation of the capitalist credit system, from a Marxian perspective. He is interested in all aspects of monetary theory, and the functioning of the capitalist financial system *per se*.

Nick Potts is a reader at Southampton Solent University and completed his PhD in 2005, on the integration of the productive and financial systems, using a Marxian sequential and non-dualistic interpretation of value (LSE, supervisor Lord Meghnad Desai). Nick is interested in the relevance of Marx to current economic issues and, has been a member of the editorial board of *Capital and Class* since 2005.

Professor **Rodney Shakespeare** is the internationally recognized leading authority on the development of *Binary Economics* that builds on the seminal work of Louis Kelso in the 1950s. He is also visiting professor at Trisakti University, Jakarta, Indonesia.

1
Introduction

Simon Mouatt and Carl Adams

This book explores the transformation of money and banking, since the industrial revolution, and its implication for the global economy and society. The changes taking place affect us all in areas as diverse as healthcare, employment, education as well as the Dollar, Yen, Pound or Euro in our pockets. Whilst money remains a claim on real resources, in recent decades it has evolved from its simple means of exchange function to appearing as a commodity in its own right, as an underlying asset in the increasingly abstract securitization revolution. Indeed, we are at a very exciting time for money. The conflux of innovation within the wider banking and financial sector, for instance, is resulting in unprecedented levels of 'virtual' wealth, alongside the *real* economy development of new capabilities and activities based on more sophisticated cybersystems. In addition, the traditional banking sector appears increasingly 'divorced' from the real economy and, equally, the real economy has evolved in to something new and is not always particularly well served by the traditional banking sector processes and mindset.

As a consequence, the purpose of this book is to theoretically and empirically explore these changes and examine the key factors that have driven the process. The question is then asked whether the evolution of the global monetary system(s) has (or will) led to a more stable and sustainable capitalist order for the future. It is posited that, despite the historic ascendancy of private credit, currency-issue and banking forms, there are increasing non-bank *corporate* (and social) monies, credit and payments systems that are gradually encroaching on the core business activity of the traditional banking infrastructure leading to significant ramifications. Furthermore, a key theme emphasized in the book is that the usual dependence on a single money-form, sanctioned by the state and privately-issued, fails to provide the resilience needed for a sustainable monetary economy. Resilience in an economic system requires currency diversity.

The book is formed of three parts that deal with the theoretical, empirical and future monetary scenarios respectively. The chapter themes are, in turn, derived (and further developed) from several mainstream and heterodox sources including Hayek, Gesell, Keynes, Kondratieff and Marx *et al.* Marx, for instance, had put forward the notion that the productive sector would gradually subjugate money lent as capital, as a result of the *secondary* nature of finance to the (value-adding) production process (Marx 1971). It is suggested that this seemingly counter-intuitive theme is in contradistinction to the popular notion that the world of finance has become increasingly autonomous, or de-coupled, from the productive economy in recent decades. A key book theme, as Lietaer notes, is that complementary currencies issued for social purpose and an informal economy, have also proliferated with notable consequences (Lietaer 2001). It is suggested that both of these *privately*-driven developments have been facilitated by the information revolution and are sometimes supported by state or civic authorities. The book concludes that non-bank *corporate* monetary activity, complementary currencies and present systemic vulnerability, provides convincing empirical evidence to support the general proposition that the productive sector and social movements (rather than the state or the private banks) are driving these monetary transformations in the modern era. The book ends with an evaluation of the impact of these developments on the stability of capitalism and an exploration of possible future scenarios and reform proposals. These include a review of new information technology, asset-backed currency schemes, and a state 'interest-free' money-issue plan (without usury), that could be adopted by policy-makers.

The editors note that money can sometimes be an emotive subject arena, as William (William 1998, p.10) comments in his book on the history of money that 'writing about money can be a hazardous enterprise, and involves treading on sensitive ground. Few phenomena in human history have been the focus of so much constant and fevered attention, occasioned so many moral and religious strictures and been the cause of so much violent strife and competition between individuals and states.' Since we have added discourse on politics, global currency competition, rapid technological innovation, freedom, social change, ethics, bankrupt states and heterodox economic theory then our writing is likely to be contentious at times. Yet, serious problems often require radical thinking in order for solutions to be found.

It is hoped that this book provides fresh insights into the monetary dynamics taking place as history unfolds. This is, of course, within the context of continual change over many centuries. The book is not just about the 'current' economic crisis but hopes to provide a theoretical base for understanding the unfolding changes in the years to come. By drawing upon a historical perspective we are able to ascertain repeating structures and patterns and, surmise the likely trajectory. The book argues that we are at a significantly different place in economic, social and technological development rivalling that of the Industrial Revolution. Kondratieff in the 1920s developed the concept of Long Waves and economic cycles and explicitly tied technological innovation with financial capital, arguing that there were three such cycles beginning with the industrial Revolution. Schumpeter *et al.* in the 1930s later developed the concept of long wave economic cycles[1] and identified a total of five significant surges of technological innovation up to the end of the 20th century, supported by massive investment from financial capital. Equally, Marx *et al.* identified a cyclic process of boom and bust as a natural consequence of a capitalist society.

This book explores the current technological change that is taking place and argues that it is more than 'another technological innovation surge' – it is another revolution, the Information Revolution, that is resulting in significantly new structures and long lasting societal change. These changes will be explored more fully at a later stage. The book makes the contention, however, that we are in the throes of a 6th Kondratieff cycle or IR2 which, in the same manner as the Industrial Revolution (IR1), is changing fundamental physical and social structures in society. This IR2, or 6th Kondratieff wave, has different cyclic characteristics to previous economic cycles, namely in the time between cycle peaks and the role of technology in disseminating innovation information (and the innovation *per se*). Also, significantly, it is changing and set to change further the very nature and structure of financial institutions. In addition, these changes are opening the way for competition from within and outside the financial sector that is set to transform the existing power balance between the financial sector, industry, government and the people. In the early 1940s Hayek produced an influential work, *The Road to Serfdom*, and his later more academic work, *Individualism and Economic Order*, which both highlight the dangers of a drift towards totalitarianism from both the extreme left *and* right and, the need for individual freedom and competition for a stable society. The current high levels of indebtedness by citizens and governments, however, indicate that societies are facing a different type of serfdom in which the balance of power has shifted towards the unconstrained financial markets. If we consider, for instance, the $4 trillion (mostly speculative) daily foreign exchange trading taking place today, and its impact on spot exchange rates, it is not easy to under-estimate the social power of modern finance.

This book hopes to provide perspective on how global society became locked into financial serfdom at the behest of a private cartel of transnational mega-financial institutions and a mindset of debt, as well as providing a roadmap of how to break out of the serfdom. A key feature of the posited emancipation is the need for competition, within and to the financial sector, forming a key theme repeated throughout the book. An evaluation of Hayek's notion of competitive *free banking*, as Boyle notes (p.157), indicates that he also supported the promotion of competition to international as well as national financial systems in order to achieve overall stability (Boyle 2002). Other thinkers have also suggested developing transnational money systems as competition to volatile national currencies such as Keynes' *Bancor*, Lietaer's *Terra* or the recent calls for a revamped IMF special drawing right (Thirlwall 1985; Lietaer 2001).

Within this book it is posited that competition is as likely to come from outside the financial sector as much as within it. The move towards digital goods and services, alongside a growing need for micropayment mechanisms, is highlighting the inadequacies of support from the traditional banking sector. Furthermore, the global economic space highlights large swaths of the global community that do not have access to bank accounts – money transfers for these people are likely to involve their mobile phone[2] rather than their bank account. Whilst investment banking has been focusing attention on speculative activity in recent times, retail banking has been going through substantial change as non-banks have increasingly proven to be the catalyst for sector innovation.[3]

Financial crises

As stated, in much of the recent discourse on global finance it has been common to focus on financial sector autonomy from the productive economy. This is hardly surprising given the growing volume of capital flows, the recent securitization revolution and an increasing level of abstraction from the real economy that results from the innovation in financial products. It has also been suggested that, in the words of the editors of a book that appeared in response to the Asian financial crisis of 1998–99, global finance 'drives the world economy' (Bello *et al.*

2000). This second notion, of course, is not a new one. In the early 1900s for instance, Hilferding had emphasized the *integrated* nature of industrial and financial capital whilst simultaneously maintaining that banking personnel were the *key* instigators of strategic investment decisions and thus the trajectory of the capitalist order (Hilferding 1981). Yet, if we were to accept the notion that finance does drive the economy we are then obliged to accept that financial factors lead to general economic (plus socio-political) crises. This contradicts, of course, the mainstream *Ricardian* view of money that presents money as neutral and instead posits money as an *instigator* of economic activity (Mouatt 2008). In addition, the book argues further that the productive sector and social forces are driving change in the financial sector itself.

Money is, of course, the only real depository of value in a monetary economy, since it represents a claim on actual tangible resources. Those that hold their wealth in the form of money also, therefore, have a vested interest in the real productive economy (and its growth) since this reflects the *real* value of money. Yet, in more recent times, we appear to be witnessing systemic vulnerability in the financial sector notwithstanding economic growth. Increasing industrial output will enhance the real value of a static stock of money, of course, whereas the existence of inflation (with static production) undermines this value. As a consequence, there may be times in the economic cycle when the interests of financiers and productive capitalists fail to converge. A period of deflation, for instance, will restrict aggregate real output, and goods/services fail to sell in sufficient quantities, affecting the interests of weaker firms. This, in turn, is offset for the financial sector by falling prices which enhance the capabilities (and thus interests) of monetary wealth-holders at the expense of debtors. The subsequent reduced cost of the means of production will also restore profitability to the economy for the benefit of any future money-capital and, any bankruptcies will further increase the growth potential and market power of competitive firms. In this sense, crises can be seen as beneficial for certain groups and indispensable to the sustainability and development of the capitalist mode of production. A key argument of this book is that, due to falling rates of profitability[4] in the production structure (where value is actually created), surplus capital has migrated to the financial sector in the normal search for profit – fuelling growth in financial markets. In addition, elements of the productive sector have sought to secure larger relative proportions of surplus value[5] created which has led to increasing (previously mentioned) non-bank financial activity. Yet, since the ultimate value of money is inseparable from the real productive economy, there is an occasional need for crises in the financial sector and productive structure combined to restore the real value of money and profitability.

The book therefore explores these recent and latent corporate developments in the financial sector, and further asks whether the substantial transformation of the global financial system is leading to a more stable capitalist order. It is posited that, despite the historic ascendancy of credit and banking forms, increasing *corporate* monies, payments systems and banks are gradually encroaching on the *core* business activity of the traditional private banking infrastructure leading to significant ramifications. It is further suggested that these market-driven developments have been facilitated by the information revolution.

Book structure

The rest of this chapter examines the concept of long waves and develops the suggestion that we are going through an Information Revolution (IR2), or 6th Kondratieff, that is culminating in the evolution of significantly different structures across society similar to that of the first Industrial Revolution (IR). The discussion of these new financial infrastructures, and their attributes, is fundamental to the discourse pursued in later chapters. The remaining chapters in Part I cover theoretical perspectives and draw upon contrasting schools of thought to bring out different insights to the economic cycles and causes of instability. The second chapter, for instance, discusses one of the key theoretical themes of the book, capitalist stability, and suggests that a unitary currency system does not provide the capacity for sustainability in terms of its ability to deal with the capitalist trajectory, shocks and other random events. Bernard describes how that, in order to be sustainable an eco-system requires a measure of diversity and inter-dependence that provides a certain 'slack' enabling the system to cope with change. He describes that, in contrast, our monetary system is a mono-culture, driven by an ideology of efficiency. Whilst this works well in some contexts, it copes very badly with change or unexpected random shocks. He suggests instead that the development of complementary currencies serves to enhance the ability of the capitalist order to facilitate stability and sustainability.

Chapter 3 then reviews the potential causes of economic (and financial) crises that are generally posited and contrasts them with the explanation of Marx. Nick concludes that even if these were removed the system would still be subject to crises, resulting from an underlying tendency for the profit rate (in labour terms) to decline in times of boom. Nick then explains and illustrates this tendency with reference to a sequential and non-dualistic approach (the one used by Marx) to price and value (Kliman 2007). Nick, therefore, offers a heterodox theoretical explanation of how the productive sector can be seen to be driving the transformation(s) in the financial sector by providing a basic outline of Marx's political economy. Chapter 4 reviews the monetary system, and economic cycle, from a Marx perspective. In particular, the emerging *endogenous* nature of financial institutions, and the role of surplus capital (and its migration to the financial sector) in fictitious capital bubbles, are both explored. A (more esoteric) mathematical model of surplus capital is also provided for any interested readers in 'The Political Economy of Money, Profitability and Value' (Potts 2005).

Chapter 5 examines the erosion of (financial) state-sovereignty and argues that the state, which is viewed as an extension of industrial capital interests, has actively participated in these processes. The chapter then explores who (or what) might have gained financial capabilities at the expense of the state or, whether capability has simply evaporated. It could be that the private banking infrastructure, or corporate production structure (or some combination of the two), has gained capabilities. Yet, if financial power has been gained by bankers *and* non-monetary corporations, how do these separate entities interact and what are their particular interests, aims and capabilities? (Mouatt 2009). Chapter 6 explores the Marx notion that the productive sector will subjugate money lent as capital, as the capitalist mode of production evolves, and discusses the processes involved. Whilst Marx had in mind the pre-capitalist lenders of the mercantilist era (as they were replaced by capitalist credit relations), this chapter argues that his depiction is analogous to (the transformation of) the current private banking infrastructure in the modern era (Mouatt and Adams 2010). It is also suggested that this is leading to more stable monetary relations in some respects but, conversely, is facilitating a centralization of social power in the larger corporations.

Part II of the book deals with the evidence for corporate and social transformation of money and banking. In Chapter 7, for instance, Carl traces the development of the so-called 'non-banks' that have emerged in recent years. It is argued that this is driven by normal capitalist competition, as the productive sector seeks to obtain a greater relative proportion of profit, which the financial sector has been enjoying. This can also partly explain the recent increasing levels of traditional bank speculative activity, as their normal sources of income have come under threat. In Chapter 8, Carl further gathers information on the emergence of corporate payment systems in the modern era. It is concluded that the information age has greatly facilitated this. In most cases these new channels of monetary circulation still rely on traditional bank back-end processing yet there are signs that circumstances are beginning to change. In Chapter 9, Carl examines the development of corporate *monies* in the information age. It is concluded that the use of information technology has a certain efficacy, in relation to traditional banking, and that this is driving the monetary changes. In Chapter 10, Bernard reviews the existing and latent complementary currencies in the world today, developed for social purposes or an informal economy. These currencies provide stability and resilience to the prevailing monetary order and contribute, of course, towards social well-being (Lietaer 2001; Lietaer 2003).

Part III presents some alternative monetary scenarios for the future. In Chapter 11, for instance, Bernard outlines proposals for various alternative commercial currencies, such as the terra and C3, and their potential role in transforming the general economic system. Some of these currencies serve to (potentially) replace the prevailing monetary order and others could complement it (Lietaer 2001; Lietaer 2003). These proposals offer an alternative to the inflation-prone credit monies of the current global monetary system. In Chapter 12 the authors present an alternative (future) monetary scenario where the present (private) fractional reserve banking system of money-issue is replaced by a sufficient quantity of circulating 'interest-free' credit money, issued from a state-managed national bank, for purposes of state expenditures (greatly reducing capital costs). The circulating credit-monies would then be acceptable for the payment of taxes and thus form legal tender. This monetary reform proposal could even be utilized to spread capital ownership and mitigate some of the other exploitative and detrimental side-effects of the capitalist mode of production (Ashford and Shakespeare 1999). In addition, the monetary reform proposal is critically contrasted with the current monetary reform movement that wishes to replace privately issued credit monies with state-issued 'debt-free' money (Zarlenga 2002).

Chapter 13 presents a future scenario of collaboration between internet search-engine firm Google and the software company Microsoft, illustrating key developments that point to possible future transformation of money and banking. Finally, in the last chapter, the editors summarize the main findings of the book and ask whether these developments are likely to lead to a more stable economic order for the future. Closer customer interaction, and a closer link with the commercial world of commodities, for instance, may lead to greater stability. Conversely, an increased centralization of social power in the corporations has implications for the democratic deficit in modern society (Adams and Mouatt 2010). In addition, a plethora of complementary currencies should serve to give the capitalist order more resilience for the future.

Business cycles, the information revolution and the 6th Kondratieff wave

The discourse on economic cycles is well established and hotly contested in economic theory and, this was particularly so during the inter-war years. Hayek and Keynes *et al.* had looked at business cycles from a monetary perspective in terms of the influence of money supply, interest rate rises and investor confidence that resulted in boom-and-bust cycles (Hayek 1944; Skidelsky 2005). Hayek had further considered horizontal influences across business sectors. One of the main strands of business cycle theory, provided by Schumpeter, was the notion of cycles rooted in surges or waves of technological innovation. According to this perspective, since the Industrial Revolution there have been other distinct surges of technological innovation resulting in specific economic cycles. However, the foundations to this thinking go back to Nikolai Kondratieff in the early 1920s, a Russian economist who developed the concept of Long Waves and economic cycles (Kondratiev 1925). Kondratieff initially identified three long waves: the first starting in the early stages of the Industrial Revolution, in about 1790, the second long wave starting in the mid-1800s and the last beginning in the 1890s (Lloyd-Jones and Lewis 1998, p.1). Kondratieff did not initially attract much support for his ideas. The idea and logical implication that a capitalist economy would emerge from a financial crisis presumably did not attract much support from the Soviet leadership of the time. There was also not much support from the West with his ideas mostly criticized for a lack of explanation of the underlying forces (Lloyd-Jones and Lewis 1998). However, there was one significant main follower of Kondratieff's concept, Joseph Schumpeter who provided a more robust framework and stronger support for long wave theory (Schumpeter 1954).

Similar to Marx's view that the natural, endogenously-driven, cycle of capitalist societies will involve crashes, Schumpeter[6] had a complementary view of 'creative destruction' from cycles of *innovation* based on entrepreneurs developing new industries resulting in the obsolescence and slumps (or destruction) of older industries. Schumpeter (1911) defines the importance of entrepreneurship in the innovative cycle with entrepreneurs generating new technical (and financial) innovations within the context of mature industries facing increased competition and falling profits. Others have taken on the long wave cycle perspective, notably Freeman (1982, 1986), Lloyd-Jones and Lewis (1998) and Perez (2006).

Perez (2010) identifies five successive technological revolutions, or Kondratieff's waves, between the 1770s and 2000, the main characteristics which are represented in Table 1.1. While much of the business cycle work focuses on the generally short to medium-term fluctuations of the economy, lasting between 3–10 years, the Kondratieff cycles represent more long-term fluctuations, lasting between 30–60 years. Long wave theories are based on the cycles being triggered by landmark inventions (or Big-bang inventions in Table 1.1) that fundamentally change economies.

Wonglimpiyarat (2005), building on Perez's (2002) work and suggestions, argues that the start of the 6th Kondratieff cycle will be based on nano-technologies in a nano-revolution. Negt, whilst discussing the (life-long) educational needs across Europe argues that the age of microelectronics has already started to exhaust its power of innovation and that the 6th Kondratieff period of economic prosperity will be based on other technologies (including nano). However, Negt's analysis misses the power of ubiquitous access to the Internet and social innovations.

Our contention is that the 5th Kondratieff wave was about computing and basic communication technologies, while the sixth is about ubiquitous access to the Internet as an information *superhighway* and conduit for social and technological innovation. Attributes of the 6th Kondratieff are represented in Table 1.2. The history of the Internet, as we know it today, began with the Advanced Research Projects Agency Network (ARPANET) developed by ARPA (Advanced Research Projects Agency) of the United States Department of Defence during the Cold War period. ARPANET was based on decentralization packet switching (i.e. a method that splits data traffic into packets of data which are then routed over a shared network); where as the proprietary network systems at the time were (mostly) based on centralized control. Out of the ARPANET grew the National Information Infrastructure (NII) in the US (part of the High Performance Computing and Communication Act of 1991), also known as the 'information superhighway' which was famously coined by Albert Gore the Vice-President of the United States at the time. This, we contend, was the start of the digital 6th Kondratieff's innovation cycle. The NII was the base of the Internet consisting of a seamless web of public and private communications networks with interoperable hardware and software. The late 1990s also saw the move towards desktop PC's accessing the Internet through telephone wires via modems. There followed a rapid growth of the

Table 1.1 First five Kondratieff Innovation cycles, based on Perez (2002, 2010)

Technological Revolution *or Kondratieff Wave*	Popular Name for the period	Big-bang initiating the revolution	Year	Core country or countries
First	The Industrial Revolution	Arkwright's Mill opens in Cromford	1771	Britain
Second	Age of Steam and Railways	Test of the Rocket Steam Engine for the Liverpool-Manchester Railway	1829	Britain (spreading to Europe and USA)
Third	Age of Steel, Electricity and Heavy Engineering	The Carnegie Bessemer Steel Plant opens in Pittsburgh, PA, USA	1875	USA and Germany forging ahead and overtaking Britain
Fourth	Age of Oil, the Automobile and Mass Production	First Model-T comes out of the Ford plant in Detroit, MI, USA	1908	USA (with Germany at first vying for world leadership), spreading to Europe
Fifth	Age of Information and Telecommunications	The Intel Microprocessor is announced in Santa Clara, CA	1971	USA (spreading to Europe and Asia)

Table 1.2 Attributes of the 6th Kondratieff Wave, the Information Revolution

Technological Revolution *or Kondratieff Wave*	Popular Name for the period	Big-bang initiating the revolution	Year	Core country or countries	Commodities
Sixth	The Information Revolution	NII's Information Superhighway, in the United States	1991	US, then developing across Europe, Japan and the far East – and then Globally	Digital and Social Innovation Information Products and Services

Internet in the technologically developed countries (particularly the US, Europe and Japan), along with much hype about new business models and new businesses. However, the reality of the infrastructure did not meet the hype and in 2000, following over-zealous investor confidence, the dot.com bubble burst and share prices collapsed. However, since that time there has been steady growth in e-commerce activity. Corporations have moved their expertise and operating activity from the centralized network systems to the more decentralized Internet infrastructure. Having an Internet presence is the norm for corporations in the richer technologically developed countries. The Internet presence expands to cover internal operations, interaction with business partners and government as well as the customer base. More currently, there is push towards more mobility in the seamless access with wireless connections to laptop computers (via Wifi and WiMax) and mobile access to the Internet via mobile/cell phones, PDAs and other powerful mobile devices. At the same time there has been a rapid increase in access to the Internet by the poorer technologically developing countries. The Internet is truly global. Often this is the results of technological 'leapfrogging' where poorer countries use cheaper wireless infrastructure to provide access to Internet resources, indeed we are facing the time when, in certain countries, the predominant means of accessing the Internet will be over wireless infrastructure. A key stage in the next development of the Internet is the introduction of 'super broadband', moving from just a few megabytes/second (MBs) of bandwidth to 100's MBs of broadband access to Internet users. There is also discussion within the telecommunications industry of 4G (4th generation), or B3G (beyond 3G) technologies, that will offer bandwidth of 100MB (one of the first trials of which was in Shanghai, China, in January 2007). There is also discussion in the e-commerce industry of Web 2.0 Cloud computing and, the move to Web 3.0, offering even more seamless access to rich information sources.

Is there any basis and evidence for the 6th Kondratieff Wave to be based on the Information Revolution? The rate of change that we have been going through in recent decades could, arguably, be described as revolutionary. Perhaps it is useful to draw upon previous times of rapid change, such as through the Industrial Revolution, to make comparisons and understand some of the change processes. Professor Phyllis Deane's book, 'The First Industrial Revolution', provides a good historical evaluation of the context and environment during the so-called (first) Industrial Revolution (IR). The aspects of the IR that Deane covered include the demographic, agricultural, commercial and transport revolutions. It also included case studies of the cotton and iron industries, banking, trade, innovation and general macroeconomic conditions. At this time fundamental new business and social structures emerged.[7] Commerce and production were mainly focused on steel, coal and cotton commodities. New production facilities called factories, emerged which enabled the mass production of goods. New types of towns also emerged to accommodate migrating farm workers as they moved towards industrial employment. New banking and capital structures also emerged to finance the development of factories and global commerce. In addition, new transportation also emerged, such as canals, rails, better road networks and steam power. So for a comparable Information Revolution, and 6th Kondratieff wave based on information commodities, there should be examples of new structures across society of a similar scale to the Industrial Revolution. For identifying these we will have to examine some current trends in social and business practices across society.

One of the key writers arguing that we are going through a prolonged set of rapid revolutionary changes is Toffler (1984). Toffler describes the transformation of humanity into three phases of innovation-led changes (Toffler 1981). The First Wave occurred when peasant-centred economies supplanted hunter-gather societies. The Second Wave was the Industrial Revolution that gave us factory-based systems and mass production for wealth generation. The Third Wave of civilization is the current set of revolution(s), where wealth creation is marked by 'de-massification' (less mass production), hyper-competition, successive technological revolutions and associated social dislocation. In the Third Wave, information and knowledge become the primary factor of production for wealth creation (Toffler and Toffler 2003, p.x). Toffler continues stating that 'vertical integration, synergy, economies of scale and hierarchical, command-and-control organization is giving way to a fresh appreciation of outsourcing, minimization of scale, profit centres, networks and other diverse forms of organization. Every shred of industrial-era thinking is now being re-scrutinized and brilliantly reformulated. It is precisely when an old paradigm crumbles and the new one is not yet fixed in place that we get great bursts of creative thinking. This is such a moment.' (Toffler and Toffler 2003, p.ix). Toffler's Third Wave ties in with the concept of an Information Revolution, the basis of a 6th Kondratieff wave, but where is the infrastructure that defines the revolution comparable to the Industrial Revolution? The Internet is certainly a base for these new infrastructures, but more is needed for a direct comparison to IR1.

Global electronic interaction and commerce has become the normal business practice for much of the technologically developed nations, as it is fast becoming a significant part for the generally poorer less technologically developed nations. Kotter (2003, p.165) argues that we have been through a new economic era for a decade or two, driven by global competition – a state that is set to continue. Similarly, Porter (2003, p.54) argues that we are going through a new paradigm of competitiveness based on technological innovation and upgrading, requiring continual change to be competitive. Business activity is conducted in an interlinked global working environment, an increasingly competitive environment as corporations are open to new opportunities from the global market space. In addition to the global opportunity for corporations there is also an increase in the number and variety of competitors from the same global market space. In such a global and competitive market-space, creativity and innovation become more important for corporations and nations. The message is that nations and corporations need to innovate just in order to survive.

If we are going through a further revolution similar to that of the Industrial Revolution, then the focus is on electronic infrastructures and technologies which dictate the rate and focus of change. Information in its wider sense, along with information-based services is the main commodity. New production practices have emerged based on virtual collaboration, supply chains, eco-nets and outsourcing, all supported by electronic infrastructures. Production activity has moved towards mass customization, supported by mobile, ad-hoc and virtual working teams using seamless access to information resources over the Internet. Companies can conduct business solely within the virtual operating environments – and increasingly are. Indeed, some of the biggest and fastest growing companies are based on virtual operating activity and simply moving electronic data (such as Amazon, e-bay and Google). The main new structure that has emerged is the information *superhighway* (both fixed-line and mobile), and from this variety further structures have emerged. One significant current example is the evolving social networking infrastructure. Social networking has always been a part of human activity however, the emergence of Web 2.0 technologies, in the wider sense, has enabling new forms of communication at unprecedented levels. Facebook, for instance, has some impressive statistics. There are over 400 million active users (i.e. who have returned to the site in the last 30 days), more than 3 billion photos are uploaded to the site each month and more than 5 billion pieces of content (such as web links, news stories, blog posts, notes, photo albums) are shared each week (from http://www.facebook.com/press/info.php?statistics, accessed 14/04/10). One 100 million users access Facebook via a mobile device. In five years an electronic community has emerged that is equivalent in size the fourth largest national population and 20 times bigger than the largest city.

The technology-enabled networking sites, act as *conduits* for both disseminating information about a digital product or service innovation as well as distributing the innovation itself. This speeds up the rate of diffusion of digital innovation. The FarmVille social networking game developed by Zynga is a good example. The game is based around players developing their own virtual farm by growing crops and animals. There is a farm market, where seeds, plants, tress and animals are purchased using 'farm coins' (tokens based on a micro-payment mechanism). Players can earn farm coins by selling crops or gaining experience levels. Players can also buy FarmVille coins from Zynga, using US dollars, but the majority of farm coins are generated by the users 'working' on their virtual farms. Zynga was founded in July 2007, and as of 7th March 2010, FarmVille had over 83 million monthly active users (from http://www.facebook.com/apps/application.php?id=102452128776).

Visual Measures, a company that monitors and measures the distribution of electronic media over the Internet, maintains a '100 Million Views Club' (see http://www.visiblemeasures.com/hundred) and, as of April 2010, there were 65 entries. For instance, Susan Boyle the star from Britain's Got Talent TV programme reached 9th with over 347 million downloads. The Information Revolution is seeing the emergence of the 'one billion club'. In July 2009, the Mozilla Foundation celebrated the one billionth download of the Firefox browser after only five years (see http://www.onebillionplusyou.com/ accessed 14/4/2010). This is equivalent to one-sixth of the world population. In March 2010, the comparative newcomer to the music industry, Lady Gaga, was the first person to reach one billion downloads – from just three records ('Poker Face', 'Bad Romance' and 'Just Dance'). Apple, the manufacturer of computers, iPods and iPhones, reached over one billion downloads from its store in nine months (http://www.apple.com/itunes/billion-app-countdown/accessed 14/4/2010). In February 2010, Apple had already reached its 10 billionth download of music from iTunes.

A further set of structures based on the information superhighway is the Open-Global Sourcing, or 'crowdsourcing', phenomena (Surowiecki 2004; Howells *et al.* 2008; Adams and Ramos 2010). The change towards an on-line outsourcing mindset has had a significant impact on traditional business practice transforming organizational structures, personnel functions, as well as the interaction with suppliers (Goo *et al.* 2008; Goo 2010). However, the command and control model of outsourcing, that was prominent in the 5th Kondratieff wave, is being challenged by

Open-global sourcing as organizations now draw upon input (ideas as well as service provision) from a vast global knowledge community. The transition to Web 3.0 technologies (Lassila and Hendler 2007) is also bringing more seamless interaction and collaboration between people as well as access to global information resources (Giddens 2002; Holton 2008). In the same way that the innovation of outsourcing significantly changed business practice, open-global sourcing is having an equally significant impact. Howe (2008) notes, for instance, that 'crowdsourcing' activity can gather intelligence, create crowds, gather informed opinion and raise finance. The Galaxy Zoo, uTest and PERT provide three examples of 'crowdsourcing' *social* innovations.

UTest (see http://www.utest.com/), was formed in late 2007 and now claims to be the world's largest marketplace for software testing services with a global community of over 18,000 testers from more than 150 countries. UTest builds a virtual testing team for each customer, putting the call for 'testing' open to their community. The Galaxy Zoo project (see http://galaxyzoo.org/), also launched in 2007 (July), shows how open-global sourcing can tackle very large problems, such as robustly classify over one million galaxies from images collected through the Sloan Digital Sky Survey (SDSS) telescope. The initial expectation was that it would take a few years for visitors to the site, along with cosmologists, to work through the million images. However, within 24 hours of launch, the site was receiving 70,000 classifications an hour. More than 50 million classifications were received by the project during its first year from almost 150,000 people from the global general public. To date there has been over 60 million classifications with input from 200,000 people. One of the best examples of social innovation that continues to have a significant impact on business working practices is the Program Evaluation and Review Technique (PERT), used for the Polaris submarine (Gabor 1970, p.6). PERT enables the management and coordination of large and complex projects by providing the ability to plan the collaboration of many different contributors with very many components, within a guideline budget and timeframe. Indeed most of the information systems produced for governments and corporations will have followed a PERT-type management approach as a result. The information revolution now means that these types of activity can take place on-line greatly enhancing efficacy.

The impact of social innovations can be subtle but far reaching (Adams and Ramos 2010). They do not translate to a specific 'technological' innovation as such although they may be closely related, providing new thinking or changes to working or social practices. The power of the Internet is not the hardware and software systems *per se* but, rather, how businesses, governments and people use it. Wikipedia, as an example of social innovation, is probably the largest ever repository of human knowledge and has been created in a short space of time with contributions from hundreds of thousands of people all over the world. It is accessed daily by millions of people from all over the world. As a knowledge sharing repository it is unsurpassed. Wikipedia, and the corresponding competing wiki's, are equivalent in terms of human time and effort to the development of the pyramids or similar very large-scale monuments in history – Wiki's are our own modern global monuments, monuments to knowledge creation and sharing on a global scale, our own modern day 'wonders' of the world.

There are significant new structures emerging around the information superhighway as part of the 6th Kondratieff, characterized by large user-numbers, a global presence and speed. It also appears that corporate, digital and social innovation has provided the basis for fundamental change to the traditional financial sector. In addition, much of the *real* economy has moved towards a digital operating space, based on social innovations and digital products and services. The best placed competition to the financial and banking arena, in order to service this evolving real economy, is therefore coming from outside of the traditional financial sector. As with the Industrial Revolution, new financial institutions and infrastructure have evolved to accommodate, support and fuel the high levels of innovation, so too with the Information Age. Indeed, everything appears ready for the new financial support structures to support the next step change in innovation. It is the contention of the editors that this will be provided outside the traditional banking and financial services arena if, of course, they fail to adapt.

Notes

1 The reader should note that others have provided a more robust framework and stronger support for long wave theory. See Kuznets (1940), Freeman (1982, 1986), Lloyd-Jones and Lewis (1998), and Perez (2006, 2010).
2 There are more people in the world with a mobile phone than with a bank account.
3 It is recognized that modern banking institutions blur the boundaries between investment and retail banking.
4 This is measured in abstract social labour not nominal monetary terms according to Marx.
5 In Marxist analysis, surplus value refers to the profit derived from labour.
6 A history of Joseph Schumpeter can be found at History of Economic Thought website (see http://homepage.newschool.edu/het//profiles/schump.htm, accessed 29/03/10).

7 Further excellent resources covering aspects of the Industrial Revolution, including the technologies and the resulting societal changes, can be found in Fahie (1884, 1902), Chant (ed.) (1988), Roberts G. (ed.) (1988), Standage (1998), Ashton (1986), Deane (1988) and Marshall (1982).

References

Adams, C. and Mouatt, S. (2010) 'Evolution of Mobile Business and Services: Government Support of M-Payment Services', *International Journal of E-Services and Mobile Applications*, 2(2).

Adams, C. and Ramos, I. (2009) 'Crowdsourcing: A Social Networking Approach to Outsourcing', *Cutter IT Journal*, 22(10).

Adams, C. and Ramos, I. (2010) *The Past Present and Future of Social Networking and Outsourcing: Impact on Theory and Practice.* Oxford: UK Association Information Systems Conference.

Ashford, R. and Shakespeare, R. (1999) *Binary Economics: The New Paradigm.* Lanham, Maryland: University Press of America.

Ashton, T. S. (1986) *The Industrial Revolution 1760–1830.* Oxford: Oxford University Press.

Bello, W., Bullard, N., Malhotra, K. and Mezzera, M. (2000) 'Notes on the Ascendancy and Regulation of Speculative Capital', *Global Finance: New Thinking on Regulating Speculative Capital Markets.* W. B. Bello, Nicola & Malhotra, Kamal. Malaysia: Zed.

Boyle, D. (ed.) (2002) *The Money Changers.* Ebbw Vale: Earthscan.

Chant, C. (1988) *Sources for the Study of Science, Technology and Everyday Life 1870–1950, Volume Two.* London: Hodder & Stoughton.

Deane, P. (1988) *The First Industrial Revolution.* Cambridge: Cambridge University Press.

Fahie, J. (1884) *A History of Electronic Telegraphing to the Year 1837.* London: Spone E. & F.N. Publishers.

Fahie, J. (1902) *A History of the Wireless Telegraph.* New York: Dodd, Meade & Company.

Freeman, C. (1982) *The Economics of Industrial Innovation.* London: Francis Pinter.

Freeman, C. (ed.) (1986) *Design Innovation and Long Cycles.* London: Francis Pinter.

Gabor, D. (1970) *Innovations: Scientific, Technological and Social.* Cary, NC: Oxford University Press.

Giddens, A. (2002) *Runaway World.* London: Profile Books.

Goo, J. (2010) 'Structure of Service Level Agreements (SLA) in IT Outsourcing: The Construct and its Measurement', *Information Systems Frontiers*, 12(2), pp.185–205.

Goo, J., Huang, D. C. and Hart, P. (2008) 'A Path to Successful IT Outsourcing: Interaction Between Service-Level Agreements and Commitment', *Decision Sciences*, 39(3), pp.469–506.

Hayek, F. (1944) *The Road to Serfdom.* London: Routledge & Kegan Paul.

Hayek, F. (1948) *Individualism and Economic Order.* United States: University of Chicago Press.

Hilferding, R. (1981[1910]) *Finance Capital: A Study of the Latest Phase of Capitalist Development.* London: Routledge and Kegan Paul.

Holton, R. J. (2008) *Global Networks.* Basingstoke: Palgrave Macmillan.

Howe, J. (2008) *Crowdsourcing: Why the Power of the Crowd is Driving the Future of Business*. USA: Crown Business.
Howells, J., Gagliardi, D. and Malik, K. (2008) 'The Growth and Management of R&D Outsourcing: Evidence from UK Pharmaceuticals', *R&D Management*, 38(2), pp.205–19.
Kliman, A. (2007) *Reclaiming Marx's Capital: A Refutation of the Myth of Inconsistency*. United States: Lexington.
Kondratiev, N. (1925) *The Major Economic Cycles*. Moscow: Richardson and Snyder.
Kotter, J. (2003) 'Rethinking Leadership', in Gibson, R. (ed.) *Rethinking the Future*, pp.166–7. London: Nicholas Brealey.
Kuznets, S. (1940) 'Schumpeter's Business Cycles', *American Economic Review*, 30(2).
Lassila, O. and Hendler, J. (2007) 'Embracing Web 3.0', *IEEE Internet Computing*, 11(3), pp.90–3.
Lietaer, B. (2001) *The Future of Money – Creating New Wealth, Work and a Wise World*. Guildford: Random House.
Lietaer, B. (2003) 'A World in Balance?', *Reflections: The Journal of the Society for Organisational Learning* (Summer: Special Issue on 'The Feminine Approach to Leadership').
Lloyd-Jones, R. and Lewis, M. J. (1998) *British Industrial Capitalism since the Industrial Revolution*. London: University College London Press.
Marshall, D. (1982) *Industrial England 1776–1851*. London: Routledge.
Marx, K. (1971) *Theories of Surplus Value: Part Three*. Moscow: Progress.
Mouatt, S. (2008) 'Evaluating Stephen Zarlenga's Treatment of Historical Monetary Thought', *International Journal of Social Economics*, 35(11).
Mouatt, S. (2009) *The Dissolution of the Financial State*. Miliband: 40 Years On, Leeds Metropolitan University.
Mouatt, S. and Adams, C. (2010) 'Marx, Subjugated Banking and an Emerging Corporate Monetary System', *Southampton Solent University Discussion Paper*.
Perez, C. (2004) 'Finance and Technical Change: A Long-Term View', in Hanusch, H. & Pyka, A. *The Elgar Companion to Neo-Schumpeterian Economics*. Cheltenham: Edward Elgar.
Perez, C. (2006) *Technological Revolutions and Financial Capital: The Dynamics of Bubbles and Golden Ages*. Cheltenham: Edward Elgar.
Perez, C. (2010) 'Technological Revolutions and Techno-Economic Paradigms', *Cambridge Journal of Economics*, 34(1), pp.185–202.
Porter, M. (2003) 'Creating Tomorrows Advantages', in Gibson, R. *Rethinking the Future*, pp.48–61. London: Nicholas Brealey Publishing.
Potts, N. (2005) *The Political Economy of Money, Profitability and Value*. London School of Economics. London: University of London.
Roberts, G. (1988) *Sources for the Study of Science, Technology and Everyday Life 1870–1950, Volume One*. London: Hodder and Stoughton.
Schumpeter, J. (1911) *The Economics of Development*. Cambridge MA: Harvard University Press.
Schumpeter, J. A. (1954) *History of Economic Analysis*. Guildford: Routledge.
Skidelsky, R. (2005) *John Maynard Keynes 1883–1946 Economist, Philosopher, Statesman*. USA: Penguin.
Standage, T. (1998) *The Victorian Internet*. London: Weidenfeld & Nicolson.

Surowiecki, J. (2004) *The Wisdom of Crowds: Why the Many Are Smarter Than the Few and How Collective Wisdom Shapes Business, Economies, Societies and Nations.* United States: Random House.
Thirlwall, A. P. (1985) *Keynesian Economic Development 7th Keynes Seminar*. Hong Kong: Macmillan.
Toffler, A. (1984) *Future Shock*. London: Bantam Books.
Toffler, A. (1981) *The Third Wave*. New York: Bantam Books.
Toffler, A. and Toffler, H. (2003) Foreword to Gibson, R. (ed.) (2003) *Rethinking the Future*. London: Nicholas Brealey Publishing.
William, J. (ed.) (1998) *Money: A History*. London: British Museum Press.
Wonglimpiyarat, J. (2005) 'The Nano-Revolution of Schumpeter's Kondratieff Cycle', *Technovation*, 25(11), pp.1349–54.
Zarlenga, S. (2002) *The Lost Science of Money – The Mythology of Money: The Story of Power*. United States: The American Monetary Institute.

Part I

Theory

2

Monetary Monopoly as Structural Cause for Systemic Financial Instability?

Bernard Lietaer[1]

The first telltale sign that there could be a systemic cause for financial and monetary instability is its repetitive nature. Indeed, even before the huge 2008 banking crash, the World Bank has identified more than 96 banking crises and 176 monetary crises since President Nixon introduced the floating exchange regime in the early 1970s (Caprio and Klingebiel 1996). Even before that period, financial booms and bust cycles were, in Kindleberger's words, a remarkably 'hardy perennial' (Kindleberger 1978). He inventories no less than 48 massive crashes between the 1637 tulip mania in Holland and the 1929 crash on Wall Street.

The general tendency is to attribute these crashes to some proximate cause, which often varies from case to case. For instance, the large scale use of derivatives during a US real estate bubble is seen as the proximate cause for the 2008 crash; the inflexible link between the national currency and the US$ is purported to be the proximate cause of the Argentinian Peso collapse in 2001; or the Asian crash of 1999 affecting a dozen countries was claimed to be due to 'crony capitalism'.

My own view is that such repeated breakdowns, in very different countries and times, under different regulatory environments, and in economies with very different degrees of development, signal some underlying *structural* problem. If there is a structural issue, the various proximate causes can indeed play a role as a trigger; but if that particular trigger had been avoided, another 'cause' would have played out a bit later. If one deals with a house of cards, does it matter that much which specific card provokes the collapse? Does it matter that it is the collapse of the Kreditanstalt in Austria that triggered the crash of 1929, or a US real estate bubble that set off the one of 2008? What will be demonstrated in this chapter is that what really matters is that the system itself is an unstable 'house of cards' looking for an excuse to collapse. Furthermore, if such a deeper mechanism is involved, it could explain why each new set of regulations achieves, at best, only a reduction in the frequency of banking and monetary crises, without getting rid of them and their horrific economic and socio-political consequences.

Here is another metaphor. You are given a car without brakes and with an unreliable steering wheel. And you are sent across the Alps or the Rockies. When you crash, you are told that you are a bad driver; or that your road maps are out-of-date. And everybody is endeavouring to get that same car back on the road, with as little change as possible... predictably until the next crash. Indeed, such a car is not fit for driving; it has structural problems which, if not fixed, will predictably cause other crashes. There are now plenty of proposals for new road maps ('regulatory changes') and even some changes of drivers ('management changes' in derelict financial companies). However, what we will show is that none of such changes will permanently solve the problem: only structural solutions can genuinely address structural problems. Therefore, a helpful starting point would be to identify the nature of the structural problem that is plaguing our financial and monetary system.

When a general cause is identified that applies to all such crises, it tends to be so vague that there isn't a lot one can do about it. For instance, Alan Greenspan, former governor of the Federal Reserve, admitted after the banking collapse of 2008 that 'the world will suffer another financial crisis' but he blamed 'human nature' for this state of affairs.[2] In this he followed Isaac Newton's footsteps when he was supposed to have said after the collapse of the South Sea Bubble that 'I can calculate the motions of heavenly bodies but not the madness of men'.[3] While human nature may indeed play a role, the problem with these interpretations is that waiting for a change in human nature isn't a very realistic basis for attaining global financial stability any time soon.

Barely more helpful is the claim that such crashes are part of Schumpeter's 'creative destruction', considered a (useful) characteristic of capitalism (Schumpeter 1942). However, all the examples Schumpeter himself was referring to are about the rise and fall of individual business units, not of an entire monetary or financial system. Furthermore, he saw the destruction as due to innovations by newcomers that replace the old institutions that are not adopting the better ways. This isn't what is happening in the financial or monetary domain: after each crash, the banking system is being bailed out at government's expense, and the old way of doing business is starting all over, with some fine tuning of the regulatory or managerial environment.

There is clearly a 'destructive' part in such a financial crash. It is even played out with a vengeance, but it affects the rest of the economy, when large numbers of otherwise sound businesses go bankrupt because of insufficient funding from the financial system.[4]

What will be shown in this chapter is that there indeed exists a structural flaw in our Modern monetary system, a flaw that has been with us for centuries. Actually, it was already 'doing its thing' when the Dutch tulip bubble burst in 1637, and played an unacknowledged role in every crash since that time, including the one we are experiencing now! The proof for this claim comes from fundamental laws that govern all complex flow systems, including natural ecosystems, economic and financial systems. It is based on a recent theoretical breakthrough which makes it possible to measure the sustainability of any complex flow system with a single metric as an emergent property of its structural diversity and interconnectivity. Furthermore, it is discovered that whenever diversity is being sacrificed because of too much emphasis on efficiency, systemic collapses are a predictable consequence.

From this perspective, it is obvious that we have been living worldwide with a monoculture of the same type of media of exchange, in the form of a single national currency monopoly in each country, created everywhere through bank debt. As we will see at the end of this chapter, both Marxist and capitalist schools of thought have been blind to this issue: they both have fallen into the same trap of imposing a monopoly of a single national currency. The main difference in this respect between communism of the Marxist-Leninist variety on the one side, and capitalism on the other, was that in the former governments were the owners of the banks, while in the latter private investors are normally supposed to be in control. But the money system itself is in fact the same: a single national currency created through bank debt...The structural solution to economic and financial sustainability becomes also clear, even if it will appear shockingly unorthodox to most economists: we need to diversify the types of currencies available in a society and the types of agents that are creating them, specifically through complementary currencies of which a series of examples will be provided in two later chapters (respectively, Chapter 10 for systems already operational today; and Chapter 12 for proposed systems for the future.

Sustainability of complex flow systems

We now can prove that a structural fault is indeed involved in generating financial crashes. The theoretical breakthrough that backs this claim is the capacity to measure with a single metric the sustainability of complex flow systems, which include natural (among others) ecosystems and economic or financial systems. Understanding and empirical substantiation of this mechanism has arisen from quantitative ecological research. The mathematical demonstration can be found in Appendix A. For those desiring a fully documented step-by-step technical proof of what will be claimed here, please refer to the seminal paper (Ulanowicz *et al.* 2009). The most relevant points are summarized hereafter.

A recent and surprising insight from systems ecology is that sustainability is at least as much about 'what is not' as about 'what is'. How can this be? Conventional science investigates what is apparent – the things that are present in our world; it ignores or understates the absence of things. This seems hardly surprising and, on the face of it, of no consequence. Even if absence can make the heart grow fonder, this surely has nothing to do with the real world. Or does it?

Information is any 'difference that makes the difference' (Gregory Bateson) and, as the binary logic of the digital age has popularized, such difference almost always involves the absence of something. In coming to terms with the working of whole systems, information theory (IT) is a means for apprehending and quantifying what is missing. The key point is that if one is to address the issue of sustainability, then the inchoate, undetermined 'potentiality' of a system also becomes an indispensable focus of inquiry, because it is the source of the resilience that allows the system to persist (Conrad 1983).

What IT tells us is that a system's capacity to undergo change (H) has two components: order and the absence of order ($H = X + \psi$). The first component, called 'mutual constraint', quantifies all that is regular, orderly, coherent and efficient. It encompasses basically all the concerns of conventional science. This X, is an analogue of Newton's Third Law of motion, or of the Chinese *Yang* construct. By contrast, the second component (ψ) represents the lack of those same attributes, or the irregular, disorderly, incoherent and inefficient potential behaviours that have escaped the scrutiny of science mainly because they cannot easily be described, and even less readily repeated or measured, or all of the above. It corresponds to the Chinese *Yin*.

In the jargon of IT, this second, overlooked component of system change ψ is called 'conditional entropy'; it can also be thought of as uncommitted potential. Critically what this says is that the very absence of order (even if its potential is never activated, and therefore unnoticed and unmeasured) plays the key role for a system to persist over the long run, to adapt to changing environment, or survive unexpected challenges. We know this intuitively and also from our experience of day-to-day living, exemplified in the familiar expressions 'laid-back', 'I can cope with that' and 'slack in the system'; but we rarely recognize it in our collective affairs, much less acknowledge its importance for sustainability. I will next show why this happens to be even more significant than the first variable, order, if we are to understand sustainability.

Separately, order (mutual constraint) and disorder (conditional entropy) tell us nothing about the vitality of a system. Is it healthily working, furiously spreading a cancer, moribund or even dead? When scaled by the activity of the system – quantified as its total system throughput (TST) – the property of mutual constraint converts into the measure of a system's 'throughput efficiency'[5] (A), so-called because it measures the capacity of a system to process volumes of whatever that particular system deals with (e.g. biomass in an ecosystem, electrons in an electrical distribution system, or money in an economy). On the other hand, scaled conditional entropy becomes a measure of a system's resilience (Φ), because it captures the capacity of a system to change and adapt. Thus the total capacity for system development (C) can be expressed as both order and disorder, or $C = A + \Phi$ (Ulanowicz *et al.* 1996).

A living system adapts in homeostatic fashion to buffer performance by expending what Odum called 'reserves' (Odum 1953). The reserve in this case is not some palpable storage, like a cache of some material resource. Rather, this second variable Φ is a characteristic of the system structure that reflects its flexibility both to survive change and to adapt to new circumstances – and it usually requires some loss of efficient performance (Ulanowicz 2009). Systems that endure – that is, are sustainable – lie in dynamic balance somewhere between these two poles of order and disorder, efficient performance and adaptive resilience.

We now have the basic elements for a more complete description of complex living systems. That it possesses throughput efficiency (A) means that the system is capable of exercising sufficient directed power to maintain its integrity and growth over time. Autocatalysis plays a key role among those processes: autocatalysis is a type of self-perpetuating (positive) feedback process capable of exerting a centripetal pull upon materials and energy, drawing more and more resources into its orbit.

So crucially, as we have seen, throughput efficiency is definitely not sufficient for sustainability. Also necessary is that it possesses a resilience, Φ, of undefined and contingent responsiveness to the unpredictable challenges thrown up by its own workings and its environment. It is thanks to this Φ that a resilient ecosystem can withstand shocks and adapt itself when necessary.

A Chinese insight

> *'When Yang and Yin combine, all things achieve harmony.'*
>
> Lao Tzu[6]

This dialectic between efficiency and resilience is the 'go and get' and the 'let go and give' of life. In the Chinese philosophical tradition, respectively *yang* and *yin*, characteristics were assigned to all natural systems.

In short, to our knowledge for the first time, Western science is able to encompass in a quantitative way the validity and depth of this yin-yang insight. So let us give credit where it is due.

These concepts, always combined as *Yin-Yang,* as necessary complements to each other, have a history of several thousands years, with its origins traced back to the *Yi Jing* (the *Book of Changes),* attributed to King Wen of Zhou (1099–1050 BC). The explicit *Weltanschauung* in Chinese philosophy is precisely the necessity of an appropriate balance between *Yang* and *Yin* energies, in all aspects of nature and life.

C. G. Jung was one of the first to express regret that our Western culture is not more familiar with this concept: 'Unfortunately, our Western mind, lacking all culture in this respect, has never yet devised a concept, nor even a name, for the "union of opposites through the middle path", that most fundamental item of inward experience, which could respectably be set against the Chinese concept of Tao.'[7]

If we are using the Yin-Yang vocabulary, at the risk of appearing exotic, it is simply because we don't have precise equivalent words in our Western languages.

Oriental philosophers have developed an infinite number of ways to describe the Yin-Yang relationship and polarity. The following figure offers those selected as most relevant for our purpose.

Figure 2.1 Yin-Yang Coherences and Polarities

This figure can be read vertically, emphasizing the internal coherences. Or it can be read horizontally, emphasizing the polarity between them. One advantage in using the Yin-Yang vocabulary is that Taoists never separate such polarities. They emphasize the connection between them – their *complementarity*. In clear: both are indispensable!

The Yin-Yang ways of looking at reality are not competing ways to relate and interpret reality, not more than your right eye competes with the left one. Instead, because of their differences, together they provide you with range and depth of vision, something which neither one can do by itself.

For the past millennia, all patriarchal societies have tended to impart legitimacy to the vision contributed by only the male half of its 'eyes'. We have thereby projected a hierarchical duality on concepts such as activity/passivity, creative/receptive, culture/nature, mind/senses, spirit/matter; invariably claiming the former to be somehow 'better' than the latter. What matters here is not to deny the qualities inherent in the masculine viewpoint, but to empower the feminine to an equal level. A shift in consciousness towards giving equal emphasis on both views is about more than fairness; it may be the key to provide a synergistic impulse towards the sustainability of our species.

'The feminine and the masculine are not objects, not things, not simply biological bodies we are attempting to unite, but rather complex, archetypal organizations of consciousness...What is needed is a recognition of the synergy between these polar opposites. Synergy is evident everywhere in nature, and is an important source of causation in the ongoing evolutionary process. Since the relationship between male and female is fundamentally synergistic, it is essential that we rethink and recreate our cultural and symbolic understanding of the feminine and its relationship to the masculine to increase the possibility that the human species will co-create an evolutionary change that is advantageous to the entire biosphere. If we do not, we are in danger of bringing about our own extinction.'[8]

Not surprisingly, in all patriarchal societies a Yang bias is accepted as normal, and when applied in the scientific domain positivism is its natural predisposition.

In contrast, the poet John Keats coined the term 'negative capability' for the often overlooked *yin* trait of human personality and experience: the capacity to hold uncertainty without angst – the capacity to live with the unknown as an ally rather than something to be eliminated. Such 'undecideness' is not hesitant fence-sitting, indifference or laziness; nor is it a skill in the usual sense of the word, although it can be cultivated. It is more like a connection to an undifferentiated ground that resists form, which continually invokes questions and reflection and is potentially multi-dimensional, a space of "both-and" and *neti-neti*, the Hindu concept literally meaning 'neither this, nor that'.

In summary, natural ecosystems exist because they have *both* sufficient self-directed identity *and* flexibility to change. The polarities necessitate each other in an appropriate balance in harmonious complementarity. Over time nature must have solved many of the structural problems in ecosystems (otherwise, these ecosystems simply wouldn't still exist today). They are our best living examples of large scale sustainability in action.

Empirical evidence

Moving beyond information theory, ecologists have measured the transfer of biomass and energy ('trophic exchanges') within ecosystems. For example, using a web-like network approach, they have estimated the magnitude of carbon transfers within a freshwater cypress wetland community leading from prawns to the American alligator via three intermediate predators: turtles, large fish, and snakes (Ulanowicz *et al.* 1996); or estimated the trophic (nutritional) transfers of energy in the Cone Spring community, a small freshwater ecosystem comprising primary producers (algae and higher plants), detritus, bacteria, detritivores (annelids and molluscs) and carnivores (insects) (Tilly 1968).

Ecologists have also found ways to derive values for an ecosystem's throughput efficiency and resilience by estimating network size and network connectedness in terms of two variables: (1) node-to-node pathway steps (n, which gauges the effective number of trophic levels in the system and is directly related to throughput efficiency and (2) links per node (c, which measures the effective connectivity of the system in terms of links per node which is directly related to resilience).[9] It turns out that there is a specific zone of optimal robustness, into which all observed natural ecosystems fall. This zone has been named the 'window of viability' in ecological literature the 'window of vitality').[10]

The key conclusion is that nature does not select for maximum efficiency, but for a balance between the two opposing poles of efficiency and resilience. Because both are indispensable for long-term sustainability and health, the healthiest flow systems are those that are closest to an optimal balance between these two opposing pulls. Conversely, an excess of either attribute leads to systemic instability. Too much efficiency leads to brittleness and too much resilience leads to stagnation: the former is caused by too little diversity and connectivity and the latter by too much diversity and connectivity.

Sustainability of a complex flow system can therefore be defined as the optimal balance between efficiency and resilience of its network. With these distinctions we are able to define and precisely quantify a complex system's sustainability in a single metric. However, the object of our interest involves in reality four dimensions, and is therefore hard to visualize mentally or graphically. What we can show here is a simplified graph that provides a conceptually valid illustration, as shown in Figure 2.2.

Observe that there is an asymmetry: in natural ecosystems optimality requires more resilience than efficiency! (The optimal point lies closer to resilience than efficiency on the horizontal axis).

Until recently, total throughput and efficiency have been the only means for us to identify the relative success of a system, whether in nature or in economics. For example, in ecosystems, as in economies, size is generally measured as the total volume of system throughput/

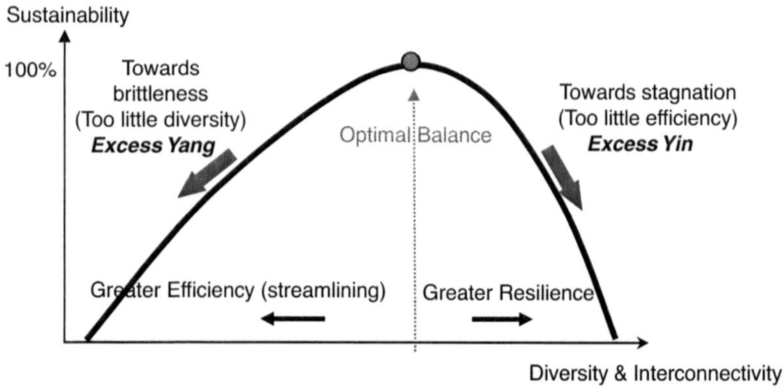

Figure 2.2 The Sustainability Curve: The curve is mapped between the two polarities of efficiency and resilience. Nature selects not for a maximum of efficiency, but for an optimal balance between these two requirements. This fundamental insight is at the core of the Taoist worldview: Chinese philosophy described this as the optimal balance between *Yin-Yang*, with excess *Yin* and excess *Yang* forms of imbalance.

activity. Gross Domestic Product (GDP) measures size this way in economies and Total System Throughput (TST) does so in ecosystems. Many economists urge endless growth in size (GDP) because they assume that growth in size is a sufficient measure of health. GDP and TST, however, are both poor measures of sustainable viability because *they ignore network structure*. They cannot, for example, distinguish between a resilient economy and a bubble that is doomed to burst; or between healthy 'development', as Herman Daly (1997) describes it, or explosive growth in monetary exchanges simply due to runaway speculation.

Now, however, we can distinguish whether a particular increase in throughput and efficiency is a sign of healthy growth or just a relatively short-term bubble that is doomed to collapse.

As explained above, it is also interesting that ecosystems have their most critical parameters within a very specific and narrow range, which can be computed empirically with precision and which we call the 'Window of Viability' (see Figure 2.3).

Application to other complex systems

The question will undoubtedly be raised whether what we learn from ecosystems still makes sense when applied to other systems, such as economic or financial systems.

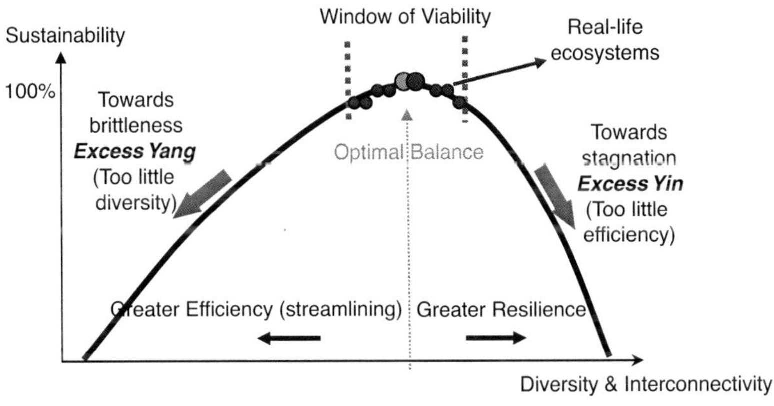

Figure 2.3 The Window of Viability: The window is where all sustainable natural ecosystems operate. Complex natural ecosystems invariably operate within a specific range on each side of the Optimum point.

It is critical to understand that the findings described in natural ecosystems arise from the very *structure of a complex flow system*, and therefore that they remain valid for any complex flow network with a similar structure, regardless of what is being processed in the system: it can be biomass in an ecosystem, information in a biological system, electrons in an electrical power network, or money in an economic system. This is precisely one of the strong points of using a web-like network approach instead of machine-like metaphor.

The fields of engineering, business and economics have all been focusing almost exclusively on efficiency, and therefore constitute a wide-open field to explore the validity of the proposed metrics to improve sustainability. For example, electrical power grids have been systematically optimized for decades towards ever greater technical and economic efficiency. It has come as a surprise to many engineers that, as they have approached higher efficiencies, suddenly large-scale blackouts have been breaking out with a vengeance 'out of nowhere'. For instance, a few decades ago several blackouts hit large areas of the United States and Northern Germany. The data should be available to model these systems as flow networks, because that is what they literally are. One could then quantify their efficiency and resilience, and their Window of Viability. The solution on how to rebalance such a system to make it less brittle, and to determine its optimal sustainability, would be an obvious 'hard science' test application of the concepts and metrics described here.

The point being made here is truly profound and has wide-reaching implications for all complex systems, natural or human-made. Placing too much emphasis on efficiency tends to automatically maximize flows, size and consolidation at the expense of choice, connectivity and resilience until the entire system becomes unstable and collapses.

Application to financial and monetary systems

Applying the above complex flow framework to financial and monetary systems, we can predict that excessive focus on efficiency would tend to create exactly the kind of bubble economy which we have been able to observe repeatedly in every boom and bust cycle in history, including the biggest bust of them all, the one that we are experiencing today.

If we view economies as flow systems, this ties directly into money's primary function as medium of exchange. In this view, money is to the real economy like biomass in an ecosystem: it is an essential vehicle for catalysing processes, allocating resources, and generally allowing the exchange system to work as a synergetic whole. The connection to structure is immediately apparent. In economies, as in ecosystems and living organisms, the health of the whole depends heavily on the structure by which the catalysing medium, in this case, money, circulates among businesses and individuals. Money must continue to circulate in sufficiency to all corners of the whole because poor circulation will strangle either the supply side or the demand side of the economy, or both.

Our global monetary system is itself an obvious flow network structure, in which monopolistic national currencies flow within each country (or group of countries in the case of the Euro), and interconnect on a global level. The technical justification for enforcing a monopoly of a single currency within each country is to optimize the efficiency of price formation and exchanges in national markets. Tight regulations are in place in every country to maintain these monopolies. Banking institutional regulations further ensure that banks tend to be carbon copies of each other both in terms of their structure and behaviour. This was demonstrated among the world's bigger banks, most recently and with a vengeance, with the simultaneous crisis in 2008.

Furthermore, in a seminal 1953 paper, Milton Friedman proposed that letting markets determine the value of each national currency would further improve the overall efficiency of the global monetary system (Friedman 1953). This idea was actually implemented by

President Nixon in 1971, to avoid a run on the dollar at that time. Since then, an extraordinarily efficient and sophisticated global communications infrastructure has been built to link and trade these national currencies. The trading volume in the foreign exchange markets reached an impressive \$3.2 trillion *per day* in 2007, to which another daily \$2.1 trillion of currency derivatives should be added (BIS 2008). Over 95% of that trading volume is speculative, and less than 5% is in fact used for actual international trade of goods and services.

Speculation can play a positive role in any market: theory and practice show that it can improve market efficiency by increasing liquidity and depth[11] in the market. But current speculative levels are clearly out of balance. Although over half-a-century old, John Maynard Keynes' opinion has never been as appropriate as it is today. 'Speculators may do no harm as bubbles on a steady stream of enterprise. But the position is serious when enterprise becomes the bubble on a whirlpool of speculation. When the capital development of a country becomes a by-product of the activities of a casino, the job is likely to be ill-done.' (Keynes 1936, p.159)

Nobody questions the efficiency of these huge markets; but their lack of resilience has also been amply demonstrated, for instance during the Asian crisis of the late 1990s, and dozens of other monetary crashes. In short, our global network of monopolistic national moneys has evolved into an overly efficient and dangerously brittle system. This system's lack of resilience shows up not in the technical field of the computer networks (which all have backups), but in the financial realm. Such a crisis, particularly a combined monetary and banking crash, is arguably – other than war – the worst thing that can happen to a country.

Even more ironically, whenever a banking crisis unfolds, governments invariably help the larger banks to absorb the smaller ones, believing that the efficiency of the system is thereby further increased. When a failing bank has proven to be 'too big to fail', why not consider the option to break it up into smaller units that can be made to compete with each other? This was done in the US, for instance, with the breakup of the Bell telephone monopoly into competing 'Baby Bells'. Instead, what tends to be done is to make banks that are "too big to fail" into still bigger ones, until they become 'too big to bail'. This whole process is illustrated in Figure 2.4.[12]

Similarly, the substance that circulates in our global economic network – money – is also maintained as a monopoly of a single type of currency – bank-debt money, created with interest. Imagine a planetary ecosystem

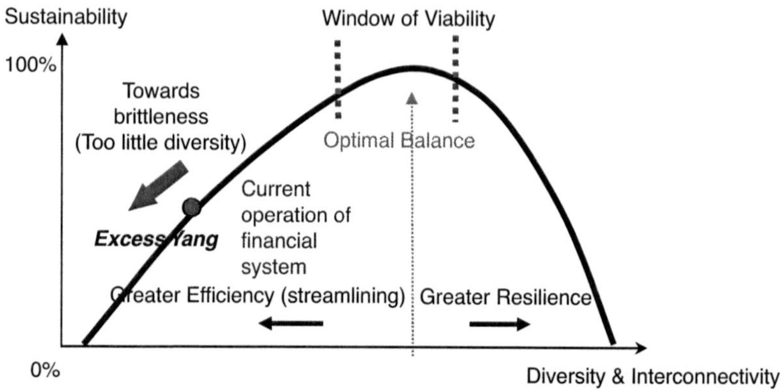

Figure 2.4 The Monetary Eco-System: Today's global monetary ecosystem is significantly overshooting the optimal balance – the Window of Viability – because of its exclusive emphasis on efficiency. It is careening toward brittleness and collapse because a general belief prevails that all improvements need to go further in that the same direction (thick downward arrow) of increasing growth and efficiency. For instance, the global monoculture of bank-debt money as legal tender is technically justified on the basis of efficiency of price formation and exchanges within each country. Internationally, floating exchanges were also justified because they are 'more efficient'. This is part and parcel of how we are building up an 'Excess Yang' deviation.

where only one single type of plant or animal is tolerated and artificially maintained, and where any manifestation of diversity is eradicated as an inappropriate 'competitor' because it would reduce the efficiency of the whole.

An overly efficient system as the one described in Figure 2.4 is 'an accident waiting to happen', condemned to a sudden crash and collapse however many competent people dedicate time and heroic efforts to try to manage it. After a collapse, in both natural ecosystems and in monetary systems, the same process takes over. Let us take as example the most extreme cases of total meltdown: Real life cases: a massive fire burns a forest down to ashes, or a complete meltdown of a financial system. In the monetary domain this happened in Germany in 1923 and again at the end of World War II, the United States during the Great Depression, or in Argentina in 1999–2002. Such a total failure means that sustainability has dropped to close to 0%. A dollar crash could make it part of our immediate future.

The first step towards recovery is an extreme fragmentation without much collaboration. In a forest, this takes the form of seedlings of any type struggling for survival. In a financial system, this would take the form of a return to primitive barter: survival exchanges without any standardization or organization. This stage can be seen at the extreme as each person having his or her own commodity currencies. The next step is the emergence of a multitude of organizations, that start to introduce some standards and some agreements on dates and places where the exchanges take place. In Argentina this took the form of the multiplication of local exchange mechanisms, under the names of '*ruedes de trueque*' in which *creditos* were exchanged in organized markets. Assuming that the designs of these systems were sound (which wasn't the case in Argentina), then the better systems would tend to emerge as winners, reshape more efficient exchange systems, and rebuild a more diversified and more interconnected economy.

Graphically, this whole process is illustrated in the next illustration (Figure 2.5).

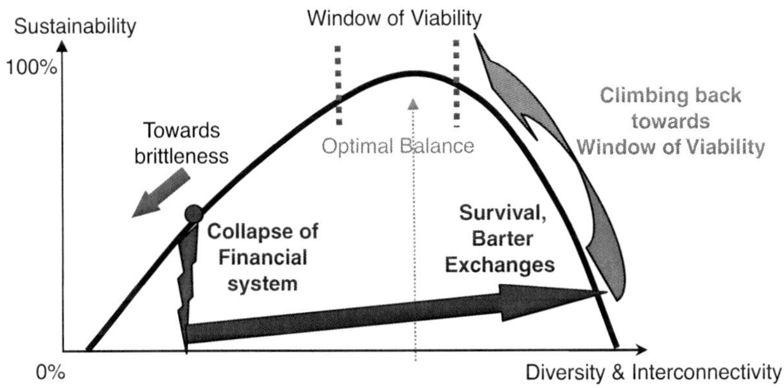

Figure 2.5 The Lack of Currency Diversity: The dynamics of an artificially enforced monoculture of currencies and banks in a complex system where efficiency is the only criterion considered relevant. The only possible outcome is systemic financial collapse. The way an economy recovers from such a collapse is first survival exchanges, at the limit down to primitive barter. Followed by a re-emergence of gradually more efficient systems, until we are back into the 'window of viability'.

In practice, however, what tends to happen is that as soon as possible, the monetary orthodoxy of a monopoly of bank debt money as the only medium of exchange is re-established back with a vengeance. This took the form in Germany in the 1920s, and in the US in the 1930s, of the outlawing on any 'emergency currencies'; or in Argentina through the massive falsification of *credito* paper currency. What we now know is that a monoculture is not a sustainable structure, so we are overshooting the window of sustainability, and get back on the next cycle of pushing for more efficiency within a monoculture environment, which will lead to the next crash.

This process is illustrated in Figure 2.6.

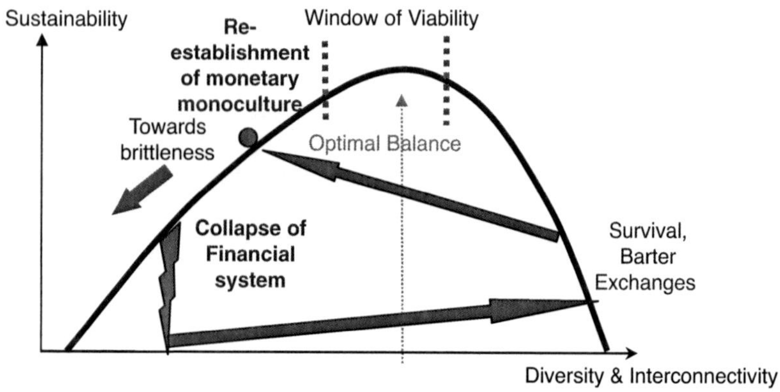

Figure 2.6 Monetary Monopoly: Under the pressure of the monetary orthodoxy, the monopoly of bank-debt money as medium of exchange is re-established. The pressures towards more efficiency in such a monoculture will invariably tend to push the system to its next crisis.

As stated earlier, nature has over billions of years selected the conditions under which complex ecosystems are sustainable, otherwise they wouldn't exist today. In contrast, humanity still struggles with the issue of how to create sustainable economies. We know that the theoretical framework applies to both natural and man-made complex systems. Has the time not come to learn in this domain from nature?

A structural monetary solution

A full inventory of the options on how to deal with a systemic banking crisis has been explained in another paper (Lietaer *et al.* 2009). Here we will focus only on the solution which aims at increasing structurally the resilience of the monetary system, even if at first sight that may be less efficient.

Conventional economic thinking assumes the *de facto* monopolies of national moneys as an unquestionable given. The logical lesson from nature is that systemic monetary sustainability requires a diversity of currency systems, so that multiple and more diverse agents and channels of monetary links and exchanges can emerge.

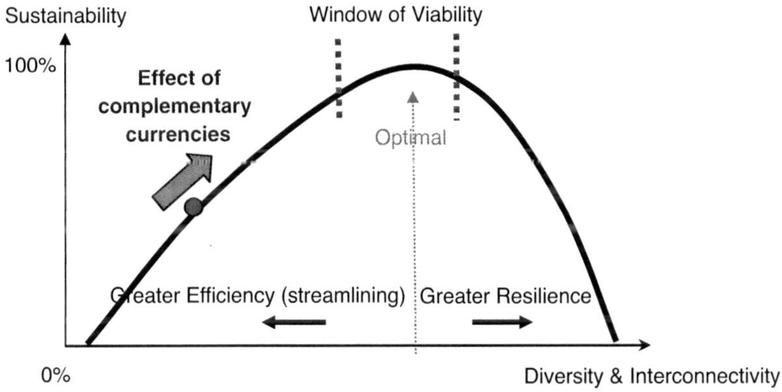

Figure 2.7 The Effect of Diverse Complementary Currencies
The operation of complementary currencies of diverse types enables the economy to flow back towards greater sustainability (thick upward arrow). While this process clearly reduces efficiency, which is the price to pay for increased resilience of the whole. Complementary currencies facilitate transactions that otherwise wouldn't occur, linking otherwise unused resources to unmet needs, and encouraging diversity and interconnections that otherwise wouldn't exist.

There is another way to get back towards the window of vitality than waiting for a total crash. That other way is to let complementary currency system grow, or even encourage the soundest of them to blossom, and gradually and gently push back the excesses of the monoculture, as seen in Figure 2.7.

This is the practical lesson from nature: allow several *types* of currencies to circulate among people and businesses to facilitate their exchanges, through the implementation of complementary currencies. Let us start by defining a currency as whatever a community is accepting as medium of exchange. A complementary currency is therefore any standardized instrument, other than national money, that is actually used in exchanges. These different types of currencies are called 'complementary' because they are designed to operate in parallel with, as complements to, conventional national monies.

What is most surprising and interesting is that, below the radar beams of officialdom and most academics, there has been a spontaneous emergence over the past decades of precisely the kind of instruments that would be relevant to correct the problem of currency monopoly. Notice that if the problem is the monopoly of one type of currency; replacing one monopoly with another isn't the solution. Monetary reforms which aim at substituting one monopoly by another would therefore be insufficient.

The very idea of allowing different types of currencies to co-exist will certainly appear shockingly unorthodox to conventional monetary thinking, but in fact there are already hundreds of thousands. By far the most common are commercial complementary currencies, such as Airline Miles, or the many thousands of other loyalty currencies issued by companies, chains and individual shops at different scales around the world. They have demonstrated that people are willing to change behaviour (e.g. return to the same vendor) in order to obtain and use them. If that weren't true, businesses wouldn't continue to issue them.

However, the more interesting behaviour changes can be found in the so-called social purpose complementary currencies. They are much less common than the commercial loyalty systems, but they have grown in number to total several thousand in a dozen countries.

Just in the social domain, a wide variety of complementary currencies have become operational, as shown in the following graph. Such

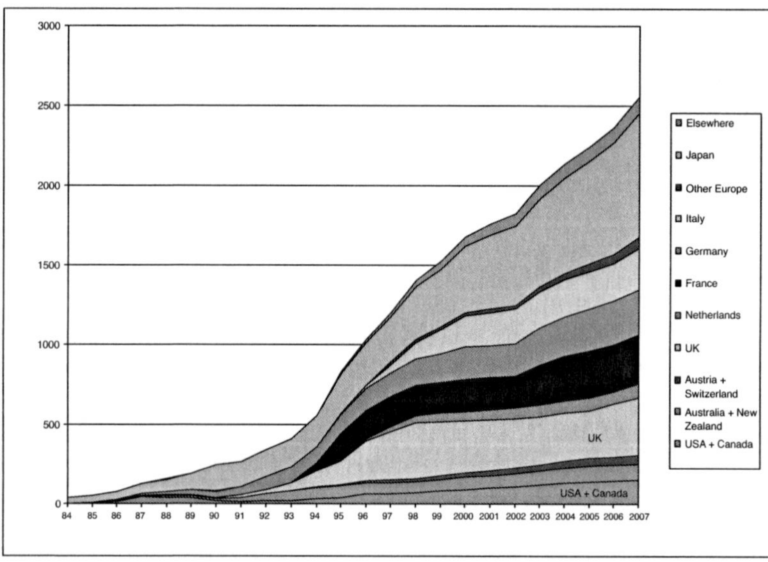

Figure 2.8 Number of Social Purpose Complementary Currencies Operational in a Dozen Countries (1984–2007)
These estimates are purposely very conservative. They include only systems that were operational during the corresponding year and whose existence was verified by one of the authors through the net or in personal contact. Many more systems exist that don't feel the need to advertise their existence.

systems have been described extensively (Lietaer 2001; Greco 2003; Kent 2005) and the *Journal of Community Currency Research* a specialized peer-reviewed journal has emerged to track academic research in this burgeoning field (see www.uea.ac.uk/env/ijccr/)

All this research has documented that people have significantly different attitudes towards different types of currencies. Even more importantly, it has proven that behaviour change can be generated systematically when incentive schemes are designed involving specialized currencies circulating in parallel with the flow of conventional national money. Evidence has accumulated in dozens of countries that complementary currency systems can be designed, for instance, to successfully improve solidarity among neighbours; to support cooperation rather than competition in a community; to encourage intergenerational elderly care; or to induce a consumer life-style that reduces carbon emissions.

As Edgar Cahn's work in Time Dollars demonstrates (reviewed in Chapter 10), whenever complementary currencies begin flowing through a community, there is an increase in the degree of diversity and interconnectivity in the system. This is due to the ability of complementary currencies to catalyse business processes and individual efforts that are too small or inefficient to compete for national currencies in a global market place (Cahn 2004).

In short, both in the commercial and the social domains, the monopoly of conventional money as medium of exchange has already technically died without most people taking notice. But most of this has been happening on too marginal a scale to make policy makers aware of the potential of such tools to address the huge breakdowns that we know we will have to face in the 21st century.

Most of those systems are too small and/or too recent for us to be able to empirically measure their macro-economic impact. One important exception is the WIR, which has been operational since 1934, involves today about 70,000 Swiss businesses, and has an annual volume of about US$2 billion (Studer 1998). It will be examined in detail in Chapter 10. Because of its 75 year history and the quality of the data gathered over this time, the stabilization effect of this system on the mainstream economy has been able to be proven quantitatively (Stodder 1998, 2000, 2009). Exactly as our theoretical framework would forecast, the Stodder studies empirically demonstrate that the WIR system spontaneously behaves counter-cyclically with the mainstream economy, and thereby helps rather than hinders the efforts of the central bank to stabilize the economy. However, both conventional monetary theory and central banking practice still consider such 'unorthodox' commercial currency systems as either irrelevant as long as they remain small; or as a nuisance that could perturb monetary policy if they were to grow to any significant size (Rösl 2006).

Application to economic theory

The issue of diversity matters not only in types of money, but also in economic agents. Too little diversity, or too much, can precipitate instability. For example, a town that has but one very large employer will find it harder to adapt if that company goes under, than a town with several medium-sized employers and many more small ones.

Theoretical ecology has shown us that the dynamic balance between an efficient (streamlined, compact) network and a resilient network (looser, more diverse, with redundant pathways) provides a measure of sustainability for any complex flow system. It provides a single metric of overall system health, which reflects how efficiently the network circulates materials and energy throughout the system, while simultaneously staying resilient enough to survive normal vicissitudes and flexible enough to adapt, develop and evolve. More efficient performance implies less latent potential, and a rather fixed structure with little scope to innovate and adapt when challenged by novel disturbances. At the other extreme, a system with too much slack and diversity may possess ample buffers, but lack the coherence and purpose to grow. Somewhere in between these extremes lies healthy sustainable development.

Current economic theory fails to differentiate healthy development from cancerous growth. Policies that promote positive-feedback growth in an economy may result in a wealth-concentrating vortex that breeds brittleness and bubbles in the same process.

The most recent banking/financial crisis shows how this works in practice. It was initially precipitated by the mortgage derivative bubble, the latest of several previous bubbles in a supersaturated, force-fed economy. Deregulated bankers in search of new sources of income, stockbrokers in search of hot new products to sell, and big financial investors in search of higher gains, formed a self-amplifying circuit in which gains in any segment naturally fed gains in the others. This autocatalytic loop grew rapidly by pulling in resources from the broader economic network and concentrating wealth in the hub. The result in the major economies was that, during the two decades leading up to the crash of 2008, profits in the financial sector roughly doubled as a percent of total corporate profits. It also evolved ever more efficient (if dangerous) 'pull' techniques and a kind of rigid group-think that dismissed traditional risk assessments precisely because selection pressures were intense, with those who increased gains being lavishly rewarded, and those who didn't being out of a job. While the derivative bubble triggered the crisis, the erosion of other sectors created an underlying brittleness (from debt burden, for instance) that made the broader economy susceptible along with the epicentre banking/financial circuit as well (Goerner *et al.* 2009).

Hence the mantra of forever increasing efficiency has become misguided and counterproductive. The quest for greater economic efficiency, for example by downsizing or by 'just in time' deliveries or other ways to continually increase the efficiency of value chains, has reduced the stability of the overall economic system. This phenomenon of autocatalysis can also precipitate system collapse through implosion. Examples are the dot.com bubble and the hollowing-out of small town high streets and urban neighborhoods by 'big-box' retailers (Goerner *et al.* 2009).

The message is we must rebalance. We now have scientific proof of why a single-minded push for greater efficiency will predictably generate systemic inflexibility to the point of brittleness and failure. Equally, policies that only tweak at the edges of a senescent system do not address the structural flaws of the current system. We must understand, cultivate and nurture the complex and adaptive components of our economic system. The end of the Industrial Era is coinciding with a convergence of an unprecedented series of challenges. Global issues such as climate change, energy and resource supply squeezes, rising underemployment and a rapidly aging population come to mind. The expectation with the dawning of an Information Age is that just about everything will change in our society, but with one critical exception; that is, we are supposed to meet those challenges with the monetary tools that were designed several centuries ago: a monopoly of bank-debt money.

Policy implications

Ironically, our financial system is so fragile because it has become too efficient. Our modern monetary system is based on a monoculture of a single type of money (all our national currencies have in common to be generated as bank-debt money). This monoculture is legally imposed in the name of market efficiency. Furthermore, governments enforce this monopoly by requiring that all taxes be paid exclusively in this particular type of currency.

Unlike natural systems ('you cannot negotiate with a living cell ...'), economic systems are completely manageable because we built them. But 'manageable changes' like new regulations, or changed personnel at the top of our financial institutions, will at best only reduce the frequency of the crashes, not eliminate them. This doesn't mean that managerial changes are not justified, useful or even necessary; but we claim that whatever is done at that level will, in the end, reveal itself to be insufficient.

This is *not* a management problem, it's a *structural* problem. So, the good news is that the repeated financial and monetary crises are avoidable. However, that will happen if, and only if, we are willing to revisit the structure of our money system. Specifically, different types of currencies issued by different types of institutions would provide the diversity and the higher interconnectivity that a resilient financial system would require.

Economists have long recognized, usually for ethical reasons, the need to factor in 'externalities' that serve to brake the effects of the market, that remains otherwise blind to anything but efficiency. In our model such brakes become necessary internal elements of the system – not an artificial externality. Furthermore, the study of 'input-output' networks has been out of fashion for several decades. Perhaps this exercise will motivate a few to dust off some of the large data sets of cash flows in input-output networks in an effort to scope out the dimensions of the economic counterpart to ecology's window of vitality. This could provide a relatively easy way to test how the concepts proposed here play out specifically in economics.

In any case, making the monetary system sustainable will require a new balance between efficiency and resilience in economics, in a way similar to what occurs naturally in ecosystems. Humanity has become, involuntarily and reluctantly, the steward of this planet's biosphere. Ultimately, we have no choice but to learn how to make our global civilization sustainable, or it will cease to exist.

Next steps?

Possibly the most urgently critical economic application of the findings presented here should be in the monetary domain. The technical justification for monopolies of national currencies is to optimize the efficiency of the price formation and exchanges in national markets. During the past few decades an extraordinarily sophisticated and efficient global communication infrastructure has been built on top of that national level, to link and trade these currencies internationally. The trading volume in the foreign exchange markets has reached an impressive 3.2 trillion dollar *per day* in 2008, to which another daily 2 trillion dollars of currency derivatives should be added (BIS 2008). Nobody questions the efficiency of these markets. However, this system's lack of resilience (not technical, but financial) has also been demonstrated spectacularly.

All the evidence points out that the monopolistic national moneys have evolved into an overly efficient and dangerously brittle system. The solution towards monetary sustainability will be a surprise for conventional economic thinking which invariably assumes monopolies for national monies as an unquestionable given. Monetary sustainability will require a diversity of currency systems, so that multiple and more diverse channels of monetary links and exchanges can emerge. Complementary currencies currently already operational at the margin of the official system today play such a role on a small scale, and they potentially could contribute to sustaining the global economic system tomorrow if they are allowed to grow to a scale necessary for them to make a difference.

The most valuable role for government in implementing the approach proposed here could limit itself to specifying the kind of currency other than conventional bank-debt national money it would accept in payment of fees and taxes. Interestingly, Uruguay has been the first country to follow precisely such a strategy by accepting an electronic business-to-business generated currency called C3 (for Commercial Credit Circuit) for all payments of fees and taxes, in addition to the conventional national money. Their reasoning: it is a very effective way to increase employment through the small and medium-sized enterprises (which represent over 90% of private employment in that country), because it provides working capital to the participating businesses without costing anything to the government. A bank plays the role of converting the C3 units into national currency when requested, at a cost borne by the participating business making that request. More information about this example, and other complementary currencies already operational today, will be provided in Chapter 10.

So why this approach not already generalized? The answer is that the prevailing monetary paradigm is suffering from a general, and institutionalized, blind spot.

The biggest obstacle: A monetary blind spot?

The human eye has a biological blind spot, i.e. the spot where the optical nerve enters the eyeball corresponds to an area where we literally can't see anything. The way that money enters the economy and our social system seems to suffer from a similar blind spot. There are four layers to this phenomenon. They are respectively: the patriarchal value coherence; the capitalist *vs.* communist ideological war; an institutionalized *status quo*; and finally an academic taboo. Here, we will only briefly summarize each of these layers.

Patriarchal value coherence

All patriarchal societies in history have had the tendency to impose a monopoly of a single currency, hierarchically issued, naturally scarce or artificially kept scarce, and with positive interest rates. This was for instance the case in Sumer and Babylon, in Greece and Rome, and from the Renaissance onwards in Western societies all the way to today. The form of these currencies has varied widely, ranging from standardized commodities, precious metals, paper or electronic bits. But what they all have in common is that governments accepted only that specific currency for payment of taxes, that this currency could be stored and accumulated, and that borrowing such currencies implied payment of interest. They all have in common Yang characteristics as illustrated in Figure 2.1.

In contrast, matrifocal societies have tended to use a dual currency system: one currency (typically identical to the surrounding patriarchal societies) for trading long distance with people one doesn't know; and a second type of currency for exchanges within one's own local community. This second type of currency, with Yin characteristics, was usually created locally (often by the users themselves); was issued in sufficiency; and didn't have interest. In the most sophisticated cases, this currency even had a demurrage fee – a negative interest equivalent to a parking fee on money –, which would discourage its accumulation. In short, it would be used as a pure medium of exchange, not as a store of value. This was the case, for instance, with the corn-backed currencies that lasted for well over a millennium in Dynastic Egypt that was one of the secrets of the wealth of that ancient society (Preisigke 1910; Lietaer 2000).

Notice that we are talking about 'matrifocal' societies, not matriarchal ones, because there is no evidence that genuine matriarchal societies have actually existed in reality. In a purely matriarchal society, the only role for a male would be procreation. The Amazons are an example of such a society, but they have only existed in the imagination of the Greeks, as no historical or archeological evidence for such an Amazon society has ever shown up. In contrast, matrifocal societies, defined as those where feminine values are honoured, while less frequent than patriarchal ones, *have* existed in various parts of the world. The easiest way to detect them is to look at their vision of the divine.

In a matrifocal society, it is a goddess or goddesses that play the most important roles, such as being a 'Co-Creator' or a 'Savior'. In comparison, in patriarchal societies it is invariably a male god that plays this role; and in monotheistic religions a single male God plays even all the divine roles.

Examples of matrifocal societies include Dynastic Egypt (where Isis was the Savior), or the Central Middle Ages in Western Europe (roughly from the 10th to the 13th century, the period of Courtly Love, also called the Age of Cathedrals which were most frequently dedicated to Our Lady). In both these historical societies, a dual currency system prevailed. Detailed evidence for these claims is provided elsewhere (Lietaer 2000).

Ideological warfare between capitalism and communism

Over more than a century, and particularly since the end of World War II, an intense ideological warfare has been waged worldwide between communism and capitalism. This has affected practically all social and political sciences, including economics. Within each of these ideologies,

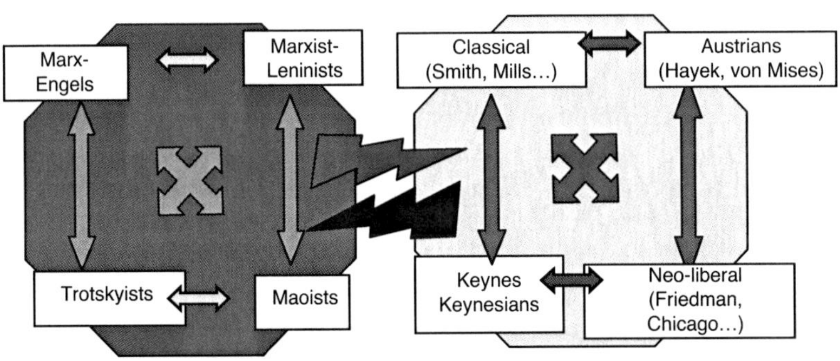

Figure 2.9 Ideological Polarization between Communism and Capitalism

there are even a number of different schools each with their own particular take on the corresponding ideology (see Figure 2.9). There are literally hundreds of thousands of books written about the smallest differences between these ideologies and schools.

However, what they have in common is almost completely overlooked. Specifically, they all consider normal a monopoly of a centralizing currency. Could the reason for this be that both ideologies were at their root two different expressions of industrial age, patriarchal societies?

This ideological split, by bringing the focus on everything *except the money paradigm,* has substantially reinforced the monetary blind spot.

Institutionalized status quo

Increasingly between the mid 17th and the end of the 19th century, a decision was made that the paradigm of a monopoly of a single currency issued through bank debt should be institutionalized. Each country's national bank plays that role, and since Bretton Woods the International Monetary Fund (IMF) and the World Bank have been added to the panoply. All these institutions have important and useful tasks in terms of preserving the integrity of the system. But they also are the guardians of monetary orthodoxy which continues to prevail: the idea that achieving the objective of monetary stability requires the safeguarding of the monopoly of the existing money creation process. This orthodoxy is part of the powerful auto-catalytic forces that engender and protect banks that become 'too big to fail'. As a consequence the orthodox idea – that we need to enforce a monopoly of a single national currency, one in each country or group of countries – remains firmly in place, despite the massive systemic collapse in 2008. Let us please remember that it is also orthodoxy that got us into this trouble.

Let us also express sympathy to financial regulators and policy makers who find themselves in the uncomfortable role of trying to control the defective car sent over a mountain range that was described in the metaphor at the beginning of this paper.

Academic taboo

Challenging a paradigm in any field is always a risky business. In particular, challenging the monetary paradigm can be interpreted as violating an academic taboo. It somehow gets in the way in being invited to the top conferences or getting published in the most prestigious 'peer-reviewed' journals. Let us take as example the most prestigious award of all, the 'Nobel Prize in Economics'. Many people ignore that there is a significant difference between that economics prize and the other five established in 1901: respectively in physics, chemistry, medicine, literature and peace. The Economics prize is the only one that wasn't created by the will of Alfred Nobel, nor is it funded by the Nobel Foundation. Its technical name is the 'Sveriges Riksbank Prize in Economic Sciences in Memory of Alfred Nobel', and it was first awarded in 1969. Its laureates are selected exclusively by the Board of the Swedish central bank, and its funding is coming from the central bank. Is it surprising that none of the 64 Nobel Laureates in economics so far have made the mistake of challenging the monetary paradigm?

Conclusions

The four layers that generate the blind spot in the monetary paradigm reinforce each other to the point of locking us into a pretty tight straightjacket around what is perceived as 'normal' or 'acceptable' in the monetary domain. We should therefore not retain too many illusions that a monetary ecology, involving a variety of different types of currencies, is going to be easily embraced by either academics or policy makers.

One crucially important lesson from any ecology is that it should include systems that can operate at different scales, and involve institutions of different types than banks. Specifically, that could include at one end of the spectrum local currencies such as most of the social currencies represented in Figure 2.4, and which are typically created by local non-profit making groups and destined to remain small-scale. At the other end of the spectrum, it should include a global currency that is nobody's national currency, such as the Terra (described in Chapter 11), which is created by major multinational raw material producers. In between we could have regional Business-to-Business currencies run mainly by Small and Medium-sized enterprises (such as the C3 described in Chapter 10); and today's national currencies operated by the banking system.

Together, these systems would form a diversity of currency types and monetary actors. If such a richer monetary ecosystem were in place, if any component were to get into major trouble, that may still be disturbing. However, other systems would be able to kick in and amortize the resulting shock. Just like what happens in a natural ecosystem: if one type of tree gets wiped out in a forest, others trees and plants will quickly fill in the vacuum, and limit the damage to the forest as a whole.

It should be clear that in such a more diverse financial institutional environment, if a banking crash like the one of 2008 were to occur, it would become more realistic to follow the advice given by Nobel laureate Joseph Stiglitz to the UK government in 2009: let your banking system sink, and build up a new one from scratch.

Five thousand years of monetary history confirm that significant changes in monetary systems don't take place preventively, they occur instead only after the collapse of the previous system. Furthermore, governments learned in the 1930s that they can't let the banking system sink, without risking a collapse of the entire economy. The rescue operations for the institutions that are 'too big to fail', and governmental help for them to absorb their smaller competitors when they get in trouble, lead therefore automatically to further concentration of power into fewer hands. As this chapter has shown, this reduction in diversity is in fact worsening the structural problem that drives the instabilities in the first place.

The trillion-dollar question becomes therefore: how many more banking and monetary crashes do we have to live through before we have the humility to learn from nature in this domain? Could it be that governments may have to learn from the next crisis that they can't afford to save the banking system?

Notes

1 The author wants to thank particularly Robert Ulanowicz, Sally Goerner and Nadia McLaren for their direct or indirect contributions to substantial parts of this chapter. We were all co-authors in an article published under the title 'Is our monetary structure a systemic cause for financial instability? Evidence from Nature' in the special issue about the financial crisis of the *Journal of Future Studies* February–March 2010. Some parts of this paper are repeated in this chapter, with permission from that Journal.
2 Interview of September 8, 2009 on BBC2 http://news.bbc.co.uk/2/hi/8244600.stm
3 First claimed in, *The Romance of Trade*, by HR Fox Bourne Cassell 1876, p.292. Internet archive http://www.archive.org/details/romanceoftrade00bouruoft. However, it is unlikely that the attribution of this quote to Isaac Newton is valid, because we know that Newton himself lost a fortune in the South Sea Bubble.

4 It is sufficient that banks reduce the volume of new credit compared to the previous year to have a serious strangulation effect on the real economy. In other words, any fluctuation in the amount of credit created in a given year (even if the amounts remain positive all the time) is transmitted in an amplified way to the real economy. It is generally (and erroneously) believed that if bank borrowing increases by any amount, that should be sufficient to boost the economy. However, what is important is not the growth or contraction in outstanding debt, but rather the change in the levels of new credit. For instance, in 2008 in the US new borrowing was still 4% of GDP, but that didn't have any positive effect on the economy. The reason is that in 2007 new borrowing was at 15%, and the drop from that level to 4% in 2008 was sufficient to provoke the massive contraction in the economy that was observed in 2008 and 2009.

The silver lining in this phenomenon is that it is also possible to have the economy grow when credit is not. If an economy is deleveraging, then a slowdown in the pace of deleveraging will be sufficient to boost demand growth. Swedish private sector credit, for instance, contracted by 4% in 1994, after having fallen by nearly 20% during the previous year. This slowdown in the rate of deleveraging generated rapid growth, even as the governmental stimulus was reduced.

See Michael Biggs, Thomas Mayer and Andreas Pick 'Credit and Economic Recovery' *DNB working paper* #218/2009 July 2009 available for download on http://www.dnb.nl/binaries/Working%20paper%20218_tcm46-220409.pdf

5 We will abbreviate this variable simply as efficiency. The original ecological literature refers to this variable as 'ascendency'.

6 Mitchell (translator) *Tao Te King* number 42.

7 Jung, C. G. *Collected Works* (translated by R. F. C. Hull) Vol. III, p.203.

8 Dwyer, Molly 'Complexity and the Emergent Feminine: A Cosmological Inquiry into the Role of the Feminine in the Evolution of the Universe' (Winning Paper of the 1999 Vickers Award International Society for the Systems Sciences, Asimolar, CA).

9 Mathematically $n = 2^{A}$ and $c = 2^{\Phi/2}$.

10 The zone of viability is defined on one axis by a measure of path length of between 2 and 5 nodes (with optimum performance at around 3) and on the other by a node/link density of between 1 and 3. The geometric center of the window (n = 3.25 and c = 1.25) suggests the best possible configuration for sustainability under the information currently available. In essence, this says that systems can be either strongly connected across a few links or weakly connected across many links, but configurations of strong connections across many links and weak connections across a few links tend to break up or fall apart, respectively (Zorach and Ulanowicz 2003).

11 'Liquidity' and 'Depth' of a financial market refers to the possibility of moving large volumes of money without significantly affecting prices. In a deep market, a lot of people are buying and selling. By contrast, in a thin market, because fewer people are trading, even one single large transaction could significantly affect prices.

12 We have not yet been able to formally quantify the window of viability of the global monetary system, although such an exercise would be achievable if the data about global flows by currency and institution are available.

However, we are clearly dealing with a monoculture of bank-debt money worldwide. A monoculture is by definition lacking the diversity of any natural ecosystem, and pushes us away from the resilience pole. The institutional pressure on efficiency further pushes in the same direction.

References

Bank of International Settlements (BIS) (2008) *Triennial Central Bank Survey of Foreign Exchange and Derivatives Market Activity 2008 – Final Results.* Washington, DC.

Cahn, E. (2004) *No More Throw Away People*. Washington, DC: Essential Books.

Caprio, G. Jr and Klingebiel, D. (1996) *Bank Insolvencies: Cross Country Experience.* Policy Research Working Papers No.1620. Washington, DC: World Bank, Policy and Research Department.

Conrad, M. (1983) *Adaptability: The Significance of Variability from Molecule to Ecosystem*. New York: Plenum Press.

Daly, H. E. (1997) *Beyond Growth: The Economics of Sustainable Development.* Boston: Beacon Press.

Friedman, M. (1953) 'The Case for Flexible Exchange Rates', in *Essays in Positive Economics*, pp.157–203. Chicago: University of Chicago Press.

Goerner, S. J., Lietaer, B. and Ulanowicz, R. E. (2009) 'Quantifying Economic Sustainability: Implications for Free Enterprise Theory, Policy and Practice', *Ecological Economics*, 69(1), pp.76–81.

Greco, T. (2003) *Money: Understanding and Creating Alternatives to Legal Tender.* Vermont: Chelsea Green Publishing.

Kent, D. (2005) *Healthy Money, Healthy Planet: Developing Sustainability through New Money Systems*. New Zealand: Craig Potton Publishing.

Keynes, J. M. (1936) *The General Theory of Employment, Interest and Money*, p.159. London: Macmillan.

Kindleberger, C. P. (1978) *Manias, Panics and Crashes* (3rd edn). New York: Wiley & Sons.

Lietaer, B. (2000) *Mysterium Geld: Emotionale Bedeutung und Wirkungsweise eines Tabus*. Munich: Riemann Verlag.

Lietaer, B. (2001) *The Future of Money*. London: Century.

Lietaer, B., Ulanowicz, R. E. and Goerner, S. J. (2009) 'Options for Managing a Systemic Bank Crisis', *Sapiens*, 2(1). Available online at http://sapiens.revues.org/index747.html.

Odum, E. P. (1953) *Fundamentals of Ecology*. Philadelphia: Saunders.

Preisigke, F. (1910) *Girowesen im griechischen Ägypten enthaltend Korngiro, Geldgiro, Girobanknotariat mit Einschluss des Archivwesens*. Strassburg.

Rösl, G. (2006) *Regional Currencies in Germany: Local Competition for the Euro?*. Discussion Paper, Series 1: Economic Studies, No. 43/2006, Deutsche Bundesbank Eurosystem. Available for download at http://www.bundesbank.de/download/ volkswirtschaft/dkp/2006/200643dkp_en.pdf

Schumpeter, J. (1942) *Capitalism, Socialism, and Democracy*. New York: Harper and Row.

Stodder, J. (1998) 'Corporate Barter and Economic Stabilization', *International Journal of Community Currency Research*, 2.

Stodder, J. (2000) 'Reciprocal Exchange Networks: Implications for Macroeconomic Stability', in Conference Proceedings, International Electronic and Electrical Engineering (IEEE), Engineering Management Society (EMS), Albuquerque, New Mexico. Available for download at http://www.appropriate-economics.org/materials/reciprocal_exchange_networks.pdf. An updated version (2005) is available at http://www.rh.edu/~stodder/Stodder_WIR3.htm

Stodder, J. (2009) 'Complementary Credit Networks and Macro-Economic Stability: Switzerland's *Wirtschaftsring*', *Journal of Economic Behavior and Organization*, 72, pp.79–95. Available for download at http://www.rh.edu/~stodder/BE/WIR_Update.pdf

Studer, T. (1998) *WIR in unsere Volkswirtschaft*. (English translation: *WIR and the Swiss National Economy*). Available at http://www.lulu.com/content/268895

Tilly, L. J. (1968) 'The Structure and Dynamics of Cone Spring', *Ecol. Monographs*, 38, pp.169–97.

Ulanowicz, R. E. (2009) *A Third Window: Natural Life Beyond Newton and Darwin*. West Conshohocken, PA: Templeton Foundation Press.

Ulanowicz, R. E., Bondavalli, C. and Egnotovich, M. S. (1996) *Network Analysis of Trophic Dynamics in South Florida Ecosystems, FY 96: The Cypress Wetland Ecosystem*. Annual Report to the United States Geological Service Biological Resources Division University of Miami Coral Gables, FL 33124.

Ulanowicz, R. E., Sally, J., Goerner, B. L. and Rocio, G. (2009) 'Quantifying Sustainability: Resilience, Efficiency and the Return Of Information Theory', *Ecological Complexity*, 6(1), pp.27–36.

Wray, R. L. (1998) *Understanding Modern Money: The Key to Full Employment and Price Stability*. Northampton, MA: Edward Elgar Publishing.

Zorach, A. C. and Ulanowicz, R. E. (2003) 'Quantifying the Complexity of Flow Networks: How Many Roles are There?', *Complexity*, 8(3), pp.68–76.

3
Marx's Big Idea

Nick Potts

> The *true barrier* to capitalist production is *capital itself*. It is that capital and its self-valorization appear as the starting and finishing point, as the motive and purpose of production; production is production only for *capital*, and not the reverse, i.e. the means of production are not simply means for a steadily expanding pattern of life for the *society* of the producers. The barriers within which the maintenance and valorization of the capital-value has necessarily to move – and this in turn depends on the dispossession and impoverishment of the great mass of the producers – therefore come constantly into contradiction with the methods of production that capital must apply to its purpose and which set its course towards an unlimited expansion of production, to production as an end in itself, to an unrestricted development of the social productive powers of labour. The means – the unrestricted development of the forces of social production – comes into persistent conflict with the restricted end, the valorization [sic] of the existing capital.
>
> Marx (1981, pp.358–9)

Introduction

In the above quote Marx is condemning capitalism as an inherently flawed system. Moneymaking, the valorization/self-expansion of capital, is the sole purpose of the capitalist system, with the workers' (the society of producers) interests being completely secondary. Production is not simply for consumption; production is an end in itself. Capitalism does deliver technological progress, but, rather than this simply improving all's wellbeing, the means of production are concentrated in the hands of capitalists, increasing inequality. Furthermore as capital expands it comes up against a barrier of its own making, as we shall explain, in the form of a tendency for the rate of profit to fall as capital is accumulated in boom. Cyclical crises are inevitable, capital must be sacrificed to restore the profit rate and again allow capital to be accumulated at a faster rate. Capitalism is historically necessary to create the material foundations (level of development/technology) on which a superior form of society can be created, with capitalism's life span being limited precisely because of its inherently flawed nature. Marx's economics certainly leads Marx to a revolutionary conclusion, and, given that we have not moved on to a superior form of society, economists *must* have *scientifically* superseded Marx's analysis in the 125 years since his death?

It is impossible to model our world 'completely'; we must simplify our task by abstracting from elements of reality, while hoping to retain the essential features of our world. The test for any economic theory is, or rather should be whether it accurately predicts how the real world tends to behave. Scientific progress should mean that economists accept the most plausible theory that currently exists, until a superior theory is developed that clearly better explains reality as we observe it. But economics is too politically sensitive to follow such a scientific method, Marx (1976, pp.96–7):

> Let us take England. Its classical political economy belongs to a period in which the class struggle was as yet undeveloped. Its last great representative, Ricardo, ultimately (and consciously) made the antagonism of class interests, of wages and profits, of profits and rent, the starting-point of his investigations, ... With the year 1830 there came the crisis which was to be decisive, once and for all. In France and England the bourgeoisie had conquered political power. From that time on, the class struggle took on more and more explicit and threatening forms, both in practice and in theory. It sounded the knell of scientific bourgeois economics. It was thenceforth no longer a question whether this or that theorem was true, but whether it was useful to capital or harmful, expedient or inexpedient, ... In place of disinterested inquirers there stepped hired prize-fighters; in place of genuine scientific research, the bad conscience and evil intent of apologetics.

In this and my next chapter, I shall argue that Marx's economics is the most plausible explanation of our system, precisely because the tendencies Marx predicted have, and continue to, best explain the world we actually live in. The economy does cycle from boom to bust. Concentration has tended to increase the size and reduce the number of firms in each industry, with new industries springing up with initially smaller firms. Inequality has relentlessly grown (Freeman 2004).

Determination of commodities' values by labour-time – The basic idea

Marx (1976) Chapter 7 explains how in all forms of society labour processes must occur to produce commodities; concrete things must be combined with real people with real skills for production to occur. What makes capitalism different to other social systems is the fact that labour processes are not directly controlled by people, as they were in the feudal world by aristocrat, church and guild; rather it is the market that ensures that only profitable activities can continue to occur. Production is for exchange value not direct consumption. The valorization process, the advancement of capital/value to production with the aim of expanding this capital/value through producing and selling commodities, is both unique to capitalism and the system's sole purpose. Capital/value is expressed in money, and realized in units of money, but in sequence takes the form of money capital (M), means of production (productive capital, C), produced commodities (commodity capital, C′), and then money capital again (M′), over the circuit of capital (Marx 1978, Part 1). Capital/value is not simply money; it is a social process. Marx (1976) Chapter 1 explains how the one thing that capitalistically produced commodities have in common is that they are all the product of human labour, in the form of workers' living labour and the dead/past labour of the means of production used up in production. Human labour, which can be expressed in units of money or labour-time, is the substance and sole source of value. The produced value of a commodity is the average (social) labour-time necessary to reproduce that commodity over all producers of that commodity. Labour-time is measured in units of 'simple' labour, Marx (1976, pp.304–5 and then p.135),

> in the valorization process it does not in the least matter whether the labour appropriated by the capitalist is simple labour of average social quality, or more complex labour, labour with a higher specific gravity as it were. ... labour-power whose production has cost more time and labour than unskilled or simple labour-power, and which therefore has a higher value.

> More complex labour counts only as *intensified*, or rather *multiplied* simple labour.

Marx is developing an abstract and complex concept of value, so when he introduces his concept of value in Marx (1976), to simplify, he assumes that all commodities exchange at, have appropriated values equal to, their produced values. Marx knows this is not the case in reality (Marx 1976, p.421), but wishes to focus on the process of production as whole. At the aggregate level Marx is working at, the total produced value of commodities must equal the total appropriated value of commodities if the human labour applied in production is to be the sole source of value; pure acts of exchange can neither create or destroy value.[1] Individual exchanges may leave one party worse off and another better off, but exchange at the aggregate level must be a zero sum game. By assuming appropriated values equal produced values Marx is assuming, for simplicity, that all exchanges are fair. With all exchanges being fair, how can capitalists expand their capital?

The means of production are bought by capitalists at prices equal to their values, and, to the extent they are used up in production, pass this value to the commodities produced in that period. As means of production simply transfer their value Marx terms this form of capital constant capital. If constant capital is entirely used up (circulates) in the production period it passes its entire value to the value of commodities produced that period. If some of the constant capital remains intact at the end of production (is fixed), it only passes value equal to the proportion of itself that is used up in production to the value of commodities produced that period. Total capital at the end of production equals the value of newly produced commodities, plus the remaining value of fixed capital. In either case constant capital (c) only transfers its value to newly produced commodities, preserving value, but not creating new value. Living labour is also applied to production, workers are 'fairly' paid the value of their labour-power, but this does not represent their entire labour, Marx (1976, pp.280, 731 and 274–5).

> The sphere of circulation or commodity exchange, within whose boundaries the sale and purchase of labour-power goes on, is in fact a very Eden of the innate rights of man. It is the exclusive realm of Freedom, Equality, Property and Bentham. ... When we leave this sphere of simple circulation or the exchange of commodities, ... He who was previously the money-owner now strides out in front as a capitalist; the possessor of labour-power follows as his worker. The

> one smirks self-importantly and is intent on business; the other is timid and holds back, like someone who has brought his own hide to market and now has nothing else to expect but – a tanning.

> The fact that this particular commodity, labour-power, possesses the peculiar use-value of supplying labour, and therefore of creating value, cannot affect the general law of commodity production. ... The law of exchange requires equality only between the exchange-values of the commodities given in exchange for one another. ... its result is:
> (1) that the product belongs to the capitalist and not to the worker;
> (2) that the value of this product includes, apart from the value of the capital advanced, a surplus-value which costs the worker labour but the capitalist nothing, and which none the less becomes the legitimate property of the capitalist;
> (3) that the worker has retained his labour-power and can sell it anew if he finds another buyer.

> The value of labour-power is determined, as in the case of every other commodity, by the labour-time necessary for the production, and consequently also the reproduction, of this specific article. ... If the owner of labour-power works today, tomorrow he must again be able to repeat the same process in the same conditions as regards health and strength. His means of subsistence must therefore be sufficient to maintain him in his normal state as a working individual. ... must include the means necessary for the worker's replacements, i.e. his children, in order that this race of peculiar commodity-owners may perpetuate its presence on the market.

The main focus of Marx (1976) is to make this central point, capitalism may appear to be moral and fair on the surface, but as soon as we enter production we reveal that capitalism is simply based on the exploitation of workers. Workers work L hours, receive wages/firms advance variable capital (v) with a value below L, ensuring a surplus-value (s) is extracted from labour, allowing capital to expand.

$$M = C = c + v < c + L = C' = M' \qquad \text{because } L - v = s,$$

The total surplus-value extracted from labour represents the maximum profit capitalists can realize/the total amount capital can expand. Productive capitalists extract this surplus-value, and distribute some of it by paying rent, interest and tax, while circulation, and other unproductive activities, consume another part of surplus-value, with the remainder being capitalists' profit of enterprise. Workers may also pay tax, and be charged usurious interest and excessive rents, suffering further secondary exploitation (Marx 1981, Chapter 36). But, abstracting from all these particular features of capitalism to focus on production alone, reveals surplus-value to be the sole source of profit, and living labour ($L = v + s$) to be the sole source of new value.[2] Although Marx (1976) introduces many concepts, and in Chapter 25 considers the process of capitalist accumulation as a whole, Marx does not, or rather does not need to in the context of what he wishes to explain, develop his concept of value further. Likewise, when focusing on circulation in Marx (1978), Marx simply again assumes appropriated values equal produced values, that is, takes an aggregate approach to focus on the matter in hand.

Determination of commodities' values by labour-time – Capitalist competition

Marx further develops his theory of value in Marx (1981) Part 2. If appropriated values always equalled produced values industries with a higher ratio of constant capital to variable capital (value or organic composition of capital) would have a lower profit rate, $s/(c + v)$, than industries with lower ratios of constant to variable capital. But, in the competitive capitalist market, capital would tend to flow to industries with higher profit rates, increasing supply, and away from industries with lower profit rates, decreasing supply. Prices/appropriated values must consequently deviate from produced values to tendentially equalize the profit rate across industries. Marx (1981, p.264),

I.	$80_C + 20_V + 20_S$.	Rate of profit = 20%. Price of the product = 120. Value = 120.
II.	$90_C + 10_V + 10_S$.	Rate of profit = 20%. Price of the product = 120. Value = 110.
III.	$70_C + 30_V + 30_S$.	Rate of profit = 20%. Price of the product = 120. Value = 130.

In this second, and simplest, illustration of the transformation procedure in Marx (1981) Chapter 9 Marx assumes all constant capital circulates, transferring its entire value to the output of each industry. The average ratio of constant to variable capital for the economy as whole is 80 to 20 (240 to 60 in aggregate), and the average rate of profit for the economy as a whole is 20% (s = 60 divided by c = 240 plus v = 60). For all three industries to share this average profit rate they must price their output 20% above its cost price of c plus v, which is equal to 100 for all three industries. The resulting prices of production of 120 for each industry ensure all three industries have a 20% profit rate. Industry I appropriates the value it produces because it has the economy's average ratio of constant to variable capital. Industry II, with a higher ratio of c to v, appropriates ten more units of value than it produces at the expense of industry III, which has a lower ratio of c to v and consequently appropriates ten less units of value than it produces. Although commodities appropriated values deviate from their produced values, surplus-value is maintained as the sole source of profit and total appropriated value (360) equals total produced value (360). So, profitability will tend to equalize across competitive industries, with this process being both dynamic and imperfect. Fluctuations in supply and demand will ensure market prices deviate from prices of production, causing profitability to be uneven, but profitability will tend to equalize through market prices tending to move to prices of production (Marx 1981, Chapter 10). Whether profitability is equalized or not, total appropriated value always equals total produced value and total profit always equals total surplus-value. Marx (1981, p.1001) explains how monopoly industries are not subject to the transformation process. Through setting a high monopoly price they appropriate more value than they produce, reducing the total amount of surplus-value available to distribute across the competitive sectors of the economy.

With his theory of value now further developed Marx (1981) Part 3 moves on to consider how the process of competition between capitalists creates a tendency for the profit rate to inevitably fall in boom. Although profitability tends to equalize across industries, within industries profitability is not, and does not tend to be, equalized. Leading producers will have higher profitability than average and laggard producers because they are more productive, that is, produce more units of output per unit of capital applied. Competition ensures a single market price is established for the output of each industry. Assuming profitability is equalized across industries, the 'average' producer in each industry will appropriate sufficient value, price times units of output produced, to realize the economy's average rate of profit on the capital they advance. An above average productivity producer produces more units of output per unit of capital advanced, and sells them all at that industry's single market price, and hence enjoys above average profitability. Conversely, laggard producers, producing less units of output per unit of capital applied than the industry average, will earn below average profitability. If in an industry leading producers become even more productive, average productivity in that industry will rise, reducing the price necessary for the 'average' producer to earn the economy's average profit rate. But the 'average' producer is merely a statistical concept; as particular producers improve profitability, by increasing productivity, all other producers, who have not increased productivity, earn less profit than they previously did, with the least productive tending to continually drop out of the industry altogether. Marx (1981) Part 3 explains how leading producers tend to increase their productivity through growing larger by applying more machinery, increasing their ratio of constant to variable capital, Marx (1981, pp.325–6),

> The course of the development of capitalist production and accumulation requires increasingly large-scale labour processes and hence increasingly large dimensions and increasingly large advances of capital for each individual establishment. The growing concentration of capitals (accompanied at the same time, though in lesser degree, by a growing number of capitalists) is therefore both one of its material conditions and one of the results that it itself produces. Hand in hand with this, in a relationship of reciprocity, goes progressive expropriation of the more or less immediate producers. In this way a situation comes about in which the individual capitalists have command of increasingly large armies of workers (no matter how much the variable capital may fall in relation to the constant capital), so that the mass of surplus-value and hence profit which they appropriate grows, along with and despite the fall in the rate of profit. The reasons that concentrate massive armies of workers under the command of individual capitalists are precisely the same reasons as also swell the amount of fixed capital employed, as well as the raw and ancillary materials, in a growing proportion as compared with the mass of living labour applied.

By 'more or less immediate producers' Marx means people who have traditionally produced directly themselves, such as peasant farmers. The process of competition between capitalists provides the tendential basis for growing inequality, both within countries and between countries. Developed countries tend to have more leading producers, more monopolies (witness the developed world's push for intellectual property rights/the creation of 'intellectual' land) and industries with higher ratios of constant capital to variable capital. All these factors cause them to receive surplus-value from 'developing' countries with more laggard producers, less monopolies and industries with a lower ratio of constant to variable capital.[3] This provides the state in developed countries with the tax base to fund a welfare state to limit the growth of inequality if they wish/are politically pressurized to do so. In contrast, the state in 'developing' countries, which gift developed countries much surplus-value, struggle to provide their populations with basic welfare services, causing inequality to relentlessly grow within 'developing' countries/the vast majority of the world (Freeman 2004).

The process of capitalist competition has a further and profound consequence. If capitalists tend to invest in constant capital more than they expand employment, as living labour is the sole source of new value and surplus-value, the profit rate will tend to fall as capitalists accumulate/compete, as normal, in boom. Marx (1981, pp.373–4),

> No capitalist voluntarily applies a new method of production, no matter how much more productive it may be or how much it might raise the rate of surplus-value, if it reduces the rate of profit. But every new method of production of this kind makes commodities cheaper. At first, therefore, he can sell them above their price of production, perhaps above their value. He pockets the difference between their costs of production and the market price of the other commodities, which are produced at higher production costs. This is possible because the average socially necessary labour-time required to produce these latter commodities is greater than the labour-time required with the new method of production. His production procedure is ahead of the social average. But competition makes the new procedure universal and subjects it to the general law. A fall in the profit rate then ensues – firstly perhaps in this sphere of production, and subsequently equalized [sic] with the others – a fall that is completely independent of the capitalists' will.

Capitalists, inexplicably to themselves, defeat themselves; the contradictory system inevitably endogenously generates its own instability. Although the tendency is for the rate of profit to fall, there are counter-tendencies, which can slow down, even temporally reverse, this tendency. The rate of exploitation of labour may rise. Exploitation may, potentially at any time, rise through the production of absolute surplus-value (lengthening the working day, or reducing wages, Marx 1976, Part 3), but, as we shall explore, Marx thinks this is more likely to occur in crisis than in boom. In boom exploitation is more likely to rise through workers' means of subsistence becoming cheaper, Marx (1976, pp.436–7),

> Capital therefore has an immanent drive, and a constant tendency, towards increasing the productivity of labour, in order to cheapen commodities and, by cheapening commodities, to cheapen the worker himself.

This production of relative surplus-value (Marx 1976, Part 4) reduces the proportion of the working day necessary to reproduce the worker, the value of labour-power, allowing the proportion of the working day that produces surplus-value for capitalists to rise. However, this boost to profitability is occurring precisely because a rising ratio of constant capital to variable capital is increasing productivity, and thus acting to drag profitability down. Furthermore the decline in the value of labour-power is limited. If workers could live off air alone surplus-value could only grow by the growth rate of living labour applied, which tends to fall below the growth of constant capital, as capitalists invest in constant capital/labour-saving techniques to increase their productivity. The growth of constant capital also faces a limit, in the form of the decline in the profit rate that faster growth of constant capital than variable capital tends to deliver.

Rising productivity also cheapens means of production, helping to boost the profit rate. But a cheapening of means of production, produced this production period, does not cheapen the means of production employed this period, as if they were magically produced this period (as we shall explore in the next section replacement cost valuation implies). The profit rate is calculated by dividing the surplus-value the capitalist appropriates by the value of the capital they advance, when it was advanced, at the start of the production period.[4] Cheaper means of production act to boost the profit rate in the next period, by reducing the unit value of means of production applied next period, but, again, this cheapening occurs precisely because capitalists are investing more in constant capital than variable capital, Marx (1981, p.318),

> There corresponds to this growing volume of constant capital – although this expresses only at a certain remove the growth in the actual mass of use-values which the constant capital consists of in material terms – a continual cheapening of the product.

So, as boom progresses, profitability tends to fall, slowing growth/capitalists' drive to accumulate (making capital surplus, as we shall explore in the next chapter). Crisis is now necessary to restore profitability and return the economy to boom/a faster pace of accumulation again (we shall consider in the next chapter how stagnation may result if we attempt to postpone/limit crisis, and thus stop crisis from decisively restoring the profit rate). In crisis constant capital suffers dramatic moral and physical depreciation. As capitalists go under they are forced to either sell their operations to new capitalists, at knock down prices, or their factories are closed forever. With workers' bargaining position weakened by unemployment, capitalists are likely to significantly increase the rate of exploitation through the production of more absolute surplus-value. The working day may be lengthened. As the value of labour-power contains a 'historical and moral element' (Marx 1976, p.275), workers may be forced to adjust down their expectation of the necessities required for their reproduction. Wages may fall further than the falling value of labour-power, causing workers to live in a 'crippled state' (Marx 1976, p.277).

With constant capital sharply depreciated, and the rate of exploitation boosted, the profit rate is restored by crisis, laying the foundation for renewed boom. Growth under capitalism cannot be smooth, the economy has an in-built/endogenous tendency to cyclically boom and fall into crisis; this is why Marx thinks 'The *true barrier* to capitalist production is *capital itself*' (Marx 1981, p.358).

The controversy

I have assumed that Marx employed a sequential approach to time (production this period follows circulation at the end of the last period, with circulation following production this period, before production next period) and a non-dualistic approach to value (human labour is the substance and sole source of value, which can be measured either in units of money or labour-time). To convert between units of labour-time and money we must appropriately account for the value of money (Marx 1981, pp.236–8). To calculate the value of money at the end of production (when Marx thinks prices are established, Marx 1976, p.260), we must divide the total produced value of capital at the end of production by the total appropriated value/price of that capital expressed in money. For simplicity in Marx (1976, 1978 and 1981) Marx tends to assume the value of money is constant at one hour of labour-time equals one unit of money. For example this is the implicit assumption in the example of the transformation procedure we have considered (Marx 1981, p.264).

Interpreting Marx as following a sequential and non-dualistic approach ensures his central results hold; the transformation procedure adds up (Kliman and McGlone 1988), the tendency for the rate of profit to fall is confirmed (Kliman 1996), and surplus-value is identified as the sole source of profit (Kliman 2001). The Temporal (sequential) Single System (non-dualistic) Interpretation of Marx (TSSI) argue the fact that Marx employed a sequential and non-dualistic approach is clearly evident in his work (Freeman and Carchedi 1996). If alternative interpretations of Marx's method also confirmed Marx's central results, we would have to rely on a textual analysis of Marx's work to judge which method best represented Marx's method. However, hermeneutically (Kliman 2007), it would be completely unscientific to attribute to Marx a method which failed to confirm his central results/ensured his value theory was internally inconsistent, when an interpretation of his method does exist which confirms his central results and the consistency of his value theory. However, as Marx (1976, pp.96–7) points out, economics in practice is not a science, explaining why most 'Marxist' economists in the 20th century, and up to the present day, attribute a method(s) to Marx which both makes his value theory inconsistent and invalidates his central results.[5]

At the start of the 20th century Bortkiewicz (1952 and 1984) pioneered the application of a simultaneous and dualistic approach to Marx's theory of value. As an admirer of Walras's simultaneous approach to economics (Freeman 1996) Bortkiewicz reset Marx's transformation procedure to simple reproduction (the economy identically reproducing itself each period, Marx 1978, Chapter 20). This ensured both inputs and outputs would share the same unit values, as if they were simultaneously determined (as is conventional in mainstream economics). When I explained Marx's transformation procedure you may have noticed that I did not define the units value was being measured in. Neither did Marx, we must remember both Marx (1978) and Marx (1981) were drafts prepared for publication by Engels after Marx's death. If we have a non-dualistic concept of value this failure to define units is of little consequence; its units of value, that can be expressed either in units of money or units of labour-time.[6] Alternatively Bortkiewicz started the tradition of interpreting produced values as purely being in terms of labour-time, and appropriated values/prices being purely in terms of money (a dualistic approach to value). Once Bortkiewicz had adjusted Marx's transformation procedure to a simultaneous and dualistic approach it became impossible for both total produced value to equal total appropriated value and total surplus-value to equal total profit. Marx's transformation procedure became the transformation problem, 'Marx's' value theory did not add up, so it must be internally inconsistent.

Sweezy (1942), and then Samuelson (1971), publicized this 'scientific' conclusion, helping it to become 'mainstream' 'Marxist' economics (Desai 1979). Steedman (1977) proved that following a simultaneous and dualistic approach ensures values in labour-time are perfectly proxied by physical quantities, making Marx's value theory redundant, conventional 'real' terms are all we need. Employing a simultaneous and dualistic approach Okishio (1961) 'proved' Marx's prediction of a tendency for the profit rate to fall in boom could not hold.[7] With Marx broken, any 'Marxist' economist can fix, play pick and mix, with Marx's economics (Kliman 2010). In the next chapter we shall consider the implication of these alternative interpretations of Marx to how we explain crises. Briefly, if we rule out Marx's tendency for the profit rate to fall in boom, we must find some other explanation of crises/the cyclical instability of capitalism.

In summary, the TSSI of Marx has proved, for nearly 30 years, that a consistent interpretation of Marx's value theory exists, which confirms Marx's central results. The fact that most 'Marxist' economists reject, or rather ignore, this proof, and continue to employ approaches that do not reproduce Marx's central results, confirms the unscientific nature of modern political economy. But I don't think this would have surprised Marx at all, as economics is simply too politically sensitive to behave like a genuine science.

Conclusion

In this chapter I have set out to introduce the reader to Marx's economic analysis of capitalism. Following Marx I have abstracted from many features of the system, notably the financial system, to focus on capitalism's essential nature, as revealed in production. Marx argues that capitalism's essential nature explains why the economy must inevitable cycle from boom to bust, with inequality and industrial concentration tending to continually grow over time. With this base established in the next chapter I move on to consider the role the financial system plays in capitalism, in general, and the particular part that it plays in crises.

Notes

1 To focus on production Marx (1976) abstracts from the detail of how commodities circulate. Marx (1978) explores circulation, and explains how some value is consumed facilitating circulation; so the total produced value of

commodities exceeds the total value productive capitalists appropriate. Furthermore productive capitalists waste part of the value they appropriate on other necessary, but unproductive of value, activities.

2 Potts (2010) analyses how, if include stocks of unsold commodities or fixed capital, then, if we assume produced values equal the average labour-time necessary to produce (currently reproduce) newly produced units of commodities, value appears to arise from nowhere if productivity regresses, or disappear if productivity improves. However, as commodities values are being determined by the average labour-time necessary for their reproduction, this revaluation/devaluation effect cannot be seen to contradict the notion that commodities' values are being determined by the average labour-time necessary for their reproduction.

3 Potts (2007) explores the role of knowledge, in the form of research and development, to leading producers' ability to stay ahead. Research and development creates new use-values, in the form of new commodities and new methods of production, but a commodity's produced value depends on its cost of reproduction, not its invention. Research and development can thus be seen to be a 'waste' of surplus-value, made possible by leading producers grabbing surplus-value from laggard producers. Essentially leading producers invest surplus-value, produced elsewhere, on research and development, in order to continue to grab surplus-value from elsewhere. Additionally the state in developed countries may tax both business and workers in order to gift their capitalists free research and development and a more educated workforce.

4 As newly produced units of fixed capital cheapen, existing units of fixed capital suffer moral depreciation (Marx 1978, p.265). Their loss in value has to be (if capitalists are not to mislead themselves) written off against profit at the end of the production period newly produced units of fixed capital cheapen in, thus depressing profitability over that period.

5 Kliman (2007) provides the fullest account of the myth of Marx's inconsistency I am aware of, while Potts (2009a) considers how the TSSI's efforts to reclaim Marx economics today compare with Grossmann's attempts to defend Marx's economics from revisionism in the first half of the 20th century.

6 The TSSI of Marx define the monetary expression of labour-time (MELT), established at the end of production each period, as the total appropriated value/price of capital, expressed in terms of money, divided by the total produced value of that capital, expressed in terms of labour-time. It is the inverse of the value of money.

7 Potts (2009b) uses a common scenario of an economy in boom to show how, if we take a simultaneous and dualistic approach, the Okishio theorem is confirmed, but if we employ a sequential and non-dualistic approach the Okishio theorem is overturned.

References

Bortkiewicz, L. (1952) 'Value and Price in the Marxian System', *International Economic Papers*, No. 2, pp.5–60.

Bortkiewicz, L. (1984) 'On the Correction of Marx's Fundamental Theoretical Construction in the Third Volume of Capital', in Sweezy, P. M. (ed.) *Karl Marx and the Close of His System*. Philadelphia: Orion.

Desai, M. (1979) *Marxian Economics*. London: Basil Blackwell.
Freeman, A. (1996) 'The Psychopathology of Walrasian Marxism', in Freeman, A. and Carchedi, G. (eds) *Marx and Non-Equilibrium Economics*, pp.1–28. Cheltenham: Edward Elgar.
Freeman, A. (2004) 'The Inequality of Nations', in Freeman, A. and Kagarlitsky, B. (eds) *The Politics of Empire: Globalisation in Crisis*, pp.46–83. London: Pluto Press.
Freeman, A. and Carchedi, G. (eds) (1996) *Marx and Non-Equilibrium Economics*. Cheltenham: Edward Elgar.
Kliman, A. (1996) 'A Value-Theoretic Critique of the Okishio Theorem', in Freeman, A. and Carchedi, G. (eds) *Marx and Non-Equilibrium Economics*, pp.206–24. Cheltenham: Edward Elgar.
Kliman, A. (2001) 'Simultaneous Valuation vs. the Exploitation Theory of Profit', *Capital and Class*, No. 73, pp.97–112.
Kliman, A. (2007) *Reclaiming Marx's "Capital"*. Lanham, MD: Lexington Books.
Kliman, A. (2010) 'The Disintegration of the Marxian School', *Capital and Class*, No. 100, pp.61–8.
Kliman, A. and McGlone, T. (1988) 'The Transformation non-Problem and the non-Transformation Problem', *Capital and Class*, No. 35.
Marx, K. (1976) *Capital: A Critique of Political Economy*, Volume I. London and New York: Penguin/Vintage Publishers edition.
Marx, K. (1978) *Capital: A Critique of Political Economy*, Volume II. London and New York: Penguin/Vintage Publishers edition.
Marx, K. (1981) *Capital: A Critique of Political Economy*, Volume III. London and New York: Penguin/Vintage Publishers edition.
Okishio, N. (1961) 'Technical Changes and the Rate of Profit', *Kobe University Economic Review*, Vol. 7, pp.86–99.
Potts, N. (2007) 'Some Preliminary Thoughts on Knowledge-based Production: 49 Seconds on Mustafar', *Critique*, 35(3), pp.357–73.
Potts, N. (2009a) 'Recovering Marx: Past and Present', *Critique*, 37(3), pp.483–8.
Potts, N. (2009b) 'Trying to Help Rescue Value for Everyone', *Critique*, 37(2), pp.177–99.
Potts, N. (2010) 'Valuation in the Presence of Stocks of Commodities: Exploring the Temporal Single System Interpretation of Marx', forthcoming in *Critique of Political Economy*.
Samuelson, P. A. (1971) 'Understanding the Marxian Notion of Exploitation: A Summary of the So-called 'Transformation Problem' between Marxian Values and Competitive Prices', *Journal of Economic Literature*, 9(2).
Steedman, I. (1977) *Marx after Sraffa*. London: New Left Books.
Sweezy, P. M. (1942) *The Theory of Capitalist Development; Principles of Marxian Political Economy*. London: Merlin and Augustus M. Kelly, also New York: Modern Reader Paperbacks (1970).

4
When is a Financial Crisis not a Financial Crisis?

Nick Potts

Introduction

I shall attempt to explain why Marx thinks that the behaviour of the financial system, let us imagine it as the tail, follows from the tendential behaviour of the productive economy, our dog. Marx does not think that the tail wags the dog; rather the tail merely helps the dog run faster to where it was going anyway. The productive economy is running inevitably to crisis because profitability has a tendency to fall in boom; our dog becomes fat with constant capital and begins to slow. Crisis is a crash diet/destruction of constant capital, which is absolutely necessary to restore the profit rate and let a leaner dog run free again. Attempting to cure crisis by state encouraged creation of credit is no solution precisely because crisis is necessary to restore the profit rate, so postponing crisis merely prolongs low profitability and leads to stagnation. It is akin to our fat old dog becoming lost, following its tail into various disruptive dead-ends (fictitious capital bubbles, usurious lending to people and governments, and numerous other speculative adventurous paths), unable to find the only place, the crisis, it needs to renew itself. It is for this reason that I will argue that interpreting the current crisis as an avoidable 'accident' of the financial systems own making is naïve, as no reform of the tail can hope to change the nature of the dog.

Marx and the financial system: Everything is endogenous

Marx has a Darwinian approach to the development of capitalism, all the features of the dog develop together to make the dog exploit its environment better. Marx recognizes that tails predate dogs! Marx (1981, p.729),

> Two of the forms in which usurer's capital exists in phases prior to the capitalist mode of production are particularly characteristic. ... *firstly*, usury by lending money to extravagant magnates, essentially to landed proprietors; *secondly*, usury by lending money to small producers who possess their own conditions of labour, including artisans, but particularly and especially peasants, ... Both of these things, the ruining of rich landed proprietors by usury and the impoverishment of the small producers, lead to the formation and concentration of large money capitals.

Usury is not directly leading to a change in the nature of production; it simply feeds on the existing productive structure. An extravagant magnate may be able to squeeze his peasants more, but the loan was not taken out to improve production. Small artisans and farmers, traditionally controlled by social conventions, are not usually borrowing to expand production, but to maintain it, after losing their meagre means of production through some act of nature, war or taxation. They may lose their possessions as their work normally only barely allows them to reproduce themselves, so paying off the loan will be extremely difficult. Usury was a contentious issue in pre-capitalist societies, with traditional powers, the church and the nobility, acting to limit usury and periodically persecute usurers. In contrast to usurer's capital merchant's capital, through its connection to economic activity (circulation), was far more like capital in capitalism.

As the capitalist system developed in the 18th century factory owners faced new financial problems. Capitalists were not attempting to live beyond their means; rather they had discovered the trick of expanding their means/capital in the new competitive capitalist environment. Inputs must be purchased in advance of production, wages must be regularly paid, and output had to be increasingly shipped to distant destinations to be sold. To cover this mismatch of receipts and payments and continually produce, to most efficiently use the factory would require a large reserve of money capital. Such an advance of money capital would increase the total capital advanced, depressing the profit rate. Capitalists soon learned to avoid this depression to their profit rates by granting credit to each other in the form of commercial bills of exchange. Banks endogenously developed to provide cash, in either coin or their own banknotes, to capitalists when they needed it in return for accepting capitalists' bills of exchange at a discount. Capitalist A would go to the bank and swap a promise from capitalist B to pay him £1,000 in a month's time for £950 in banknotes. The bank makes £50 profit for essentially lending capitalist A £950 for a month. Unlike usury it's a completely victimless crime, or rather it is a service and not a crime at all! The bank captures £50 from the capitalist, who can afford to pay this as they extract surplus-value from their workers, say £150 in total. This depression to the mass of profit is no problem to the capitalist as this credit service allows the total capital they advance to be much lower, say £500, instead of a £1,000, boosting the capitalist's profit rate (100/500 = 20% > 150/1,000 = 15%). More simply, if we consider interest bearing capital in its simplest form, a productive capitalist operating with capital lent by a monied capitalist, the productive capitalist can afford to 'justly' pay the monied capitalist their interest as long as the rate of interest is below the rate of profit. Borrowing does not tend to ruin capitalists as they are borrowing to support production, that is, to exploit a third party, the workers.

The tendency to concentration within industries, and for more constant capital, much in the form of fixed capital, to be applied relative to variable capital, created further opportunities for the financial system to develop. To raise the capital to fund increasingly large enterprises, notably early on railways, joint-stock companies developed. Shares represented a loan for an infinite period, with a second-hand market for these shares, the stock market, endogenously developing to magically provide the shareholder with liquidity. Specialist financial institutions developed to buy, sell, issue, and gamble on, the general explosion of 'fictitious capital' capitalism brought forth as it developed. Marx (1981, p.595, pp.597–8 and p.596),

> The form of interest-bearing capital makes any definite and regular monetary revenue appear as the interest on a capital, whether it actually derives from a capital or not.
>
> The formation of fictitious capital is known as capitalization. Any regular periodic income can be capitalized by reckoning it up, on the basis of the average rate of interest, as the sum that a capital lent out at this interest rate would yield. For example, if the annual income in question is £100 and the rate of interest 5 per cent, then £100 is the annual interest on £2,000, and this £2,000 is then taken as the capital value of the legal ownership title to this annual £100. ... Even when the promissory note – the

security – does not represent a purely illusory capital, as it does in the case of national debts, the capital value of this security is still pure illusion. We have already seen how the credit system produces joint-stock capital. Securities purport to be ownership titles representing this capital. ... the capital does not exist twice over, once as the capital value of the ownership titles, the shares, and then again as the capital actually invested or to be invested in the enterprises in question. It exists only in the latter form, and the share is nothing but an ownership title, *pro rata*, to the surplus-value which this capital is to realize. ... The independent movement of these ownership titles' values, not only those of government bonds, but also of shares, strengthens the illusion that they constitute real capital besides the capital or claim to which they may give title. They become commodities,

Moving from the capital of the national debt, where a negative quantity appears as capital – interest-bearing capital always being the mother of every insane form, so that debts, for example, can appear as commodities in the mind of the banker.

The financial system endogenously developed to both co-ordinate fictitious capital, and capture and lend out as many idle hoards of money as possible. Rather than holding capitalism back, this necessary, but unproductive, part of the capitalist system is 'paying for itself' by allowing total production and extraction of surplus-value to occur on a much larger scale, with the need to apply relatively less capital, than if the financial system did not exist. Marx argues that the financial system allows an already elastic system to be stretched further, Marx (1981, p.572),

If the credit system appears as the principal lever of overproduction and excessive speculation in commerce, this is simply because the reproduction process, which is elastic by nature, is now forced to its most extreme limit; and this is because a great part of the social capital is applied by those who are not its owners, and who therefore proceed quite unlike owners who, when they function themselves, anxiously weigh the limits of their private capital. This only goes to show how the valorization of capital founded on the antithetical character of capitalist production permits actual free development only up to a certain point, which is constantly broken through by the credit system.

> ... credit accelerates the violent outbreaks of this contradiction, crises,

Abstractly, with no financial system, capitalists could still dynamically expand production because they extract surplus-value from their workers. Even if most of this surplus-value was simply wasted, if the remainder was added to the value of the capital preserved through production and circulation this period, total capital applied next period would grow/the economy would grow. Demand is not balanced on a knife-edge. Furthermore growth may simple entail producing more means of production/constant capital, which requires no increase in 'consumer' demand at all. Say at the start of production total capital advanced equals £100, £80 on constant capital and £20 on variable capital. Assume £20 of surplus-value is extracted (a profit rate of 20%) and is invested in raising constant capital input to £100 next period, with a variable capital input of £20 again. Let us again assume a surplus-value of £20 is extracted from workers in production next period. The profit rate falls to £20/£120 = 16⅔%, but production did expand, and is still profitable, just a bit less so, without the need to assume any increase in 'consumer' demand at all.

In capitalism production can thus simply be for production's own sake. The reason demand is high in boom is precisely because the profit rate is sufficiently high to induce capitalists to productively invest sufficient surplus-value to ensure demand is high/the economy is in boom. It is this already inherently elastic process the financial system speeds up. Furthermore, the financial system cannot simply take away capitalism's ultimate limit, as the tendency for the rate of profit to fall is rooted, already exists, in the very nature of the productive economy.

Surplus capital

Essentially the idea is very simple (see Potts 2010a), as the profit rate on productive investment of capital tends to fall capitalists cut back on productive investment and invest their, now 'surplus', capital in a wide range of unproductive activities. Capital is surplus to capitalists' desired level of investment in the productive economy, Marx (1981, pp.349–50 and p.359), followed by Marx (1969, p.484),

> the rate of profit, is the spur to capitalist production (in the same way as the valorization of capital is its sole purpose), a fall in this rate slows down the formation of new, independent capitals and

> thus appears as a threat to the development of the capitalist production process; it promotes overproduction, speculation and crises, and leads to the existence of excess capital alongside a surplus population.

> As the profit rate falls, so there is a growth in the minimum capital that the individual capitalist needs ... This growing concentration leads in turn, at a certain level, to a new fall in the rate of profit. The mass of small fragmented capitals are thereby forced onto adventurous paths: speculation, credit swindles, share swindles, crises. The so-called plethora of capital is always basically reducible to a plethora of that capital for which the fall in the profit rate is not outweighed by its mass.

> more capital is accumulated than can be invested in production, and for example lies fallow in the form of money at the bank. This results in loans abroad, etc., in short speculative investments.

Potts (2009) sets out to model the process of capital becoming surplus, simulating a growing economy, with firms having shares, fictitious capital, and paying half their profits as dividends on these shares. Share prices are simply calculated by dividing the dividend on the share by the interest rate, abstractly, like the number of shares, kept constant throughout our simulation.[1] The total return from holding shares over a period equals the dividend paid, plus any capital gain over the period, divided by the total price of the shares at the end of the previous period. Surplus-value grows each period through assuming living labour input grows each period, and by assuming that wages are held constant in use-value terms, causing the rate of exploitation to rise as productivity improves each period. To ensure value is the same in nominal and labour-time expression I set the value of money constant at £1 equal to one hour of labour-time. The nominal rate of return on shares grows as total surplus-value grows. With the value of money constant at £1 equal to one hour of labour-time the nominal money profit rate simply equals the profit rate in value terms, which declines, as input of constant capital grows faster than input of variable capital each period. With the rate of return on shares rising and the profit rate falling, a point is reached, in my simulation period 13, when the return from investing in shares is greater than the return from investing in production. I now assume productive capitalists increasingly switch to investing in shares themselves, pushing up the return on this fictitious capital further, and slowing the growth of the productive economy as their productive investment declines. If I introduce inflation into my model, assuming a constant 2% rate of inflation each period, both the nominal profit rate and the nominal rate of return from holding shares rises each period. But the return on holding shares rises faster, and exceeds the return from productive investment from period 13 onwards, just as when I held the value of money constant. Inflation, or rather the falling value of money, is distorting the picture, but does not prevent the underlying situation in value terms from manifesting on the nominal surface of the economy.[2] This result essentially follows from assuming the price of fictitious capital depends on the mass of profit, whereas the rate of profit depends on the mass of profit divided by the total capital advanced.

Notably Grossmann (1929) employed Marx's notion of surplus capital to predict recession would soon occur in the United States, Grossmann (1992, the English translation of Grossmann 1929, p.79 then pp.191–3),

> A classic illustration is the United States today (March 1928) where, together with a superfluity of capital, shortage of investment opportunities and massive speculation in real estate and shares, there is a surplus working population of 4 million unemployed workers. This not because too much surplus value has been produced but because in relation to the accumulated mass of capital too little surplus value is available.

> superfluous capital looks for spheres of profitable investment. With no chance in production, capital is either exported or switched to speculation. ... Despite the optimism of many bourgeois writers who think that the Americans have succeeded in solving the problem of crises and creating economic stability, there are enough signs to suggest that America is fast approaching a state of overaccumulation. ... The depressed state of industry is reflected by an expansion of speculative loans and speculative driving up of share prices. ... Today America is doing its best to avert the coming crash – already foreshadowed in the panic selling on the stock exchange of December 1928 – by forcing up the volume of exports. ... When these efforts are matched by a similar drive by the Germans and the British, the crisis will only be intensified.

Grossmann points out how banks could only take a leading role in co-ordinating industry, as Hilferding's (1910/1981) notion of finance capital imagined, if capital was short in supply. Grossmann (1992, pp.199–200),

> Hilferding's exposition contradicts the actual tendencies of development of capitalism. It is also incompatible with the fundamental ideas of Marx's theory. For if Hilferding were right in arguing that the banks dominate industry, this would only shatter Marx's theory of the crucial importance of production itself to the structure of capitalism. The crucial role would then be played not by the production process but by finance capital, or structures in the sphere of circulation. ... At more advanced stages of accumulation industry becomes increasingly more independent of credit flow because it shifts to self-financing through depreciation and reserves. ... In countries like Britain, France and especially the USA, it is simply not possible to speak of industry being dependent on the banks. ... According to Vogelstein, this is one of the reasons why banks have been turning to the stock exchange by way of investments.

Rather than explaining bubbles in terms of pure speculation, the concept of surplus capital explains why such bubbles should cyclically reoccur. It is not a matter of irrationality; it is simply a consequence of supply and demand. If productive capitalists wish to productively invest less, the financial system is left with more capital to invest elsewhere. The fact that the financial system may overextend itself by trying to employ surplus capital as intensively as it possibly can is as rational/irrational as productive capitalists causing the rate of profit to fall by investing more in constant capital than variable capital. From an overall point of view it seems irrational, but just as competition compels capitalists to invest more in constant capital than variable capital, financial institutions must competitively try to maximize their investors' returns. The more idle money is the lower its return, with completely idle hoarded money in the form of cash earning no return at all. Until liquidity becomes a problem the super-liquidity of cash is of no significance at all. Eventually the over-extended system drops into crisis. Marx (1981, p.621),

> In a system of production where the entire interconnection of the reproduction process rests on credit, a crisis must evidently break out if credit is suddenly withdrawn and only cash payment is accepted, in the form of a violent scramble for means of payment. At first glance, therefore, the entire crisis presents itself as simply a

> credit and monetary crisis. ... It is clear that this entire artificial system of forced expansion of the reproduction process cannot be cured by now allowing one bank, e.g. the Bank of England, to give all the swindlers the capital they lack in paper money and to buy all the depreciated commodities at their old nominal values.

Although Marx thinks that all the swindlers should not be bailed out, in Marx (1981) Chapter 34, he ridicules the 1844 Currency School inspired legal limit to how many banknotes the Bank of England could issue. The Currency School, the monetarists of their day, believing in a simple causality between the amount of money and prices, argued for the 1844 Bank Act to safeguard the value of money. But when crisis hit in 1847 and 1857, under pressure from the Bank of England and the financial system, the government rapidly suspended the Act to allow the Bank of England to release sufficient liquidity into the financial system to prevent its systematic collapse. So it would appear that Marx does not think preventing the systematic collapse of the financial system is the same as attempting to avoid crisis by bailing out all the swindlers. Marx (1981, p.649),

> A devaluation of credit money (not to speak of a complete loss of its monetary character, which is in any case purely imaginary) would destroy all the existing relationships. The value of commodities is thus sacrificed in order to ensure the fantastic and autonomous existence of this value in money. ... As long as the *social* character of labour appears as the *monetary existence* of the commodity and hence as a *thing* outside actual production, monetary crises, independent of real crises or as an intensification of them, are unavoidable. It is evident on the other hand that, as long as a bank's credit is not undermined, it can alleviate the panic in such cases by increasing its credit money, whereas it increases this panic by contracting credit. ... The suspension of cash payments by the so-called national banks, which is resorted to as the sole expedient in all extreme cases, shows that even now no metal money is needed at home.

The central bank has the ability, as long as it does not completely undermine the value of money, to act to alleviate financial crisis. But assuming the crisis is not a 'monetary crises, independent of real crises', crisis is necessary to restore the profit rate; constant capital must be heavily depreciated and workers conditioned to a higher rate of exploitation. The situation 'cannot be cured' (Marx 1981, p.621) by state-supported credit creation, as avoiding the crisis would avoid a restoration of the profit rate and subsequent renewed boom. The economy would simply stagnate in a state of postponement, with low profitability and continual generation and adventurous employment of surplus capital.

Evidence from America

Kliman (2009) estimates the post-war profitability of the US corporate sector, explores in general the issues surrounding attempting to calculate profitability, and criticizes recent estimates of profitability in the US. Kliman records how Moseley (2009) estimates that US profitability rebounded in the 2000s to near its 1960s peak, with Duménil and Lévy (2005) finding a similar result for the US corporate sector. But these results rely on firstly cherry picking the data (Kliman 2009, pp.35–7) and secondly on employing replacement cost valuation (Kliman 2009, p.37). Kliman explains how the profit rate has a short-run cycle, from recession to recession, and a long-run trend. If we compare the trough of a short-run cycle with the peak of another short-run cycle we mislead ourselves over the long-run trend. When, in my previous chapter, I considered the controversy over Marx's value theory, I pointed out how taking a simultaneous approach leads to valuing inputs at their replacement cost. The value of advanced capital is revised at the end of the period to its replacement cost, as if it had magically been produced at the end of the period it acted as input for! Undervaluing advanced capital boosts the profit rate, Kliman (2009, p.4),

> I measure trends in the rate of profit by comparing one trough to another – in order to ascertain whether a *sustainable* recovery in profitability took place. I also measure the rate of profit as the ratio of profit to the original, historical cost of capital assets, the actual sums of money spent in the past to acquire capital assets (net of depreciation). I employ two different measures of profit and two different measures of advanced capital in order to measure the rate of profit in four different ways. I find that the rate of profit either increased very slightly (by 1.1 percentage point) between the trough of 1982 and the last trough before the current crisis, that of 2001, or it failed to rise, or it continued to fall.

Kliman (2009, pp.52–3) presents for US corporations, from 1947 to 2007, 'Before-tax Profits as a percentage of Historical Cost of Fixed

Assets' and 'Property Income as a percentage of Historical Cost of Fixed Assets'. These profit rates are presented in nominal terms, real terms and, by adjusting nominal terms by his estimation of the monetary expression of labour-time, value terms. Both profit rates in real terms are higher than they are in value terms (as we would expect, with real terms missing the effect of productivity improvement reducing commodities values, see endnote 2), but have very similar trajectories in real and value terms. The trend is for both profit rates, in both real and value terms, to sharply decline from 1947 to the 1970s. Since the 1980s the trend for 'Before-tax Profits as a percentage of Historical Cost of Fixed Assets' has been flat, at lower average rates in real and value terms than experienced in the 1970s. 'Property Income as a percentage of Historical Cost of Fixed Assets' has in both real and value terms continued on average to gradually decline from the 1970s to the 2000s. The result is strikingly clear; *the US corporate sector has been in a state of stagnant low profitability for over 30 years!*

Before I consider this result further I should point out how Kliman (2009) recognizes that estimating profitability is a very difficult task. Data is not recorded to match Marx's categories, while as capitalism is a global system calculating statistics for any one part of it is problematic. We are simply deluding ourselves if we think that we can calculate Marx's 'definitive' rate of profit, so researchers should employ a range of methods to calculate a range of estimates of profitability to help them interpret events. Kliman (2009, p.20),

> I note that Marx never estimated a Marxian rate of profit and that he was able to explain movements in profitability and economic crises quite well without one.

Kliman (2003) argues that the reason why profitability has remained low is that since the 1970s governments throughout the developed world have continually encouraged the creation of credit to postpone/limit crises. Crises have been insufficient to decisively restore the profit rate, causing the economy to stagnate at a much slower growth rate. Conventional estimates of GDP confirm growth has slowed (Freeman 2004). With profitability low we would expect much capital to be surplus, and take adventurous paths. From the 1970s onwards we have experience dramatic rises in capital exports to developing countries (so-called globalization), an explosion of usurious lending to the public in developed countries and governments throughout the world, and in general many bubbles in fictitious capital.[3] Finally, in 2008, the bursting of the latest, and greatest, fictitious capital bubbles seems to have dragged the world economy into sufficient crisis to decisively restore the profit rate, and so return us to boom again in the future. However, if western governments' rescue of the financial system and Keynesian attempts to fight the crisis simply ensure crisis is again too small to decisively restore the profit rate, we will be condemned to further stagnation. New bubbles, fuelled by persistently surplus capital, will again arise, again, in the end, leading us to apparently purely financial crisis.

Alternative theories of crisis

In general I reject theories that suggest the economy is purely held back by a deficiency of demand. As I have already explained, appreciating that surplus-value is extracted in production takes us away from imagining that demand is balanced on a knife-edge. Understanding that production can be for production's sake takes us away from imagining that demand is held back by the limited purchasing power of the public. Realizing that the economy is dynamically in motion from boom to slump (with postponement of slump representing stagnation) rules out conventional notions of the economy having an optimal equilibrium, which it tends towards or cycles around. Accidental/random explanations of crises/disruption of ideal equilibrium are, in my opinion, by definition, devoid of any theoretical depth. Focus on human imperfections, from information problems to biological animal spirits, may appear to address specific phenomenon as they arise. But such particular/partial explanations of the surface of the world simply fail to identify that such phenomenon can be explained, and linked to other phenomena, by employing a deeper theory of the economy, such as Marx's. However, as I pointed out in my previous chapter, Marx predicts that economics will not proceed like a science, as the social function of economics is to justify capitalism, rather than actually trying to explain it.

Turning to radical attempts to understand events, in my opinion one factor stands out in importance above all others. If like 'mainstream' simultaneous Marxists we, by adopting conventional real terms (a physical concept of value), turn our back on Marx's tendency for the profit rate to fall, we are forced to find alternative explanations of crises and the behaviour of the economy in general. Given, as the TSSI of Marx has clearly demonstrated a consistent interpretation of Marx does exist, that confirms his law of the tendential fall in the rate of profit, this search by 'Marxists' for alternative explanations purely stands in way of taking Marx's own work seriously. Marx's central point is simply ignored. Marx (1981, p.319),

> given the great importance that this law has for capitalist production, one might well say that it forms the mystery around whose solution the whole of political economy since Adam Smith revolves.

With industrial conflict rife from the late 1960s radical economists, like mainstream economists, focused on the capital labour conflict, developing conflict theories of inflation (Goodwin 1967 and Rowthorn 1977). Capital and labour were modelled as fighting over their shares of newly added value (surplus-value plus variable capital), with unemployment representing the ultimate solution to control workers' wage demands. This focus on the net product (Duménil 1983 and Foley 1986) to explain the profit rate logically follows from adopting the conventional use-value approach to value. As Okishio (1961) actually proved the profit rate in use-value terms has no tendency to fall, so if you work in use-value terms you must look elsewhere, to conflict over the net product, to 'understand' how the profit rate is determined. With labour's share of the net product apparently falling as capital gained the upper hand over labour from the 1980s onwards, high profitability, as defined by capitalists' gaining a higher share of the net product, should have led to strong growth. But growth remained subdued, so were policy makers deliberately holding back growth to keep unemployment high, so as to weaken labour and keep capitalists' share of the net product high? Rather than accident we now have conspiracy. Post-Keynesians and circuitists (notably Parguez 1996) argued that rentier-like central banks were deliberately holding the productive economy back by setting excessively high interest rates. As interest rates fell to historically low levels in the 2000s this argument, like other single phenomenon, and thus historically specific theories, passed its 'explain by' date. Alternatively Brenner (1998) argued that 'excess' competition since the end of the Golden Age has caused the relative stagnation of the world economy, missing Marx's point that, as total profit is determined by total surplus-value, competition can only determine the distribution of total profit, not its level.

Many observers (notably Fine *et al.* 1999) argued that the productive economy was somehow being held back by the behaviour of the financial system. The growing financial system was seen as a new economic force in itself, which was preying on the productive economy. Such theories do identify that capital is being switched to financial/adventurous paths. However, by not appreciating that profitability in the productive economy is low they have no real explanation for why this capital is surplus, that is, if the profit rate is fine why is capital not drawn more to productive investment? Consequently supporters of this view (notably Lysandrou 2009) are drawn back to the idea of demand constraints, resulting from increasingly uneven distribution of income, holding the productive economy back, as the financial system expands in response to the riches' growing wealth. Finally, as the crisis broke out, believing profitability to not be the problem, radical economists (notably Moseley 2008) have turned to Minsky's (1982) idea that the financial system tends to over-extend itself because of its innovative and over-excitable nature. Quite simply, if we believe profitability has not been the problem we must purely look to the behaviour of the financial system to explain the current crisis.

Conclusion

In this chapter I have tried to explain why we should look to the behaviour of the productive economy to explain our current crisis. Quite simply periodic crises are absolutely necessary to restore the profit rate, because the profit rate tends to decline in boom. Postponing crises by escalating credit creation appears to have only created stagnation in the world economy since the 1970s, with persistent surplus capital taking many disruptive adventurous paths. If the economy is to return to strong boom it must first take its crisis medicine. This is not a comforting solution, but it is what Marx means when he states 'The *true barrier* to capitalist production is *capital itself*' (Marx 1981, p.358); we cannot expect a smooth ride in an inherently contradictory system.

Notes

1 As capital becomes abundant/surplus in boom we would expect the rate of interest to fall, further pushing up the price of fictitious capital.

2 In boom, with productivity rising, the value in terms of labour-time of commodities is falling, so constant nominal prices would still cause the value of money to fall. To keep the value of money in terms of labour-time constant commodities nominal prices must fall in line with their falling values in terms of labour-time. Taking a conventional use-value approach to value, imaging units of 'physical' commodities as their unit of measurement, ensures economists miss this element of inflation/the erosion of the value of money completely.

3 Potts (2010b) analyses how surplus capital has led to a usurious expansion of lending to workers in developed countries, primarily in the form of mortgages to support private home ownership. Answering Adair Turner's suggestion that the financial system has outgrown the 'needs' of society (Parker 2009), I argue that under capitalism the financial system must support the productive economy. But modern usury is not a necessary feature of capitalism; rather it is a symptom of persistent surplus capital generated by governments' attempts to postpone capitalism as 'usual'.

References

Brenner, R. (1998) 'The Economics of Global Turbulence', *New Left Review*, No. 229.

Duménil, G. (1983) 'Beyond the Transformation Riddle: A Labour Theory of Value', *Science and Society*, 47(4), pp.427–50.

Duménil, G. and Lévy, D. (2005) 'The Profit Rate: Where and How Much Did it Fall? Did it Recover? (USA 1948–1997)', available at http://www.jourdan.ens.fr/levy/dle2002f.pdf

Fine, B., Lapavitsas, C. and Milonakis, D. (1999) 'Addressing the World Economy: Two Steps Back', *Capital and Class*, No. 67, pp.47–90.

Foley, D. (1986) *Understanding Capital: Marx's Economic Theory*. Cambridge Mass: Harvard University Press.

Freeman, A. (2004) 'The Inequality of Nations', in Freeman, A. and Kagarlitsky, B. (eds) *The Politics of Empire: Globalisation in Crisis*, pp.46–83. London: Pluto Press.

Goodwin, R. M. (1967) 'A Growth Cycle', in Feinstein, C. H. (ed.) *Capitalism and Economic Growth*, pp.54–8. Cambridge: Cambridge University Press.

Grossmann, H. (1929) *The Law of Accumulation and Collapse of the Capitalist System: Also a Theory of Crisis*, Hirschfeld, Leipzig. English translation, Grossmann, H. (1992) *The Law of Accumulation and Breakdown of the Capitalist System: Being also a Theory of Crises*. London: Pluto.

Hilferding, R. (1981) *Finance Capital*. London: Routledge and Kegan Paul.

Kliman, A. (2003) 'Value Production and Economic Crisis: A Temporal Analysis', in Westra, R. and Zuege, A. (eds) *Value and the World Economy Today*. New York and London: Palgrave Macmillan.

Kliman, A. (2009) 'The Persistent Fall in Profitability Underlying the Current Crisis: New Temporalist Evidence', posted at http://akliman.squarespace.com/presistent-fall on 15-10-09.

Lysandrou, P. (2009) 'The Link Between Global Inequality and Global Financial Crisis: A Two-Commodity Space Perspective', *EAEPE Annual Conference*, Conference Paper, Amsterdam, November.

Marx, K. (1969) *Theories of Surplus Value*, Part II. London: Lawrence and Wishart.

Marx, K. (1981) *Capital: A Critique of Political Economy*, Volume III. London and New York: Penguin/Vintage Publishers edition.

Minsky, H. (1982) 'The Financial Instability Hypothesis: Capitalist Process and the Behavior of the Economy', in Kindleberger and Laffargue (eds) *Financial Crises*. Cambridge: Cambridge University Press.

Moseley, F. (2008) 'Some Notes on the Crunch and the Crisis', *International Socialism*, No. 119.

Moseley, F. (2009) 'The US Economic Crisis: Causes and Solutions', *International Socialist Review*, No. 64, March–April.
Okishio, N. (1961) 'Technical Changes and the Rate of Profit', *Kobe University Economic Review*, Vol. 7, pp.86–99.
Parguez, A. (1996) 'Beyond Scarcity: A Reappraisal of the Theory of the Monetary Circuit', in Deleplace, G. and Nell, E. (eds) *Money in Motion: The Post Keynesian and Circulation Approaches*, pp.155–99. London and Basingstoke: MacMillan.
Parker, G. (2009) 'FSA Chief Puts Weight Behind Global Tax', *Financial Times*, 27th of August, p.1.
Potts, N. (2009), 'Back To C19th Business As Usual: A Surprise?', *Faculty of Business, Sport and Enterprise Research and Enterprise Working Paper*, No. 7, Southampton Solent University, available from Nick.Potts@Solent.ac.uk.
Potts, N. (2010a) 'Surplus Capital: The Ultimate Cause of the Crisis?', *Critique*, 38(1), pp.35–49.
Potts, N. (2010b) 'Marx and the Crisis', draft paper available from Nick.Potts@Solent.ac.uk.
Rowthorn, R. E. (1977) 'Conflict, Inflation and Money', *Cambridge Journal of Economics*, 1(3), pp.215–39.

5
The Dissolution of the Financial State

Simon Mouatt

Introduction

Which individuals or entities, control the issue, value and operation of modern money? In the popular conception these matters are the responsibility of the monetary authorities – the state. Yet, in recent times, we have experienced a reduction in the scope and size of the state generally. Does this extend to a diminishing state role in the national monetary system? Whilst some, such as Killick, have outlined the existence of restricted fiscal and monetary policy autonomy, as a consequence of international capital flows, privatization and foreign corporate investment, far less discussion has taken place regarding the existence and impact of the increasing *private* control of *money-creation* and *money-value* (Killick 1995). This is despite monetary debates, since the classical period, on topics as diverse as convertibility, neutrality or endogeneity. Also, what about the creation and operation of international monies? The dollar remains the key currency for payments and reserves yet, successful currency competition (greater usage and value) can lead to significant benefits for a nation and/or its financial institutions (Cohen 1998). Has the relative decline of the financial state led to an increased *private* ability to manipulate currency and, by implication, alter the international balance of power? Given that the *control* of money resources is a key source of social power, the question would appear to be an important one.

This chapter examines the erosion of (financial) state-sovereignty from a Marxian perspective and, argues that the state, viewed as an extension of industrial capital interests, has actively participated in these processes. The paper then explores who (or what) might have gained power at the expense of the state or, whether capability has simply evaporated. It could be that the private banking infrastructure, or the productive sector (or some combination of the two), has gained capability. Yet, if power has been gained by bankers and non-financial corporations, how do these two separate entities interact and what are their particular interests, objectives and capabilities? This latter theme is taken up in Chapter 6.

Financial power

Whilst money is often seen as significant in studies of political economy, it is not placed as the central mode of analysis. This is due, in part, to the mainstream view of money as relatively neutral in the long term. If money is neutral and, by implication, the real economy is akin to a barter economy, then money merely facilitates a more efficient operation of the economic system. Conversely a variety of heterodox economists view money as non-neutral and having a wider scope of function. From this perspective the control of financial resources is a primary source of *social power* in a monetary economy and, subsequently, the politics of money creation, value and function then become relevant and interesting arenas of study.

Power *per se* can be perhaps described as the ability to get someone (or an entity) to do that which they would otherwise choose not to do.[1] Using this definition authors have then observed the exercise of power, in the present capitalist order, and surmised on the sources of this power (Mann 1986; Strange 1988; Walter 1993; Strange 1997; Ferguson 2002; Zarlenga 2002). Arguably the *control* of money and finance (including the provision and expansion of credit) constitute a primary (but not exclusive) source of this social power and therefore (arguably) needs to be the central mode of analysis.[2] A corollary of this proposition could be that the *control* of financial resources largely determines power relations, or that shifting power relations (derived from other sources) are manifested through the medium of the *control* of financial resources. It is this definition of *financial power,* derived from Susan Strange, which is accepted and forms the basis for the whole chapter (Strange 1988). Financial power is, at first, located in the ability to *issue* currency and control its exchange value, and is derived from both the state *and* market in varying proportions (Strange 1988).

Money performs certain standard functions in the social economy, such as a means of account, store of value, enabler of exchange and a means of deferred payment. This functionality, in turn, needs a *social* acceptability that is derived from the (state) monetary authorities' ability to maintain scarcity, legitimacy and stable inflation. Yet, the often neglected quality of *fungibility* (the ability to change form) increases money's operational flexibility in relation to other assets or sources of power and endows it with certain commodity qualities. Indeed it is this quality, arguably, that is indispensable to the exercise of virtually *all* power. The controllers of assets in other forms (including near-liquid assets) simply do not possess the same abilities despite their value. In order to exercise financial power, they would need to *materialize* this by transferring their assets into a money form. Similarly, social power that is derived from other sources is limited, without the access to and control of financial resources. Monetary control, therefore, must be obtained.

The control of money is, of course, exercised through the possession of financial resources (in conjunction with associate property rights) or the control and management of the institutions and systems that determine its use. Financial power thus wielded can then manifest in the real global economy in a variety of modes through *inter alia* its (spending power) impact on global markets, new economic activity, war finance, international capital flows (and their ramifications) and the social relations between creditor and debtor. It is these social power capabilities that enable those that wield financial resources to pursue an extremely wide range of objectives and strategies in almost every aspect of life. Furthermore, the initial money-issue (and maintenance of exchange value) gives those that preside over the function, substantial social power.

Credit creation, for instance, is a key source of financial power as a direct consequence of the pervasive use (and ubiquity) of credit-money. Credit has enabled economic systems to evolve more efficiently through the recycling of money surpluses to deficit agents. Yet, in the present era, levels of debt have reached unprecedented volumes and substantial political leverage is transferred to the creditors.[3] Any principal and interest repayments required will also restrict the present spending power of borrowers and increase the financial power of lenders. Furthermore, the interest is sometimes compounded. The net effect is that as capitalism evolves there is an accumulation of the relative social power of *rentier* creditors, since the credit expansion process itself leads to an expansion of their resources. Ironically, as credit expands there is not enough circulating money (if obliged to use the current stock) to meet all of the loan contract repayments plus the interest, a phenomena known amongst monetary reformers as the 'impossibility contract', and therefore capitalist development then relies upon further credit expansion (to supply sufficient quantity of circulating money) in order to function (Kennedy 1995). In addition, as a result of modern fractional reserve banking, as described by the endogenous money paradigm, money is created *ex nihilo* by the private banking infrastructure and does *not* require the pre-existence of funds prior to the lending contract (Hawtrey 1919; Naito 2008). In addition, even the necessary liquidity to meet capital adequacy requirements (legal and operational) does not have to pre-exist in order for lending to take place (Rochon and Rossi 2007). Also, the proportion of credit-money in circulation (in relation to fiat-money) has also increased in the modern era, rising from 50% in 1945 to 97% in 2001 in the United Kingdom (Shakespeare and Challen 2002). This reflects, of course, a decline in state (financial) capability in terms of money-issue.

Credit creators can also grant or restrict spending power as well as 'manage or mismanage' currencies through the leverage they permit, which then affect consumer markets and fluctuating exchange-rates. Both activities lead to a redistribution of financial resources (Strange 1988). Strange has explained how this financial power is located in a *financial structure* that consists of two elements. Firstly the systems of credit creation, determined jointly between the state and private banks (in varying proportions), and the processes that determine exchange-rates. These rates derive from state economic policies, inter-state negotiated regimes and (private) agent activity in the foreign exchange market. The nexus between state and market consequently becomes a key factor in determining the distribution of financial power. However, since the historical expansion of the state itself has coincided with its increasing indebtedness to the private banking structure, the state could be viewed as the weaker partner in the relationship. This view, of course, necessarily implies the existence of a Marxian *bourgeois* state, which prioritizes the protection of the private ownership of capital in its many (including money) forms. Any reforming forces in the state have, in the main, been reluctant to challenge this.

Financial powers are also instrumental in impacting capital flows where, in recent years, international transactions have grown exponentially (Griffith-Jones 1998). These *private* capital flows enhance exchange-rate risk and enforce a monetary discipline on those states that are able to manipulate their macroeconomic variables enough in order to further their economic interests. Those states that are not capable find that currency devaluations lead to repressive adjustment policies and an enforced exposure to foreign direct investment that enables multinationals to purchase assets 'on the cheap'.[4] State sovereignty is subsequently reduced as the capability of *financial power* is increased (Strange 1988).

Financial power is also manifested through the use of international money. The US dollar, as the main reserve and vehicle currency, fulfils this role and US financial powers gain substantial *seigniorage*, notwithstanding periodic difficulties in practice.[5] General confidence in the dollar, imperative for international liquidity, can be maintained with both long-term balance of payments equilibria and prudent monetary management. The nature of international monetary interaction is such that all currencies (including the reserve) are ultimately valued in foreign exchange markets that, operate (it is assumed) according to the relative strengths of underlying fundamentals. This overall *currency competition,* as Cohen notes, subsequently leads to a redistribution of inter-state (or currency area) financial power and is therefore significant for the future world order (Cohen 1998).

Also, multilateral monetary regimes such as Bretton Woods, as sets of political arrangements that define the structure of the international financial system and regulate the processes, can restrict the *fungibility* of money and financial power is subsequently curtailed. Exchange rate regimes, for instance, seek to maintain currency stability amongst trading partners, which is useful for sustaining trade but may necessitate capital controls. Whilst these serve state development agendas the *capabilities* of inter-state *private* financial powers are restricted. Conversely, during the neo-liberal order, rate flexibility has become increasingly pervasive and private financial power is, therefore, then increased through global capital movement. In the same manner, of course, the various government legal and operational influences, on respective national financial systems, will also further impact the functioning of money.

As stated, the underlying assumption of this chapter is that the private control of monies is increasing at the expense of the state with presumed ramifications for (financial) power relations. Several writers have observed these developments in the present era of capital flow liberalization, financial market deregulation and private credit creation (Helleiner 1994; Killick 1995; Strange 1996; Cohen 1998; Griffith-Jones 1998). Still other authors have emphasized the strong role of political (state and non-state) factors driving these changes (Helleiner 1994; Cerny 1998; Germain 1998). Since the collapse of Bretton Woods, leveraged hedge funds, currency speculators, investment banks and private equity firms have all increased their activities in the global financial markets where there is now an enhanced incentive (and hence temptation) to manipulate market values. These financial developments, arguably, serve to undermine the capabilities of the state and also the level of potential cooperation in the international state system. A further (implicit) assumption is that a relative accumulation of money resources, by private financial 'rentiers', contributes to a *de facto* redistribution of 'financial power' towards a monied elite. The elite, in turn, consisting of both non-bank corporate and financial entities, then forms a plutocracy. Antecedents of these notions can be found in Lenin, Luxemburg and Hilferding, following the rise of the joint-stock company and, in more recent times, by several academics and monetary reformers (Hilferding 1981; Luxemburg 1971; Kennedy 1995; Lenin 1996; Shakespeare and Challen 2002; El Diwany 2003). Through the combination of the role of interest (and fees, commissions and charges), speculation, accumulation and the control of money issue, state capability is subsequently eroded to the potential detriment of the productive economy and society.

The financial state

The class conception of the state, following Marx, is that it simply represents an extension of the interests of capital (Miliband 1977). This has been theorized from the perspective of earlier competitive capitalism and, the more recent, monopoly capitalist (high degree of market concentration) form (Miliband 1969; Poulantzas 1974). These interests of the capitalist class can be considered to be *inter alia* the protection of private property (in terms of the means of production), a business legal infrastructure, state-supported (capitalist) banking, free markets, minimal regulation and competition law. If we examine the historical activities of the capitalist economies, over the last five centuries, it is difficult to convincingly argue that these core essentials have been under serious threat at any point. Furthermore, as Kliman has recently argued, the state is often involved in direct action to protect the system from crisis or collapse in what has been termed 'state capitalism' (Kliman 2008).[6] Be that as it may, the Marxist view can be separated into two distinct viewpoints, even though they amount to the same political outcome. The first, associated with the ideas of Nicos Poulantzas and Goran Therborn *et al.*, identifies a political structure where the institutional entities that constitute the state are clearly formed from class relations *per se* (Barrow 1993). The second viewpoint, conversely, suggests that the political process has a power balance, at any particular point in time, which is consistently biased towards maintaining the (key) interests of the capitalist class (Olin-Wright 2002).

The Marxist notion of the state *per se* is normally challenged with reference to the liberal democratic state that is presented as having a *pluralist* nature. The state is seen as autonomous from the interests of private capital (or any other interested party) and operates in the midst of (and consists of) a disparate plurality of powers, for example; business, banks, societal groups, external forces, and so on (Ball 1977). It is in the interactive political process that this power *mélange* determines outcomes. Yet, this (arguably) does not detract from the empirical reality which, appears to demonstrate that the *key* interests of capital have remained unchallenged (at least in a serious way) in capitalist economies since the transformation from the feudal era.

It is also appropriate to consider the modern state within the context of globalization. One of the consequences of a crude view of power, as a *possessed* capability, is the emphasis that this gives to the international society of states (and their comparison). Later Marxist thinkers, however, have developed ideas that have pointed towards an alternative view. The approach of *Gramscian* Robert Cox, for instance, enables a much broader concept of world order, which takes account of the international dimension, and is concerned about power relations at varying levels instead. Cox focuses on 'classes', rather than states, whose condition (in a Marxian sense) is determined by their material relations in the (now global) production structure. Since the production structure creates the *resources* that are indispensable to other sources of power (for example, military power) the relations (hierarchies) of production are responsible for forming the political authority – the state (Cox 1987). The state, in turn, reinforces the (same) political hierarchies of production that galvanize a 'system of accumulation'. In this sense power and wealth are accumulated by the same 'exploitation' of some groups over others – only at a global level (Strange 1996).[7]

The state has clearly discharged different functions in the monetary system, depending on historic context and place, a notion that is central to this chapter. Karl Polanyi, for instance, had pointed out that power (including financial) ebbed and flowed between state and market, depending on the historical epoch in question (Polanyi 1944). So, how is financial *control* actually discharged by the *modern* capitalist state as (commonly) determined by the professional, academic and informed (popular) sources? Clearly, as Knapp had noted in a 1905 seminal work, the authorities are responsible for the sanctioning of the legal currency (by law) which, in turn, finds its legitimacy in its *acceptability* for the payment of state taxes (Knapp 1924). Yet, the urban myth that suggests it is the government that solely issues the currency is simply not true. So, if this is the case, what does the banking, and educational literature, say on the matter?

There are, of course, exogenous and endogenous explanations of money-creation. Yet, in reality, it is a combination of the state (including the national bank as an agency) in conjunction with the private banking infrastructure that is responsible for the money-issue. One of the common difficulties is that the economics literature (for example, Pilbeam) tends to present the credit multiplier, as a demonstration of (private bank) money expansion, which necessarily depends upon the existence of a (state determined) reserve asset ratio (Pilbeam 2005). However, as Rochon has noted, this ratio has disappeared in a few western states (including the United Kingdom), and is minimal in others. This continued inaccuracy gives the impression that the state is still able to influence the overall level of (credit) money expansion. There is a real need, therefore, for the textbooks to be rewritten (Rochon and Rossi 2007). A notable exception is the Howells and Bain textbook. Here there is an explanation of the endogenous money paradigm, with reference to double-entry book-keeping and termed the 'flow of funds' model, since money is created in response to demand. The authors also note that the unreality of the alternative (monetary base) multiplier model still persists in many educational explanations (Howells and Bain 2002). Be that as it may, since the state (or central bank) sets the short-term interest rate, in an exogenous sense, it could still be argued that (depending on definition) they *are* still responsible for the overall level of monies created. Yet, this is ineffectual since they are not able to have accurate knowledge of the likely credit consumer behaviour and, therefore, no reliable indicator of the overall volume of credit money that will be established. In addition, market interest rates are not always correlated to state-managed base rates anyway.

The flow of funds model recognizes that money comes into being as a result of loans and, establishes a corresponding liability and asset. The deposit once created becomes a bank liability, and the loan itself forms an asset, since the principal (plus interest) needs to be repaid to the bank. The significant point here is that the bank has not lent pre-existing funds (as is commonly thought) but represents a fresh money-issue in the form of an accounting entry. The money has been created *ex nihilo* and then circulates as electronic bank account money until the loan is repaid. In the language of the French/Italian circuitists, this represents the creation and destruction of money (Gnos 2004). In this sense, money needs to be viewed as a flow rather than a stock. The balance sheets of the commercial banks will consist, therefore, of various assets and liabilities that are subject to any legal monitoring and audit that the modern nation-state devises. The bank ratios of reserves (liquid assets) to their loan portfolios will necessarily change as well, of course, as new lending takes place and deposits are subsequently drawn upon.

It is worth noting there has been some debate, however, between the structuralist and horizontalist view of endogenous money-issue, in response to demand at the government determined (or independent central bank) short-term interest rate. In the *horizontalist* conception, the private banks expand credit completely in response to demand at a horizontal supply, whereas in the *structuralist* notion it is suggested that the banks require higher interest rates (compensation) at larger volumes of credit expansion (Wray 2004). Notwithstanding, it is assumed in both of these viewpoints that the government (or delegated agency) sets the interest rate with regard to prevailing priorities. Yet, as Wray notes, even an exogenous interest rate has a measure of endogenous determination since, the policy-makers are responding to certain factors derived from the market (Wray 2004). In addition, the state has relinquished responsibility for LIBOR[8] in the current UK system, where short-term (often overnight) inter-bank lending is determined by a consortium of big banks, notwithstanding some state-influence (from central bank open market operations), and private banks set their own rates for lending, albeit in a competitive financial market (Ackrill and Hannah 2001). Meanwhile, the central (or national) bank operates amongst the commercial bank network and, provides their daily need for reserves as required. However, this requirement is usually satisfied through inter-bank lending these days. So, according to the informed consensus, money is issued as debt (credit-money) in response to consumer demand at a given short-term interest rate, regardless of who determines the level.

According to Pilbeam, the government, via the central bank, can determine (or influence) the money supply through three methods (Pilbeam 2005). Firstly, by the buying and selling of treasury securities, known as open market operations, which then has a bearing on the LIBOR rate (and reduces or increases private bank liquidity) and, in turn, general lending. Yet, as Howells outlines (p.260), the overall determination of the money supply is *not* what the bank hopes to achieve when they engage in this activity in practice (Howells and Bain 2008). Secondly, by changing the reserve asset ratio the state can restrict or loosen any credit expansion, through the credit multiplier. However, since the reserve asset ratio no longer exists in the UK, multiplier explanations are fallacious. Thirdly, through the central lending rate and its impact on general lending

(Pilbeam 2005). Yet, as stated, market rates are only 'loosely' based on the national bank rates. Notwithstanding, there have been times when there has been a serious attempt, from the state, to monitor and determine the nominal amount of monetary growth but, this has led to substantial difficulties in practice. During the 1970s, for instance, the 'corset' (special compulsory non-interest deposits at the Bank of England in order to restrict credit expansion), cash ratios, (strictly observed) reserve asset ratios and direct credit controls were used by successive governments until finally abandoned in 1980. Most of these methods relied on monetary base control, the use of the level of liquid assets that banks have in relation to their overall lending, and this proved to be problematic (Howells and Bain 2008). Firstly, when the state used to target the monetary base (MB) it often meant fluctuations in short-term interest rates, which led to undesirable macroeconomic instabilities. Secondly, since the MB is a liability of the central bank it can cause problems for the bank officials because, they do not always know what volumes they will need in their 'lender of last resort' capacity (to the private banks or the government). They tend to prefer more certainty in their own balance sheets in practice. Thirdly, even if the central bank knew exactly how to respond to reserve needs (for example, through a precise value of bond-issue), they are not practically able to always respond *at will* to the relevant MB needs. It was these types of time lags *inter alia* that led the Thatcher administration to abandon monetary targets in the early 1980s. Fourthly, in some financial systems, there would need to be structural changes to the private banking system. In the UK, for instance, the clearing banks have overdraft facilities with one another, making it more difficult for the central bank to implement MB control by measuring private bank reserves. Fifthly, most of the assets of a typical bank consist of their non-marketable loan portfolio. It is not always possible for commercial banks to respond to reserve asset ratios, for instance, since they cannot simply just sell parts of their non-liquid outstanding loan contracts. Sixthly, private bank reserves pay no interest which, amounts to a tax on banks and this then leads to an increase in their spread (between deposit and lending rates) and, perhaps, a detrimental impact on the general economy. Finally, the 'lender of the last resort' facility might be compromised when (even solvent) banks require reserves during times of tight MB control. Would the central bank still be able to offer convertibility in these circumstances? If they do not, the stability of the entire system is undermined. So, as MB control was abandoned by the state, the financial power of private banks has been increased.

The international financial system

In the absence of global government, historic monetary cooperation has relied upon interstate negotiation and trust. During the periods that specie (or convertible paper) was accepted as international money, global trade could be expanded since the (commodity) money transcended the financial boundaries of the nation-state. The gold standard, for instance, had also benefited from the size and reach of the *Pax Britannica*, since confidence in the pound was instilled as a consequence of British international activity. In the modern era, exchange rate regimes such as the Bretton Woods system, or the European Exchange Rate Mechanism (ERM), have involved substantial collaboration and had (as stated) significant implications for the monetary sovereignty of nation-states. During Bretton Woods, for example, fixed exchange rates were backed by central bank dollar to gold convertibility (at $35 per oz), capital controls were used to engender balance of payments equilibrium (by virtually eliminating private speculation) and member countries were expected to 'adjust' their macroeconomic conditions to ensure trade compliance. Monetary policy instruments (including open market operations), and occasional IMF lending, were needed to guide states towards this purpose. Yet, it was the reluctance of (current account) surplus countries to inflate, particularly Japan and Germany, which was one of the principal causes of the breakdown of the system in the seventies. When this factor was combined with a devaluing dollar, and oil price shocks, the system collapsed. During its operation, nation-states had needed to ensure that monetary policy adhered to the necessary conditions for trade stability. The early period of the ERM (from 1979 to 1986) had also involved capital controls and, member states were restricted in their monetary sovereignty in the same manner. This erosion of (state) financial management was further accentuated when exchange controls were removed in 1986, as part of the Single European Act, and countries needed to maintain market risk premiums (in practice an interest rate above the *strong* Deutschmark) in order to prevent speculative attack and a breakdown of the system. Interestingly, Potts had convincingly argued that, as a consequence, there would be more monetary sovereignty for the UK (or any other member state) in the Euro currency than could exist whilst in the ERM without exchange controls (Potts 1997). The increased currency speculation has also, of course, served to erode the monetary sovereignty of nation-states in recent times, because individual treasuries simply do not have enough funds to conduct effective open market operations in comparison with colossal privately owned volumes.[9] This point was highlighted by Griffith-Jones in her research work on capital flows (Griffith-Jones 1998). Some critics have subsequently called for a 'Tobin' tax to deter speculation and mitigate these harmful effects – restoring a measure of sovereignty (Tobin 1978). Other forms of monetary regulation, however, which are a direct result of international cooperation, are likely to have a mitigating impact on monetary sovereignty. The BIS Basle accords for instance, particularly the 2004 (Basle 2) agreement, has led to the *de facto* reduction of state regulatory power (as stated, government reserve requirements have virtually disappeared) and contributed towards the recent financial crisis as a direct result of the greater 'self-regulation' of security risk assessment. This has led to more 'in-house' risk assessment and occasional conflicts of interest between financial agents (Rochon and Rossi 2007; Docherty 2008; Rafeeq 2008).

A further issue arising since Bretton Woods, is the use of the dollar as the main reserve currency. This has led to other nation-state financial authorities being, to a greater or lesser extent, impacted by the vagaries of American domestic monetary policy. The dollar is used as the key currency for multinational accounting, statistical measures, global commodity exchanges (including the increasingly tense oil trading platforms), multilateral institutions, capital markets, sovereign lending, commercial credit and as a *vehicle* currency for virtually all foreign exchange transactions. Fluctuations in the dollar exchange rate and general (reserve) currency demand and supply conditions, therefore, have a substantial impact on the global economy. Nation-states have found, in addition, that there are further implications for their monetary sovereignty. Benjamin Cohen, for instance, has identified a measure of inter-state competition that is engendered as nation-states seek to harness the benefits that accrue when their currency is in greater general use, for example, cheaper borrowing. The United States has certainly profited from this activity during the modern era (Cohen 1998). In a world of hard and soft currency (and fewer currencies), of course, the evolution of global monies is a constant activity, with ramifications for sovereignty, as financial power is eroded or gained.

Fictitious capital and crises

The modern state is, of course, often expected to perform a role in financial crises that is unrealistic given the volumes of monies that are privately controlled. Marx had outlined how money mediates the exchange of commodities and also, how its circulation allows hoards of money-capital to become established. In this instance, Say's law fails to hold in the real world and, crises ensue as commodities fail to sell in sufficient quantities with various capitals experiencing losses (Bottomore 1991).[10] In addition, within these disturbances, hoarding can represent an unwillingness of capitalists to advance further money when faced with the prospect of further shortfalls of demand in markets if (prospective) commodities are produced and enter circulation (Bottomore 1991). The state can, of course, engage in monetary and fiscal policies to mitigate the impact of the trade cycle but, not eliminate it entirely. A further inhibitor to the advancement of monies as capital, from funds held in reserve, is the tendency for the rate of profit (in labour terms) to fall as noted in Chapters 3 and 4. In all of these circumstances, capital migrates towards fictitious capital in the financial markets, induced by the prospects (for some) of greater returns. Yet, since the very existence of fictitious capital (nominal value in excess of the underlying abstract labour-time value) means that no *new* value has been created, the activity can be precarious for agents and simply constitutes a (re)distribution of current nominal money (and hence social power) stocks. Those that gain, therefore, do so at the expense of others. In addition, increased asset demand associated with this capital migration, directly facilitates the creation of speculative 'bubbles' and the subsequent crises that follow. The subsequent expectation of asset appreciation then contributes to the 'bubble', as a result of normal rational behaviour (profit maximization), rather than some psychological deficiency on behalf of the market participants. If greater margins were being achieved in the productive economy, of course, circumstances would (arguably) be different. Yet, given the state deregulation of finance, especially the removal of legal constraints on short-selling (leverage for speculation) that has occurred, the nation-state has eroded its financial capabilities and, therefore, arguably neglected its responsibility to maintain monetary stability.

Marx had further posited that during an upturn in the trade cycle, there will be an expansion of credit (in terms of financial capital) and capital advanced from hoards, whilst the reduced expectations of capitalists during a downturn would lead to a contraction of credit and capital advanced (Marx 1981). A severe contraction of credit, such as experienced in recent times, would inevitably lead to a crisis. In this instance (as stated), the physical quantity of monies in circulation (in a virtual pure credit-money economy) is insufficient to purchase total output as well as meet interest payments (and thus Say's law does not hold), unless there is an expansion of credit or another form of liquidity creation. A credit squeeze, therefore, leads to the inevitability of default and unsold stocks. Marx thus provides us with a convincing explanation of the present financial predicament in the global economy, as well as a theory for a *bourgeois* nation-state that is relatively unwilling (or able) to act. In this sense, governments merely serve the interests of the banking and corporate sector and, only indirectly serve the interests of the people and the society they govern.

Conclusion

This chapter has presented the view that in the modern era, the state has experienced an erosion of its financial capabilities in terms of money-issue, value and function. Many of these developments have followed, as Helleiner has convincingly posited, intensive lobbying from the private banks in the post-war era so that the neo liberal (financial) order cannot simply be passed off as a consequence of economic processes alone (Helleiner 1994). Given such developments, private agents and banks as well as non-bank entities, have found their capabilities enhanced, which are then manifested in their exercise of (financial) social power in the modern global economy. In addition, the Marx-based explanation of the political process, presents the *bourgeois* state as an extension of private sector vested interest, and, therefore, complicit in the facilitation of the developments mentioned. In the next chapter, the prospect that non-banks are increasingly encroaching on the core business activities of the traditional private banking infrastructure is investigated and provides a partial explanation of the more precarious nature of traditional bank income-earning activities in recent times.

Notes

1 There are, of course, different *modalities* of power such as coercion, manipulation, seduction or authority as well as spatial and time complexities in the *exercise* of power (Allen, J. (2003) *Lost Geographies of Power*. Bodmin: Blackwell).
2 Money is defined here as state produced *fiat* money, in note and coin form, in combination with legally-sanctioned *credit* monies in sight deposits.
3 The developed world, for instance, has subjugated the developing world to neo-liberal economics through the use of structural adjustment policies of the IMF/World Bank following widespread default (Adams, N. (1993) *World's Apart – The North/South Divide and the International System*. Guildford: Zed).
4 The Asian crisis of 1997 was an example of such a currency crisis.
5 The Triffin paradox points out that in order to ensure liquidity an international reserve currency needs be plentiful and the host currency needs to run a balance of payments deficit yet, conversely, in order to maintain

stability and confidence in the international money a surplus (or at least sustained equilibria) needs to be obtained (Triffin, R. (1960) *Gold and the Dollar Crisis*. New Haven: Yale University Press).

6 Andrew Kiman attributes the term 'state capitalism' to Ray Dunayevskaya.

7 These ideas are similar to the ideas of the French 'regulationist' school (Lipietz, A. (1983) *The Enchanted World – Inflation, Credit and the World Crisis*. Thetford: Verso).

8 The London inter-bank overnight lending rate.

9 Currency 'short-sellers' exacerbate these problems for modern national banks.

10 A further consequence of economic crises is, of course, an increasing concentration of capitals as resources are reallocated towards surviving firms from those experiencing liquidation and foreclosure.

References

Ackrill, M. and Hannah, L. (2001) *Barclays: The Business of Banking 1690–1996*. Cambridge: Cambridge University Press.

Adams, N. (1993) *World's Apart – The North/South Divide and the International System*. Guildford: Zed.

Allen, J. (2003) *Lost Geographies of Power*. Bodmin: Blackwell.

Ball, A. (1977) *Modern Politics and Government 2nd Edition*. Hong Kong: Macmillan.

Barrow, C. (1993) *Critical Theories of the State*. Madison: University of Wisconsin.

Bottomore, T. (1991) *A Dictionary of Marxist Thought: 2nd Edition*. Bodmin: Blackwell.

Cerny, P. G. (1998) 'Politicising International Finance', *Millenium: Journal of International Studies*, 27(2).

Cohen, B. J. (1998) *The Geography of Money*. London: Cornell University Press.

Cox, R. (1987) *Production, Power and World Order*. New York: Columbia University Press.

Docherty, P. (2008) 'Basel II and the Political Economy of Banking Regulation – Monetary Policy Interaction', *International Journal of Political Economy*, 37(2), pp.82–106.

El Diwany, T. (2003) *The Problem with Interest 2nd Ed*. Birmingham: Kreatoc.

Ferguson, N. (2002) *The Cash Nexus: Money and Politics in Modern History, 1700–2000*. St Ives: Penguin.

Germain, R. D. (1998) *The International Organisation of Credit: States and Global Finance in the World-Economy*. Cambridge: Cambridge University Press.

Gnos, C. (2004) 'Circuit Theory as an Explanation of the Real World', *Modern Theories of Money: The Nature and Role of Money in Capitalist Economies*. L. Rochon & S. Rossi.

Griffith-Jones, S. (1998) *Global Capital Flows*. Chippenham: Macmillan.

Hawtrey, R. G. (1919) *Currency and Credit*. London: Longmans, Green & Co.

Helleiner, E. (1994) *States and the Re-emergence of Global Finance: From Bretton Woods to the 1990's*. USA: Cornell University Press.

Hilferding, R. (1981[1910]) *Finance Capital: A Study of the Latest Phase of Capitalist Development*. London: Routledge and Kegan Paul.

Howells, P. and Bain, K. (2002) *The Economics of Money, Banking and Finance: A European Text: 2nd Edition*. Gosport: Prentice-Hall.

Howells, P. and Bain, K. (2008) *Economics of Money, Banking and Finance: 4th Edition*. Gosport: Pearson.

Kennedy, M. (1995) *Inflation and Interest Free*. Canada: New Society Publisher.

Killick, T. (1995) *The Flexible Economy*. London: Routledge.

Kliman, A. (2008) *Worse than They Want You to Think – A Marxist Analysis of the Economic Crisis*. New York City: N. Space.

Knapp, G. F. (1924) *The State Theory of Money*. London: Macmillan.

Lenin, V. (1996) *Imperialism: The Highest Stage of Capitalism*. Bristol: Pluto.

Lipietz, A. (1983) *The Enchanted World – Inflation, Credit and the World Crisis*. Thetford: Verso.

Luxemburg, R. (1971) *The Accumulation of Capital*. London: Routledge.

Mann, M. (1986) *Sources of Social Power: Volume One: A History of Power from the Beginning to AD1760*. USA: Cambridge University Press.

Marx, K. (1981) *Capital: Volume Three*. Bungay: Penguin.

Miliband, R. (1969) *The State in Capitalist Society: An Analysis of the Western System of Power*. Aylesbury: Quartet.

Miliband, R. (1977) *Marxism and Politics*. Oxford: Oxford University Press.

Naito, A. (2008) *Money, Credit and the State: Post Keynesian Theory of Credit Money and Chartalism*. Association of Heterodox Economics Annual Conference, Anglia Ruskin University: Cambridge.

Olin-Wright, E. (2002) *Seminar on Theories of the State*. Madison: University of Wisconsin.

Pilbeam, K. (2005) *Finance and Financial Markets: 2nd Edition*. China: Palgrave Macmillan.

Polanyi, K. (1944) *The Great Transformation*. New York: Octagon Books.

Potts, N. (1997) 'National Economic Sovereignty and the Single European Currency', *European Review* (January).

Poulantzas, N. (1974) *Classes in Contemporary Capitalism*. Thetford: Verso.

Rafeeq, M. (2008) *Instant Experts – Dilute to Taste*. Latticework Management Consultancy.

Rochon, L. and Rossi, S. (2007) *Monetary Policy Without Reserve Requirements: Central Bank Money as a Means of Final Payment on the Inter-Bank Market*. CEMF Conference 'Post-Keynesian Principles of Economic Policy' University of Burgundy, Dijon, December.

Shakespeare, R. and Challen, P. (2002) *Seven Steps to Justice*. Chippenham: New European Publications.

Strange, S. (1988) *States and Markets*. London: Pinter.

Strange, S. (1996) *The Retreat of the State – The Diffusion of Power in the World Economy*. Cambridge: Cambridge University Press.

Strange, S. (1997) *Casino Capitalism*. Manchester: Manchester University Press.

Tobin, J. (1978) 'A Proposal for International Monetary Reform', *Eastern Economic Journal*, 4, pp.153–9.

Triffin, R. (1960) *Gold and the Dollar Crisis*. New Haven: Yale University Press.

Walter, A. (1993) *World Power and World Money*. Exeter: Harvester/Wheatsheaf.

Wray, L. R. (2004) *When are Interest Rates Exogenous?* Working Paper No.30, Jerome Levy Economics Institute.

Zarlenga, S. (2002) *The Lost Science of Money – The Mythology of Money: The Story of Power*. United States: The American Monetary Institute.

6
The Corporate Subjugation of Money and Banking

Simon Mouatt

Introduction

In his general analysis of the evolution of capitalism, Marx had posited that industrial capital would subjugate (autonomous) financial capital, older forms of money-lending, on the grounds that interest-bearing capital derives from the capitalist production process (and is therefore ultimately dependent on it) and further that any commercial credit was a secondary function (merely concerned with facilitating circulation) to the value-adding production process (Marx 1971, p.468). It is argued in this chapter that the development of the financial sector, since the industrial revolution, has culminated in a private banking system that is analogous to the feudal money brokerage Marx had in mind. It could, therefore, be gradually subjugated by the productive sector and, any appearance of strength or autonomy would be merely illusory.

Yet, shortly after Marx, events appeared to contradict this proposition. The rise of the joint-stock firm, for instance, suggested that investment banks had gained decision-making power over the corporate(s) through integration – the Hilferding notion of *finance capital* (Hilferding 1981; Lenin 1996). Substantial tribute is also, of course, extracted from the real economy in the form of interest (and fees and charges) by private bankers and their investors. It could be argued that these financial *rentiers* are now less integrated, strengthening their position relative to productive capitalists. Hedge funds and private-equity firms that 'short-sell' leveraged funds, for instance, authorized by the decisions of bank professionals, are able to manipulate currency and stock prices that can belie the market fundamentals and bamboozle small investors. Redistributive accumulation, asset stripping, and corporate monopolization can then follow any subsequent currency (or share-price) shock. It seems that money and finance (and those that control them) have triumphed over industrial capital. Marx (p.678) had also appeared to recognize the capabilities of these plutocratic financial elites:

> Talk about centralization! The credit system, which has its focal point in the allegedly national banks and the big money-lenders and usurers that surround them, is one enormous centralization and gives this class of parasites a fabulous power not only to decimate the industrial capitalists periodically but also to interfere in actual production in the most dangerous manner – and this crew know nothing of production and have nothing at all to do with it (Marx 1981).

Yet, there are contemporary signs of systemic weakness. Traditional banks are increasingly exposed to the vagaries of international financial markets, through their own trading positions, and earn a smaller proportion of their profit from interest. In addition, (non-financial) firms are now less dependent on the bankers, as a result of retained profits, and are further developing their own monies, payment systems and banks.

This chapter traces these monetary developments and argues that, largely as a result of the information revolution, a latent corporate monetary system – derived from new monies and technologies, is emerging that challenges prevailing monetary notions. These innovations could even partially replace the present financial order, in the event of major monetary disturbances. In the final analysis, industrial capital might subjugate financial capital. If this proposition were valid, of course, this would also reinforce the classical Marx notion that social power *per se* resides firmly amongst *bourgeois* producers, since this is where the *value* (in abstract labour terms) is actually created.

Marx, money and monetary evolution

Generalized monetary discourse, as Niebyl noted in his review of the classical period, is often problematic since the theories and empirical work have predominantly pertained to specific historical contexts (Niebyl 1946). Consequently, abstract monetary theories, that can be universally applied, are often non-existent or impractical. Monetary theorists (often from the same school) have also disagreed on the origin, nature and function of money *per se*. Conversely, Marx (this chapter claims) had a more robust monetary theory that began with an abstract discussion of the *endogenous* origin of money, money *socially* established as a monetary equivalent with intrinsic *commodity* value, through to the development of complex credit forms and world money (Marx 1976; Marx 1981).[1] Surplus value is realized in circulation in money-form that, simply represents abstract social labour. Money capital is thus transformed into the means of production (including labour-power) back to commodities and finally into money-form again – the metamorphosis of capital (Marx 1978). Capital accumulation and hoards, of course, also manifest in nominal monetary-terms and, money *per se* instigates economic activity and so is therefore indispensable to production. In essence, Marx's monetary ideas are simply an extension of his 'law of value' and general political economy.

For Marx, money was the only legitimate claim on wealth and truly fungible (the ability to change form) entity, meaning there is substantial *social power* wielded by those that control financial resources. This was particularly true of the state during the mercantilist era, for instance, when the state focused on the accumulation of specie stocks in order to enhance its political aspirations. These ideas, as De Brunoff noted, were developed by Marx in the *Critique of Political Economy* but not pursued further or elsewhere (De Brunhoff 1976). Marx had perhaps wanted to focus on the material relations of production and the 'law of value', as drivers of human behaviour, and leave a fuller discussion of the implications of financial power exercise to the (more subjective) realm of political science? Yet, these ideas are (arguably) significant given that any change in the relative financial capabilities of industrial and financial capitalists, has a direct impact on the distribution of social power. Whilst the interests of financial and industrial capital normally converge, as a result of the wealth-creation imperative, at times there are conflicts of interest. A debt-deflation, for instance, instigated by (autonomous) financial agents, directly impacts the productive economy and solely benefits wealth-holders. Money does *matter*, in heterodox political economy, in contradistinction to the mainstream which posits the general *neutrality* of money and (therefore) its irrelevance as a central mode of analysis. It is true that money performs certain *standard* functions in the social economy, such as a means of account, store of value, enabler of exchange and a means of deferred payment. This functionality, in turn, needs a *social* acceptability derived from the (state) monetary authorities' ability to maintain scarcity, legitimacy and stable inflation. Yet, money is *not* neutral (in a Ricardian sense), where money simply enables the economy to operate, since financial agents are able to determine outcomes through the *instigation* (and regulation and cessation) of economic activity. This activity might otherwise not occur, and can have long-term effects, whereas the quality of money's *fungibility* increases its operational flexibility and (therefore) utility.[2]

For Marx, the function of money follows from its nature as a commodity. In other words it is able to perform the functions of money because it *is* a commodity. In Marx's time this, of course, referred to gold – mined using human labour – that contained (dual) use-value (as money and precious metal) and hence an exchange value. There is an inference here that in order to possess the *social* acceptability, that money requires, an entity needs to possess this commodity status. Yet, as Itoh notes, it is irrelevant whether or not the money has commodity value other than its use-value as money and that, therefore, accounting prices *could* be set in value-less units of currency in an abstract sense (Itoh and Lapavitsas 1999). Marx appreciated the existence of abstract money, that transfers (labour) value into price, and *real* money that transfers price in to a 'concrete equivalent' containing the 'qualities of money', it has been generally assumed (erroneously) that Marx did not consider (or at least outline) anything other than a commodity money containing such final payment qualities (Itoh and Lapavitsas 1999; Mouatt 2008). In the modern era, conversely, we have a complete fiat money and credit money system that is not specie backed and is fully legitimized by the modern state. Furthermore, following Knapp, since (electronic) bank credit-monies are now acceptable for the payment of taxes, they can be considered money proper (Knapp 1924). Marx in his analysis, however, had utilized gold (or specie-backed paper) for illustrating payment settlement, although this does not preclude the *a priori* possibility of another (legally sanctioned) money fulfilling the same purpose.[3]

Marx also discussed the paper money of his day, created by the banking system, which he referred to as a 'money sign' (Mandel 1987). The paper money represented the money commodity nominally and could be exchanged for it. He was also sympathetic to the views of the *banking school* who felt that any excesses of (paper) money, above the necessary quantity of backing (not used for economic activity), would return to the banking system according to what is termed the 'law of the reflux' (Lapavitsas 1994; Itoh and Lapavitsas 1999).[4] Marx had thus emphasized the hoarding and paying functions of money, which tend to mitigate any inflationary impact of nominal money increases. If more money was needed to meet the circulation requirements, money could be drawn from hoards or the velocity of circulation could be increased. If less money was required, the law of the reflux would apply. In this sense, the money supply (for circulation needs) can be seen as partly endogenous and, non-neutral. This credit system, of course, served the emerging financial needs of bourgeois production relations. Marx had viewed the discounting of bills of exchange and overdraft facilities by retail banks, for instance, as *economizing* on the use of (real) money as a means of payment.[5] In the modern era, conversely, the cheque clearing system, switch payments and direct debits all use bank deposits in the same way.[6] The difference being that bank deposits actually *are* now *real* monies.

Yet, as stated, Marx did not view these (newer) credit monies as particularly autonomous from the processes of industrial capital. He assumed instead that older forms of money-lending (pre-capitalist), in the form of financial capital, would be gradually replaced by such bank provision to meet the evolving needs of industrial capital as the economic system developed (Marx 1971). He posited that as this occurred, monies lent as 'interest-bearing debt' became dependent on the expansion of value realized in the market, for continued existence, and monies advanced for purposes of circulation were secondary to it (Marx 1971). Marx (p.468) identifies the 'older' pre-capitalist forms of capital and states his case:

> The commercial and interest-bearing forms of capital are older than industrial capital, which, in the capitalist mode of production, is the basic form of the capital relations dominating bourgeois society – and all other forms are only derived from it or secondary: derived as is the case with interest-bearing capital; secondary means that the capital fulfils a special function (which belongs to the circulation process) as for instance commercial capital. In the course of its evolution, industrial capital must therefore subjugate those forms and transform them into special functions of itself (Marx 1971).

Interest-bearing capital, of course, is loaned (by the owners) at interest to industrial capitalists and therefore depends upon the production plans taking place. Marx further explains that, as capitalism developed, the subjugation of this capital form results from two processes. First, the 'violence' of the (bourgeois) state leads to an enforcement of lower interest rates, to the benefit of industrial capitalists who then gain a larger proportion of surplus value.[7] Secondly, the subjugation derives from the emerging (bourgeois) credit system that, Marx sees as a purposeful creation of the capitalist mode of production, in order to gain the surplus value traditionally extracted by the usurers (Marx 1971). The key driver, of course, is the competitive search for profit by (financial) entrepreneurs. He further predicts this credit system evolving as the scale of manufacture increases. Marx had also explained how commercial money-lending would be subjugated, as the feudal merchant became transformed into the industrial capitalist. In the former, the merchant (and 'interest-bearing' commercial capital) had dominion over the 'producing' guilds, or peasant craftsman, since they chose (or not) to purchase their wares. In the capitalist mode of production, the producer is himself the merchant and commercial capital becomes simply an 'intermediary only in the circulation process' and is therefore more subject to the industrial capitalist (Marx 1971). These overall processes, of course, become even more apparent as large-scale production emerges, since the market power of the firm is enhanced. The banking industry indeed experienced a major transformation, through the industrial revolution, and new financial structures were one of the main features. Deane, for instance, explored the role of the banks during this time and concluded that the emergent banking structures enabled capital to be raised, to fund the development of factories, and provided a means to save and reinvest accumulated wealth (Deane 1988). It is interesting to note that much of the prevailing (mainstream) monetary thinking, which pervades the economics discipline, has been loosely based upon these classical (Marx *et al.*) ideas formed during the industrial revolution and its immediate aftermath. In a similar way, in the modern era, the information revolution is resulting in its own set of changes to monetary structures, in order to meet the needs of the emergent electronic and virtual interactions. As new forms of banks, payment systems and money became a key industrial revolution facilitator, the emergent financial structures are likely to be a cornerstone of the new information revolution. This chapter argues that these new financial structures constitute a paradigm of the gradual subjugation of the traditional retail banking infrastructure, in the modern era, which itself had subjugated older forms of lending during the classical period.

As modern banking developed then, with (at least in appearance) a degree of autonomy from industrial capital, it was therefore analogous to the pre-capitalist lending activities that Marx had in mind above. Regardless of form, however, these financial capitalists, create no real *value* (since the labour is unproductive in Marxist terms), but nevertheless share in the distribution of surplus value and, as the relative dividends from financial and non-financial stocks have testified, the share has been (historically) quite substantial. It is concluded, therefore, that it is the *normal* competition for profit between capitals that has been the key driver of general transformation of the financial system during the capitalist mode of production.

Marx's general discussion of bank credit, is found in volume two and three of Capital, although the remaining parts of volume three were completed by Engels (Marx 1978; Marx 1981). Marx initially presents money hoards, as reserve funds of latent money-capital, derived from the (previous) expansion of value from production. Marx had (Chapter 17) further argued that accumulation is the normal *modus operandi* for a capitalist economy, which takes place when part or all of the surplus value is advanced as new capital instead of being spent on consumption or the increase of hoards (Marx 1981). This accumulation then makes the increase of hoards possible, as surplus capital is directed towards them. Marx viewed (following Tooke) these hoards as regulators of monetary circulation, as they were withdrawn and released from use (Lapavitsas 1994). Marx had also recognized the *social* power of these hoards of monetary resources, for those that controlled them, and further recognized their (Chapter 17) *de facto* claim on the annual produce (Marx 1978). In addition, Marx had posited that it was the capitalist ability to draw from these reserves that constituted a key defining feature separating the *bourgeoisie* from the *proletariat* (Marx 1848). This is an important point, since it is the *current* capability of industrial capital to draw on its own hoards that has diminished its dependency on the traditional bank provision. Marx had stated, as Itoh explains, that the existence of reserves then enabled capitalists to accept promissory notes (discounted by the banks), since the spare monies could be utilized to ensure the efficient continuation of the production process during the time period before the debt settlement date (Itoh and Lapavitsas 1999). Yet, has Marx presented a realistic explanation of the credit-system for the modern era?

Notwithstanding the efficiency that credit affords the capitalist mode of production, Marx's foundation for the operation of the credit-system was the existence of idle funds – 100% fractionally backing. Nowadays, conversely (as the endogenous money paradigm convincingly posits), money is created *ex nihilo* by the private banks and does *not* require the pre-existence of funds prior to the lending contract (Hawtrey 1919; Wray 2004). In addition, even the necessary liquidity to meet capital adequacy requirements (legal and operational) does not have to pre-exist in order for lending to take place (Pettifor 2006; Rochon and Rossi

2007). However, it could be argued that Marx's theoretical treatment of the credit system does not preclude the possibility of monies created in such a fashion, if money is defined in a certain way. Bills of exchange (and associated banknotes) that function as monies, for instance, could be conceived as contributing to the quantity of circulating currency (if banknotes are defined as money) or (as Marx perhaps implied) simply *economizing* on the use of (real) money that exists in the form of a commodity. If banknotes *are* money, then the monies could be conceived as being created *ex nihilo*, it all depends on definition. Yet, in contradistinction to the modern era, it was perhaps more rational for Marx (with the commodity money of his day) to make the separation between real (commodity) and credit monies.

Finance capital, the financial state and liberal finance

As capitalism evolved, following the death of Marx, the provision of equities, bonds and loans from the private banking infrastructure all came to be considered as *financial capital* – provided for the purposes of the industrial capitalist. Yet, the Hilferding argument was that, as the joint-stock firm enabled much larger-scale production and monopolization, the financial arrangements that facilitated this ceased to be conducted at 'arms length'. The banking 'decision-makers', therefore, became *integrated* with the industrial capitalists as a result of corporate shareholdings by banks, social links (bank directors appointed to corporate boards) and the detailed (bank) knowledge of corporate financial transactions. Hilferding considered that, in this context, bankers had the 'upper hand' in decision-making and effectively determined the future trajectory of capitalism (Hilferding 1981). If this view was valid it meant that circumstances were (or appeared) to move away from Marx's prediction and the financiers, rather than becoming subjugated, were forming a *de facto* plutocracy. To complicate matters further, later in the 20th century, the state enhanced its role in the financial system.

The classic Marxist (class) conception of the state, of course, is that it simply represents an extension of the interests of industrial capital (Miliband 1977). This has been explained from the perspective of earlier (more) competitive capitalism and, the recent, monopoly capitalist (high degree of market concentration) form (Miliband 1969; Poulantzas 1974). These interests of the capitalist class can be considered to be *inter alia* the protection of private property (in terms of the means of production), a business legal infrastructure, state-supported (private) banking, free markets, minimal regulation and competition law. If we examine the activities of the state in western civilization, notwithstanding occasional divergence of interest, it is difficult to convincingly argue that these core capitalist essentials have been under serious threat at any point in the last two centuries. In addition, as recently witnessed, the state is often involved in direct action to protect the system from economic crisis or collapse in what could be termed 'state capitalism'. The immediate aftermath of the depression and WW2 had led to calls for the state to play a larger role in the financial system. Friedman had, for instance, identified a central bank-driven credit squeeze as the root cause of the thirties deflation and argued for state action (Friedman 1956). In addition, monetary reformers like Keynes, Wicksell and Fisher, had long been advocating increased (state) monetary policy to combat the increased magnitude of the trade cycle oscillations of the early 20th century (Skidelsky 1995). So, the Bretton Woods 'golden age' era began, characterized by low interest rates, state-intervention, a fixed exchange-rate regime and a dollar-exchange anchor. Yet, as Helleiner has noted, the (private) banking lobbyists almost immediately began to pressurize post-war governments towards financial liberalization, in the form of capital control removal and market deregulation, eager to profit from prospective changes (Helleiner 1994). As soon as the dollar came under pressure (towards the end of the 1960s), coupled with OPEC oil price rises, currencies floated and exchange controls were later removed.[8] There are several calls in the present era, of course, to re-establish the multilateral regulation of the international financial system in order to mitigate harmful speculation, and avert the continuation of the currency crises, but with limited success.[9] As the profit margins of the private banks began to increase, after the 1970s, it appeared to many that the financial sector was becoming more autonomous from industrial capitalists (Griffith-Jones 1998; Strange 1998). Yet, whilst the discourse on financial matters had often lamented unregulated monies circulating around international financial markets, and the autonomous nature of (private) financial agents, the focus *now* seems to be on the vulnerabilities of commercial and investment banks to the vagaries of the money-system. If the financial capabilities of the state have declined, and the private banking infrastructure is showing signs of a profit-squeeze, then which entities have gained financial power at their expense? The central argument of this chapter, of course, is that emerging corporate monies, payment systems and banks (*corporafinance*) have encroached on the traditional activities of the banks (driven by the profit-motive) in the same manner that Marx had described the emerging credit system of his day. Indeed, even recent state intervention to deal with financial crises has not substantially mitigated the decision-making capabilities of private (bank and non-financial corporate) agents, and these processes (outlined above) are continuing unabated.

The rise of non-banks

Even if we reject the Marxian notion of the capitalist trajectory, where firms seek to realize increasingly more surplus value to offset the falling rate of profit (in abstract labour terms), the generally accepted corporate imperative is still the pursuit of profit. Yet, as previously stated, there are fresh challenges for firms since the information age and, corporate innovation has led to new channels of financial circulation and financial liberalization has been contributing towards a more competitive global economy. The companies likely to succeed in this environment, as Lietaer has noted, are the ones most able to combine (electronic) knowledge systems with production. If this is extended to the development of corporate monies, banks and payment systems this will further strengthen their competitive position (Lietaer 2001). It appears, therefore, that the normal *modus operandi* of competitive capitalism is driving these *corporafinance* processes.

So, nonbanks are playing increasingly significant roles in the financial world. Bradford *et al.* have examined their varied roles in payment activity, in both traditional and emerging systems. As a consequence, they have developed complex relations with the banks and payment system users. In addition, since they are rarely directly involved with final settlements, they appear (at least) to be less associated with systemic risk.

Many non-financial corporations have also experienced a relative competitive advantage during the information age. The margins on internet payment transactions, for instance, are lower than ones for traditional electronic retail banking and the non-bank corporations, through financial innovation, are therefore able to further encroach upon traditional bank business.[10] Another feature of the new financial landscape is that retailers have diversified into financial services, challenging banks in their own core markets. Since retailers have strong brands and customer responsiveness they often have stronger market knowledge. Yet, as Welch and Worthington have identified, retailers have so far adopted a selective approach to the provision of financial services and do not cover the wider range offered by banks (Welch and Worthington 2007).Notwithstanding, the retailer threat to retail banking is likely to continue. Retailers tend to have stronger customer relations than banks, provide extra services and tie-in customers with reward schemes.

In the 1990s, the Centre for the Study of Financial Innovation, a London-based think-tank, initiated an investigation into the non-bank phenomenon in Europe and how this would impact the retail banking sector. The report concluded that new entrant retail players posed a serious threat in the long term, although inroads made by retailers into the financial sector had so far been limited (Lascelles 1999). It seems that the corporate sector is, therefore, poised to make a serious impact on the retail banking sector, and its systems, facilitated by technology-led innovation and customer interaction. As stated, the current information age is resulting in the development of a new network of financial systems and structures, which are transforming and challenging the existing financial power structure, ultimately driven (arguably) by the relentless search for profit. Yet, retailing is not the only threat to the commercial and investment bank sectors. Manufacturers, for instance, have found that their development of finance houses for consumer credit, have been an antidote to tighter margins in recent years. The success of GM capital, for instance, provides an example of the rise of multinational corporate finance houses in the modern era (Houghton-Budd 2005).

In response to the threat to their core activities, there has been innovation initiated from the banking sector itself. Specific changes since the 1970s, for instance, have included automatic telling machines, call centres, telephone services and internet banking. There has also been a proliferation of new innovative instruments, serving international financial markets (such as derivatives) which offer quick returns and fungible products for large investors. The repackaging and reselling of securitized mortgages is another recent and topical example.[11] Yet, whilst the banking sector has been innovative in their core markets, an increased level of abstraction of money (and increased customer distance) has occurred as money and finance appeared more divorced from actual production during the liberal era.[12] Initially, the returns were good and banking professionals, and investors, received the rewards. Yet, this triggered (this chapter has argued) a response from industrial capitalists, eager to secure a greater proportion of surplus value through the development of *corporafinance*.

One explanation (following Marx) for the expansion and increasing autonomy (at least in appearance) of finance, during the liberal era, was the tendency for the profit rate (in abstract labour terms) to fall in the productive economy (LTFRP).[13] In these instances, capital can be tempted to migrate towards fictitious capital (Marx's term) in the financial markets, induced by the prospects (for some) of greater returns. Yet, since the very existence of fictitious capital (nominal value in excess of the underlying abstract labour-time value) amounts to a zero-sum game, the activity can be precarious for agents and simply constitutes a (re)distribution of current nominal money (and hence social power) stocks. Those that gain, therefore, do so at the expense of others and no (surplus) value has been created in the process. In addition, the financial market conditions, associated with this capital migration, directly facilitate the creation of speculative asset 'bubbles' and the subsequent crises that follow. Continued expectations of asset appreciation during the upturn, as Kregel has noted, then contribute to the 'bubbles' as a result of normal profit seeking behaviour, rather than the psychological deficiency of the market participants (Kregel 2008). If greater margins had been obtainable in the productive economy in the first place, circumstances would have (arguably) been different.

It could also be argued, of course, that the existing and latent information age *corporafinance* processes mentioned in this chapter, constitute the prospect for greater stability in a future financial system, as a result of closer customer interaction or the asset-backed nature of the new monies. This is particularly pertinent since the realm of fictitious capital in the financial markets has proven to be subject to periodic crises. If *corporafinance* and traditional banking continue asymmetrically, conversely, it could be that money competition (in a Hayekian sense), would eventually deliver a system that achieved the common trust necessary for stability, albeit with fewer currencies (Houghton-Budd 2005). This, given current circumstances, is the most likely scenario if conditions are left to the market. In order to be viable, of course, any corporate currency would require the legal sanction of the state for sustainability. If the state is merely an extension of the interests of industrial capital, this should not be a problem. However, there could be political implications if, as Marx had predicted, *corporafinance* manages to completely subjugate financial capital. The corporate sector is, as Handy noted, autocratic not democratic, since the generic company decision-making process is hierarchical (Handy 1992). In addition, there is likely to be a further concentration of *social* power in the corporations, as a consequence of the subjugation of financiers. Given the democratic deficit prevalent in western society, this is (arguably) not desirable.

Conclusion

This chapter has argued that Marx's view of industrial capital 'subjugating' the independent elements of financial capital, as capitalism evolves, seems to be a correct one. It is not claimed, however, that Marx is the sole antecedent of this contemporary notion. Edward de Bono, for instance, had posited the future possibility of corporate (asset-backed) currencies and Bernard Lietaer has suggested a similar possible future scenario (Bono 1993; Lietaer 2001). Yet, Marx can probably be considered to be the earliest proponent of these notions, which form an integral part of his overall political economy. Marx's monetary theory has been presented therefore, as an extension of his 'law of value', that illustrates the functionality of money as well as the *social* power that it confers. The emerging credit system of the classical period was also outlined, demonstrating the subjugation of pre-capitalist money capital, which was driven by the desire of industrial capitalists to secure a greater proportion of surplus value. It is concluded that these pre-capitalist lenders are analogous to autonomous (at least in appearance) financial capital that emerged in the post-Bretton Woods liberal era, which is therefore likely to be again subject to the increasing subjugation of industrial capital.

The sustainability of the bank sector, therefore, seems shakier than in previous decades. If there is a collapse or major disturbance in the banking sector then, corporate finance could step in and replace the banking infrastructure as the prime power of capital. In the absence of crises then the trend is still towards a more insular banking industry, more abstract sources of funds and a riskier monetary base. The productive sector, in this scenario, might well subjugate financial capital by stealth. Yet, it is argued, this will inevitably lead to a further democratic deficit and an increasing centralization of social power in corporate hands. We now turn to a consideration of empirical matters, where the authors hope to illustrate the changing realities of money and banking in the modern era.

Notes

1 It should be noted that Marx's notion of the historical endogenous origin of money has been contested by monetary historians (Hudson, M. (2003) *The Creditary/Monetarist Debate in Historical Perspective. The State, The Market and the Euro*. E. N. S. Bell. London: Edward Elgar).

2 This notion assumes that money (and monetary factors) is the *catalyst* for productive agents rather than the entity that merely enables economic activity, following instigation by production agents.

3 Marx had a good reason for his use of commodity money in that it could transcend the boundaries of the state, unlike fiat currency, but had also recognized its shortcomings in terms of the political difficulty of establishing a 'standard of price' (Marx, K. (1970) *A Contribution to the Critique of Political Economy*. Union of Soviet Socialist Republics: Lawrence & Wishart).

4 Lapavitsas argues that Marx had developed his monetary ideas more deeply than the Banking school by describing the different functions of commodity, fiat and credit monies (Lapavitsas, C. (1994) 'The Banking School and the Monetary Thought of Karl Marx.' *Cambridge Journal of Economics* **18**: 447–61).
5 Marx also thought that the credit facilities enhanced the velocity of circulation (Marx, K. (1970) *A Contribution to the Critique of Political Economy*. Union of Soviet Socialist Republics: Lawrence & Wishart).
6 Nowadays, economists view bank deposits as (real) money but Marx (and most of his contemporaries) thought otherwise. Marx appeared only interested in that which fulfilled the circulation functions of money (measure of value, means of exchange and world money) in the context of his time. Bank deposits *per se* simply did not fulfil the criteria.
7 However Marx sees this as pertaining to a 'lesser-developed' capitalist economy (Marx, K. (1971) *Theories of Surplus Value*: Part Three. Moscow: Progress).
8 RobertTriffin had predicted that the dollar-exchange system would come under pressure due to the conflict between liquidity needs and the maintenance of confidence in the international reserve currency (Triffin, R. (1960) *Gold and the Dollar Crisis*. New Haven: Yale University Press).
9 The Asian crisis of 1997–98 provides a good example of the damaging effects of un-regulated private capital flows.
10 This has been further enhanced by the development and licence of public key cryptography.
11 Much of this activity has derived from the blurring of the boundaries between commercial and investment banking, following financial deregulation for example, the reversal of the Glass-Steagal act in the USA (1999).
12 Ultimately, of course, all money (denominated in different currencies) is valued by its claim to entities in the real economy, and its relative value is determined by the vagaries of foreign exchange market forces.
13 It is worth noting that some Marxist economists have rejected the LTFRP, on the grounds of the transformation problem, whilst others such as the temporal single system Marxists have claimed that Marx's method is consistent and the LTFRP can be reclaimed (Kliman, A. (2007) *Reclaiming Marx's Capital: A Refutation of the Myth of Inconsistency*. United States: Lexington).

References

Bono, E. D. (1993) *The IBM Dollar*, The Centre for the Study of Financial Innovation.
De Brunhoff, S. (1976) *Marx on Money*. New York: Urizen.
Deane, P. (1988) *The First Industrial Revolution*. Cambridge: Cambridge University Press.
Friedman, M. (1956) *Studies in the Quantity Theory of Money*. Chicago: University of Chicago Press.
Griffith-Jones, S. (1998) *Global Capital Flows*. Chippenham: Macmillan.
Handy, C. (1992) *The Empty Raincoat*. London: Arrow.
Hawtrey, R. G. (1919) *Currency and Credit*. London: Longmans, Green & Co.
Helleiner, E. (1994) *States and the Re-emergence of Global Finance: From Bretton Woods to the 1990's*. USA: Cornell University Press.
Hilferding, R. (1981[1910]) *Finance Capital: A Study of the Latest Phase of Capitalist Development*. London: Routledge and Kegan Paul.

Houghton-Budd, C. (2005) *Auditorial Central Banking – Monetary Themes for the 21st Century*. New Economy Publications: Centre for Associative Economics.
Hudson, M. (2003) *The Creditary/Monetarist Debate in Historical Perspective*. The State, The Market and the Euro. E. N. S. Bell. London: Edward Elgar.
Itoh, M. and Lapavitsas, C. (1999) *The Political Economy of Money and Finance*. Chippenham: Macmillan.
Kliman, A. (2007) *Reclaiming Marx's Capital: A Refutation of the Myth of Inconsistency*. United States: Lexington.
Knapp, G. F. (1924) *The State Theory of Money*. London: Macmillan.
Kregel, J. (2008) *Using Minsky's Cushions of Safety to Understand the Sub-Prime Mortgage Crisis*, Brunei Gallery: School of Oriental and African Studies.
Lapavitsas, C. (1994) 'The Banking School and the Monetary Thought of Karl Marx', *Cambridge Journal of Economics*, **18**: 447–61.
Lascelles, D. (1999) *Europe's New Banks: The 'Non-Bank' Phenomenon*. London: The Centre for the Study of Financial Innovation.
Lenin, V. (1996) *Imperialism: The Highest Stage of Capitalism*. Bristol: Pluto.
Lietaer, B. (2001) *The Future of Money – Creating New Wealth, Work and a Wise World*. Guildford: Random House.
Mandel, E. (1987) *Karl Marx*. Marxian Economics. M. M. a. P. N. John Eatwell. Hong Kong: Macmillan.
Marx, K. (1848) *The Communist Manifesto*.
Marx, K. (1970) *A Contribution to the Critique of Political Economy*. Union of Soviet Socialist Republics: Lawrence & Wishart.
Marx, K. (1971) *Theories of Surplus Value*: Part Three. Moscow: Progress.
Marx, K. (1976) *Capital: Vol. One*. St Ives: Penguin.
Marx, K. (1978) *Capital: Vol. Two*. Aylesbury: Penguin.
Marx, K. (1981) *Capital: Vol. Three*. Bungay: Penguin.
Miliband, R. (1969) *The State in Capitalist Society: An Analysis of the Western System of Power*. Aylesbury: Quartet.
Miliband, R. (1977) *Marxism and Politics*. Oxford: Oxford University Press.
Mouatt, S. (2008) 'Evaluating Stephen Zarlenga's Treatment of Historical Monetary Thought', *International Journal of Social Economics*, **35**(11).
Pettifor, A. (2006) *The Coming First World Debt Crisis*. Chippenham: Palgrave Macmillan.
Poulantzas, N. (1974) *Classes in Contemporary Capitalism*. Thetford: Verso.
Rochon, L. and Rossi, S. (2007) *'Monetary Policy without Reserve Requirements: Central Bank Money as a Means of Final Payment on the Inter-Bank Market.'* CEMF Conference 'Post-Keynesian Principles of Economic Policy' University of Burgundy, Dijon, December.
Skidelsky, R. (1995) 'J. M. Keynes and the Quantity Theory of Money.' *The Quantity Theory of Money – From Locke to Keynes and Friedman*. G. Wood. Chippenham: Edward Elgar.
Strange, S. (1998) *Mad Money*. Guildford: Manchester University Press.
Triffin, R. (1960) *Gold and the Dollar Crisis*. New Haven: Yale University Press.
Welch, P. and Worthington, S. (2007) 'Baning at the Checkout 2007–08: Evaluating the Provision of Financial Services by Retailers', *Journal of Financial Services Marketing*, **2**(3): 230–45.
Wray, L. R. (2004) *When are Interest Rates Exogenous?* Working Paper No. 30, Jerome Levy Economics Institute.

Part II

The Evidence

7

The Emergence of Non-Banks: E-Commerce Driven Competition in the Financial Sector[1]

Carl Adams

Introduction

This chapter explores the growing importance of non-bank entities within the traditional banking system. There are two sides to this development. The first covers the increased use of technology within the banking sector, that has resulted in more expertise and functionality being used from outside. Many banking functions are now provided by non-bank institutions providing business for computer hardware or software companies, telecommunication companies, call centres and other intermediaries. The second is the growing competition to the banking sector core business by non-bank entities, including electronic payment systems, retailers, credit companies, technology companies, telecommunications companies and intermediaries. We have labeled these developments *corporafinance* and they are supported and enabled by the capabilities of electronic commerce infrastructures and practices within the information revolution. The evolution and adoption of these e-commerce technologies has even made it possible to now consider alternatives to the existing financial system, which may provide more stability.

A systemic weakness in the financial sector arose in 2007, following default in the sub-prime United States mortgage market, with knock-on effects around the globe due to general bank exposure. The issues of instability were raised early in a speech at the Philadelphia Fed Policy forum, in November 2007, where Governor Randall Kroszner discussed some of the innovations and challenges facing financial markets, particularly relevant in the wake of the crisis. Kroszner argued that sufficient *information* about financial innovations is paramount for stakeholders to aid risk assessment and for market stability: 'When market participants realize that they do not have the appropriate information necessary for [*the*] proper valuation of risk, the price-discovery process can be disrupted, and market liquidity can become impaired' (Kroszner 2007, p.4).[2] Sub-prime collateralized securities lacked information resulting in inappropriate AAA ratings given to a collection of investment products, heralding a major collapse and restructuring within the financial sectors. In the wake there have been bank-runs, failing hedge-funds, debt write-downs, bank job cuts and emergency measures from central banks (and governments) to stabilize the banking sector (Bawden 2008; Jagger 2008). In March 2008 the US Federal Reserve, for instance, responded to the deteriorating credit crisis with a $2,000bn collateral facility. In April 2008, the Bank of England offered a similar £50bn facility to support banks and interbank lending. In the EU, governments took similar actions to support their financial sectors in an attempt to stave off or reduce recession.

Modern banks are increasingly exposed to the vagaries of international financial markets, as a consequence of their increased speculative trading positions, whilst their income from interest is (relatively) reduced. Meanwhile the size of the markets has mushroomed. Lietaer (2001) has calculated and compared the volumes of currency trading over recent decades with daily transactions in 1975 in the order of $15bn, compared to $2,000bn in 2000 (it's now double). A 5% run on currency in the earlier years would have resulted in about $3bn of pressure, which most central banks could withstand, whereas in 2000 a 5% run would result in $100bn pressure which no central bank could withstand (Lietaer 2001; Boyle 2003, p.39). The financial system is now driven on speculation and gambling on the markets, which provides a risky and volatile base (Soros 1995; Boyle 2003, p.80).

Since, as stated, the current focus is on electronic infrastructures and technologies they are now dictating the rate and specifics of general business (and banking) transformation. Information in its wider sense, with information-based services, has become the main commodity. New production practices have also emerged based on virtual collaboration, supply chains, eco-nets and global outsourcing, which are all supported by electronic infrastructures and information. Production activity has also moved towards mass-customization, supported by mobile, ad-hoc and virtual working teams. Companies can now conduct business solely within the virtual operating environments. Indeed, some of the biggest and fastest growing companies are based on virtual operating activity and effectively are just moving electronic data (such as e-bay and Google). The changes have, of course, affected the financial domain as new types of banks and financial instruments have emerged such as virtual banks, electronic markets and derivatives. The information revolution, and corporate innovation, has also led to new channels of financial circulation, a key arena for non-bank activity.

Technology and function outsourcing

Writing in the late 1980s, Stenier and Teixeria (1990) captured some of the fundamental changes that were taking place in the banking sector at the time. Since the 1960s the industry had seen a significant increase in the number of employees, peaking in the 1980s. In the US, for instance, the commercial banks employed approximately 640,000 bankers in the sixties, by 1986 that had grown to approximately 1.48 million (Stenier and Teixeria 1990, p.xi). The rise in employee numbers corresponds with a significant increase in banking activity, which also continued in the 1990s. Banks also used more and more technology, automating many of the back-office business processes and (increasingly) the front-line processes that deal with customers. Much of this automation has been driven by technological changes, mostly computing, which has resulted in a restructuring and transformation across the whole of the banking industry.

Financial institutions run and are reliant on a host of information and communication technologies (ICTs). Banks now use, for instance, a variety of software applications including Business Process Management (BPM), customer relations management, security systems, portfolio management systems, application process systems, loan-tracking systems, reconcile account systems, fraud protection systems, trading systems, clearing systems, network management systems. The full range of services and financial products that banks operate is fairly large, each requiring their own software systems. As Stenier and Teixeria have identified 'Banking is very far from being a homogenous activity. In fact, it is a collection of more than 150 specific product [*or*] market services. Lines of business differ by customer – whether retail, corporate, or other financial institution. They differ by distribution channel, whether by branch, by direct salesman, or by mail. They [*also*] differ by product group, whether lending, deposit gathering, or payment product' (Stenier and Teixeria 1990, p.xv).

In terms of the customer, perhaps one of the most obvious areas of automation was the introduction of Automated Teller Machines (ATM). This development, of course, like many other innovations, resulted in considerable labour displacement as ATMs replaced bank staff. Banks have become increasingly reliant on technology to interact with customers and conduct back-office processes. The introduction of online banking services has created further reliance on technology, along with the supplying technology companies, and also at the same time further distancing the interaction with the customer. Since the 1980s banks have also been outsourcing their software production – indeed most of their software is either outsourced or consists of off-the-shelf packaged solutions provided by the larger software companies (such as IBM, Oracle or SAP). This has helped them remain competitive, keep operating costs down and be able to pick and mix from the best systems available. Yet, it has also meant that they have lost some of their capability in producing systems themselves. Banks simply do not have the expertise or man power to directly develop all the software and technology needed to participate in the electronic world. They may have had the expertise at one time but, driven by recent cost-cutting and efficiency measures they have mostly outsourced their development teams. The dominant technology provision strategy across the banking sector is to outsource based on competitive tender. The body of knowledge and expertise covering the wider range of technology developed and used by the banking industry, therefore, is now firmly lodged within technology companies rather than the banks.

In non-retail banking the situation is the same. Stock exchanges, for example, use the expertise of technology companies rather than developing and maintaining the systems themselves. The London Stock Exchange (LSE) uses TradElec software, a bespoke set of software created by Microsoft and Accenture, which provides the real-time trading system with an impressive sub-ten millisecond response time for market participants (http://blogs.computerworld.com/london_stock_exchange_suffers_net_crash, accessed 14/4/2010). Getting such speed in a consistently robust and secure environment requires high levels of technological expertise, which is outside the financial sector capability.

The rise of nonbanks: *Corporafinance*

Nonbanks are playing an increasingly significant role in the financial world. Bradford *et al.*, have examined the roles that nonbanks play in payment activity and identified that they are involved in both traditional and emerging payments types (Bradford *et al.* 2002). Since nonbanks are rarely involved in settlement activities, they also concluded that they tend be associated with limited operational and systemic risk. A follow-on study by the European Central Bank and Federal Reserve

Bank of Kansas City (ECB & FRBK 2007) confirmed the growing importance and influence of nonbanks: 'Retail payments systems throughout the world are undergoing fundamental change. Traditional chapter-based forms of payment are giving way to electronic forms of payment. Technology advances are making possible new front-end payment instruments and new back-end processing methods. New products, business models, new markets, and new alliances are an everyday occurrence. ... One key element of this new environment is the increased importance of nonbanks in the payment system. Nonbanks are making their presence felt at all stages of the payments chain. At this time, nonbanks appear most prominent in the United States, but they are prominent in many European countries as well. And, most importantly, their presence appears to be increasing in virtually all countries' (ECB & FRBKC 2007, p.45).

Welch and Worthington (2007), focusing on how retailers have diversified into financial services, identify that the multinational retailers are seen as a threat to retail banks and are challenging banks in their own core markets. Retailers have strong brands and are responsive to customer needs – including financial. However, the authors identify that, so far, retailers have adopted a selective approach to the provision of financial services and do not cover the wider range of financial services offered by banks (Welch & Worthington 2007). However, retail(er) banks can also offer financial services that are not well covered by the traditional banking sector. In the United States, for instance, community banking and accounts for people with very low income are emerging, offering an extra customer support from retail corporations.

It is worth noting that the e-payments 'industry' is not a single industry but rather a set of evolving *industries*, converging around an association with e-payments, which has clear implications for market competition since the majority of the players are new entrants. Even comparatively long-standing players, such as credit card companies like Visa or MasterCard, have few years experience in dealing with online payments. The evolution of on-line business and activity, with corresponding e-payments, is thus creating a completely new business arena. This means that the key corporate players in e-payments have evolved from different industrial sectors including the payments service sector itself (credit cards companies and payment service providers), the banking sector (banks and building societies), the telecommunications sectors (especially the mobile and fixed telecommunication operators) and the technology sector (such as software and hardware companies). In addition, there are the new Internet entrants such as Paypal, Google and

Payhound. Furthermore, the retail sector has also moved into the e-payment arena. So, the e-payments industries have become intense competitive places and the (traditional) financial institutions are facing competition from each of these evolving sectors. It is perhaps possible to describe the current e-payments industries as a *hyper competitive market place*, and it is not clear which sectors or companies within these industries are likely to emerge as successful. As a consequence, banks have been creating alliances with other banks, technology companies and telecommunication companies. This development contributes to potential instability for the traditional financial sectors and sets the scene for future systemic change.

The retailer threat to retail banking may be even more fundamental. Retailers have strong relationships with their customers, often providing ranges of services that tie in customers with reward schemes. In addition, a typical customer is more likely to meet a retail manager than a bank manager suggesting a potential efficiency saving. As stated, the trend in traditional banking has been towards ATMs, and 'distance-banking', where customers rarely get to see banking personnel. In contrast, customers regularly visit their preferred retailer for their weekly shop or for a variety of other goods such as medicines, mobile phones, kitchen items, white goods, electronics goods, books, CDs, DVDs, stationary and a variety of services such as credit cards, or pet and car insurance.

Many of the innovations in the banking and financial sector (such as ATMs, online banking, call-centers and 'distancing of the customer') have been driven mostly by cost saving, whereas innovations from the retail sector have been mostly driven by developing new services. Banks' business activity revolves almost exclusively around financial services yet, conversely, retailers' business models are more diverse and supported by the selling of physical commodities which are in daily need. If there are problems in the financial services markets, then banks are more heavily affected than retailers who can rely on their sustainable retailing activity to offset any financial instability. In addition, large retailers receive payment from customers (for their weekly shopping) often before the suppliers have been paid for the very same goods. This low-risk approach of retailers, as Subramani notes, extends to other aspects of the supply-chain relationship (Subramani 2004). Subramani has identified, for instance, that the supplier-retailer relationships is complex and uneven especially where there are technology-dominated supply chains, since a small supplier will need relationship-specific investments and are effectively locked-in to a retailer. The larger retailers, therefore, transfer much of the risk to their wider supplier network (Subramani 2004).

The Centre for the Study of Financial Innovation, a London based think-tank, at the end of the 1990s initiated an investigation into the 'non-bank' phenomenon within Europe and how this would impact the retail banking sector (Lascelles 1999). They concluded that the new entrant retail(er) players did pose a serious threat for the longer term, although the market-share impact made was currently small. It seems that the retail sector is poised, therefore, to make an impact on the retail banking sector and its financial systems. Furthermore, much of this latent retail sector activity has been supported by technology-led innovations. Similar to the first industrial revolution, our current information revolution is developing new sets of financial systems and structures, which are changing and challenging existing relationships and dominances.

Yet, the retail sector is not the only threat to the retail banking and financial sectors. Edward De Bono (1993), while at the Centre for the Study of Financial Innovation, raised the concept of an *asset-backed* 'IBM Dollar', or large corporation currency, which is directly linked to the commodity being produced.[3] Boyle has also suggested something similar to this concept of corporate money, in the form of new money systems for large urban centres such as London (Boyle 2000).[4] This would effectively form 'regional corporation' money and cover significant expenditure items within the region, such as transport and/or local economic exchanges. Current examples already exist with the Oyster card system in London and the Octopus cards in Hong Kong, which can also be used to purchase non-transport items. Similar systems are been applied in other cities around the world, one of the most recent being in Dubai (Octopus 2007). The Oyster and Octopus systems do not, however, perform the *full* functionality of a complementary currency system (envisaged by Boyle) that operates alongside existing financial systems. Perhaps the closest example of such a system is the 'Wir' system in Switzerland (covered more fully in Chapter 10). Wir, an acronym for *Wirtschaftsring* –'economic circle' Europe's oldest bartering operation, is specifically aimed at smaller companies, and is now so widespread that it amounts to a virtual currency in parallel to the Swiss franc. Wir was started in 1934 by two followers of the economist Silvio Gesell (admired by Keynes), who had urged the creation of negative interest-rate currencies in order to encourage currency circulation. Whilst the Wir scheme does not actually depreciate, by 1993 it had a turnover of £12 billion and 65,000 corporate members (Boyle 2000, p.14).

A large city can have enough social participation and economic activity to generate its own duel currency, that competes with (and complements) the existing formal currency and financial system. However, the same may also be true of all manner of dispersed groups that engage in mutual exchanges, such as commercial or socializing networks that use the internet to shrink the distances between the participants. Corporate networks have recently emerged with a host of voucher systems for *inter alia* books, music, groceries (such as Tesco Clubcard points) and travel (such as Airmiles). An interesting collaboration of 'vouchers' has also emerged in Ireland with 'The One4all® Gift Voucher' (see http://www.one4all.ie/) which uses a single voucher for 4,000+ retail outlets. This has been expanded to other regions as well, including some parts of the UK and Malta. In the same fashion, these city systems and networking systems are driven and supported by the information and communication technologies at the heart of the information revolution.

The rise of nonbanks: Competition and standardization

As stated, dual or multiple currencies already operate in a variety of different forms around the world, from social network systems to larger-scale corporate non-bank systems. There are also many non-bank players that take a leading role in developing sustainable *corporafinance* alternatives, such as technology companies (like IBM, or Google) or retail companies at the forefront of using ICT (such as the voucher-based systems of Wal-Mart, Tescos in the UK or Carrefour in France). However, these different forms on non-bank monies are mostly small scale compared to the main banking sector.

Competition seems to be the key driving force towards new currency systems from the non-bank sector. At the same time, for systems to reach critical mass requires some level of coordination and cooperation between systems is needed. Along with competition there will need to be some common standards. The later parts of Kroszner's speech cover the need for standardization. He states that 'The benefits of the development of standardization for enhancing the liquidity of financial markets have a long history ...' and he provides a few historical examples such as 'the development of exchange-traded commodities futures contracts in the mid-1800s [*which*] improved the flow of information to market participants, reducing transaction costs and fostering the emergence of liquid markets .... In the early days of the Chicago Board of Trade, in the mid-1850s, standardization took the form of creating "grades" or quality of categories for commodities ... traders no longer needed to verify that a certain quantity of grain was a sufficiently high grade' (Kroszner 2007, pp.5–6). Standardization, it is argued, will improve the information needed to support stakeholders in understanding market risks and is also practically indispensable for developing market stability. In order for *corporafinance* to provide a real alternative to the financial systems then a variety of system approaches should combine and collaborate. The notion of free banking, as Hayek had posited, will allow a variety of currencies to develop with the assumption that market forces will (after adjustment) lead to the establishment of stable and trusted monies.

Technological innovations are also set to continue making deep changes in the financial services sectors. The next technological evolution of the Internet, for instance, towards Web 2.0 and Web 3.0 technologies are set to have a substantial impact on the range and type of financial services that will emerge, as well as facilitating even more new entrants to the financial services market place (Towell *et al.* 2007). It also seems likely that the Web 2.0/3.0 (evolving) financial services market place will soon be dominated by technology companies and virtual retailers rather than the more traditional banking institutions. It is also raising, of course, the political issue of Internet 'neutrality' as certain companies seek preferential bandwidth in relation to their Internet competitors.

In Europe the EU Electronic Money directive gave member states guidelines to develop legislation for corporations to develop their own electronic monies. In the UK this has been translated in to the 'governance of electronic money-issue', by the Financial Services Association (FSA), who issue licenses for corporations that wish to issue their own money. The licenses are granted under tight rules and monitoring activity. Interestingly, Paypal was an early example of a licensee under the new EU scheme, pre-dating the issuing of licenses to many of the telecoms companies. An amendment to the directive from the EU, directive 2007/64/EC, moves further to encourage competition in financial services and e-payment markets. Fundamentally, the amended directive encourages variation and competition, specifically incorporating supermarkets, retailers and other entities, and seeks to encourage low-value or micro-payment mechanisms.

Conclusion

Money and its related infrastructures have continually evolved throughout history. As Williams *et al.* note on the development of money, 'The clearest characteristic of the modern period of world history is perhaps the rate at which change has taken place – particularly in relations to changes in technology and the sciences, in which the last 250 years have seen greater change than in the preceding 2,500. This feature is typical of the modern history of money' (Williams 1997). It could be argued that the last 50 or possibly even just 25 years has witnessed a greater transformation of money and banking than during the whole of the last 250 years. The introduction of financial derivatives and global exchanges, for instance, which dwarf the scale of any money flows preciously seen in history, are relatively new. Also, the wide-scale adoption of credit and debit cards, ATM machines, online banks accounts, online transactions and new forms of banks and institutions (e.g. PayPal, Google) are shaping consumer and commercial practice in the information economy. If we add the immense potential afforded by Internet and mobile technologies which are providing wider access (particularly in the developing world), new channels, and most importantly bringing in a whole new set of industries (with their technologies, capabilities and business models) into the (electronic) money and payments arena. The traditional banks and financial institutions are not necessarily going to emerge as the main drivers and implementers of change. Nonbanks, therefore, have the potential to provide significant competition in the evolving technology-dominated area.

The changes have also resulted in increasing levels of abstraction, creating distance between banks and customers, since they do not have all the expertise to develop new and innovative systems themselves. Indeed, their core business is increasingly reliant on technology companies. These non-banking corporations provide further risk to the banking sector since they combine the understanding of the banking industry (providing the technological services and support) and the technological capability to provide innovations. It seems that the retail and technology sectors could be poised to make a serious impact on the banking sector and its financial systems. Global systems would require cooperation and collaboration, of course, between large non-bank entities and industries. It could therefore be an interesting time for the banking sector as new innovation drives further changes.

Notes

1 Note this chapter, in part, is based on the paper (Adams, C. and Mouatt, S. (2010) 'The Rise of Complementary Currencies and Corporafinance: E-commerce Driven Competition in the Financial Sector', *Journal of Internet Banking and Commerce*, 15(1)).

2 The ideas of Krosner are reminiscent of the *market efficiency hypothesis,* first espoused by Eugene Fama (in a seminal article) where he argued that different levels of information directly impacted the reliability (in terms of the real value) of market-price signals for financial securities (Fama 1970) 'Efficient Capital Markets – A Review of Theory and Empirical Work', *Journal of Finance,* 25, pp.383–417.
3 This, of course, would be anti-inflationary.
4 Bernard Lietaer explores these potential and latent corporate currencies in Chapter 11.

References

Adams, C. and Mouatt, S. (2010) 'The Rise of Complementary Currencies and Corporafinance: E-Commerce Driven Competition in the Financial Sector', *Journal of Internet Banking and Commerce,* 15(1).

Bawden, T. (2008) 'Citigroup adds Fresh $15.2bn Writedown and 9,000 Job Cuts', *The Times,* Saturday April 19 (p.63).

Boyle, D. (2000) 'Why London Needs its own Currency'. New Economic Foundation, available from http://www.neweconomics.org/gen/uploads/wm11dn45 byfcr555ptyxzs2506042005123501.pdf, accessed 11/1/2008.

Boyle, D. (ed.) (2003) *The Money-Changers: Currency Reforms from Aristotle to e-cash.* Sterling: Earthscan Publications.

Bradford, T., Davies M. and Weiner, S. E. (2002) 'Nonbanks in the Payments System,' Payments System Research Working Chapter PSR WP 02-02, *Federal Reserve Bank of Kansas City.* Available from ideas.repec.org/p/fip/fedkpw/psrwp 02-02.html, accessed 11/1/08.

De Bono, E. (1993) *The IBM Dollar.* Pamphlet published by the Centre for the Study of Financial Innovation, in London. Extracts also in Boyle (2002), pp.168–70. See also http://www.csfi.org.uk/.

ECB and FRBKC [European Central Bank and Federal Reserve Bank of Kansas City] (2007) Nonbanks in the Payments System: European and U.S. Perspectives. Proceedings of Nonbanks in the Payments System: Innovation, Competition and Risk. Santa Fe, New Mexico, May 2–4, 2007. Available from http://www.kansascityfed.org/Publicat/PSR/Proceedings/2007/07prg.htm, accessed 3/1/08.

Fama, E. (1970) 'Efficient Capital Markets: A View of Theory and Empirical Work', *Journal of Finance,* 25, pp.383–417.

Jagger, S. (2008) 'Hedge Funds on the Brink as Fed Cash Fails to Ease Crisis', *The Times,* Thursday March 13, p.44.

Kroszner, R. S. (2007) Innovation, Information, and Regulation in Financial Markets. Speech at the Philadelphia Fed Policy Forum, Philadelphia, Pennsylvania, November 30th, pp.1–10. Available from www.federalreserve.gov/newsevents/ speech/ kroszner20071130a.htm, accessed 5/1/2008.

Lascelles, D. (1999) 'Europe's New Banks: The "Non-Bank" Phenomenon', *The Centre for the Study of Financial Innovation,* in London. Also available from: http://www.csfi.org.uk/.

Lietaer, B. (2001) *The Future of Money: Creating New Wealth, Work and a Wise World.* Guildford: Random House.

Octopus (2007) Octopus to Provide Major Transport Smartcard System in Dubai. Octopus press release 22 November 2007. Available from http://www.octopus.com.hk/release/detail/en/20071122.jsp, accessed 11/1/2008.

Soros, G. (1995) 'The Looming Crisis'. Interview on the State and Future of the Financial Systems, reprinted in Boyle (2003) (pp.80–3).

Stenier, T. D. and Teixeria, D. B. (1990) 'Technology in Banking: Creating Value and Destroying Profits.' Homewood, Illiois, US: Business one Irwin.

Subramani, M. (2004) 'How Do Suppliers Benefit from IT Use in Supply Chain?' *MIS Quarterly*.

Towell, P., Scott, A. and Oates, C. (2007) 'Web 2.0: How the Next Generation Internet is Changing Financial Services'. *The Centre for the Study of Financial Innovation*, London. September, 2007. Available from http://www.csfi.org.uk/, accessed 11/1/08.

Welch, P. and Worthington, S. (2007) 'Baning at the Checkout 2007–08: Evaluating the Provision of Financial Services by Retailers'. ECR Publishing Partnership Worthington, S., Retailers and Financial Services in the United Kingdom, *Journal of Financial Services Marketing*, 2:3, pp.230–45.

Williams, J. (ed.) with Cribb, J. and Errington, E. (1997) *Money a History*. The British Museum Press.

8
Changing Payment Systems

Carl Adams

Introduction

This chapter explores the changing nature and concepts of money and the corresponding changing infrastructures that are needed to support money and make it work. Money is intrinsically tied in with the working of an economy: Money is the 'oil' for a functioning economy enabling all the myriad of transactions to take place, providing mechanisms for people to be paid for their labour and for companies to charge for their good and services. Restricting the flow of money would restrict economic activity. Money is very much a human invention and technological innovations have enabled new forms of money to emerge. Advances in metallurgy, for instance, enabled coins to be produced; paper and the paper press enabled paper money to be widely produced. Equally though, innovation in money has also been driven by the needs of society, rulers and governments. An expanding economy and lack of copper in early China necessitated the early use of paper money there (Boyle 2002, 2003). Similarly the needs of the emerging US economy in the times of the Colonial Americas, combined with a shortage of coin money, also paved the way for paper money along with a supporting banking structure (Davies 1994, p.465) This chapter provides a different perspective on money, examining some of the drivers for change, how it changes and the evolution of corresponding support structures. First though we will have to examine some of the background to money and money concepts.

At a basic level, money functions as a (concrete payment) means of exchange, unit (and means) of account, store of value and standard for deferred payment. Yet also, as Davies notes (1994, p.27) money provides a framework for the market allocation system (prices) and also the existence of monetary factors arguably provide an instigative impact on the productive economy in general.[1] Other features of money include cultural and psychological factors. The existence of a separate currency for a particular jurisdiction, for instance, is often perceived as a sovereignty issue and a source of national pride.

To fully understand money one has to consider the context and time of its use. Generalized monetary discourse, as Niebyl noted in his review of the classical economic period, is often problematic since the theoretical development and empirical work on money has predominantly pertained to a specific historical context and cannot be universally applied (Mouatt and Adams 2010; Niebyl 1946). Furthermore, monetary theorists (even from the same school of thought) have historically disagreed on the origin, nature and function of money *per se* (Mouatt and Adams 2010). Much of the prevailing monetary thinking has been loosely based upon ideas formed during the industrial revolution and its immediate aftermath. Indeed much of the existing banking and financial infrastructures emerged from the Industrial Revolution. In the current era, as discussed above, we are arguably in the throes of an e-commerce or information revolution where the fundamental commodities are information-based. The channels of money transaction, in corporate and the traditional banking sector, are increasingly technology-based. Electronic digits have virtually replaced coins and paper money.

One of the prerequisites for successful economic activity is to have practical and usable payment systems. The attributes of money change over time as do the supporting systems and structures – such as the payment and exchange mechanisms. This continual change, innovation and evolution in monetary systems are similar to the dynamic innovation process described by Damsgaard and Goa (2004). In a similar light, Coutts *et al.* (2005) discuss an innovation spiral where technology use stimulates new innovation. Adams (2007) takes this theme further by defining an innovation cycle around a problem-solution space, or innovation space, which is continually changing. This is represented in Figure 8.1. From this prospective, in periods of rapid technological change there is likely to be continual change in user practices and expectations which fuel further change in technology. This in due course will result in new requirements, opportunities and innovations leading to new technological solutions.

The idea that payment mechanisms and systems evolve and change is not new. Adam Smith noted in his 'Wealth of Nations' that 'Many different commodities, it is probable, were successively both thought of and employed for [*the purpose of*] money. In the crude ages of society,

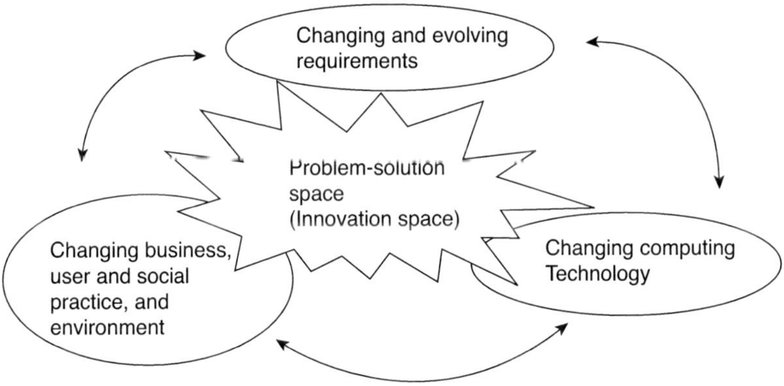

Figure 8.1 Innovation Space with Evolving Technology and User Practices
Source: Adams, 2007

cattle are said to have been the common instrument of commerce: and, though they must have been a most inconvenient one, yet in old times we find things were frequently valued according to the number of cattle which had been given in exchange for them. The armour of Diomede, says Homer, cost only nine oxen; but that of Glaucus cost a hundred oxen. Salt is said to be the common instrument of commerce and exchanges in Abyssinia; a species of shells in some parts of the coast of India; dried cod at Newfoundland; tobacco in Virginia; sugar in some of our West Indian colonies; hides or dressed leather in some other countries; and there is at this day a village in Scotland where it is not uncommon, I am told, for the workman to carry nails instead of money to the baker's shop or the ale-house ...' *but also notes* 'In all countries, however, men seem at last to have been determined by irresistible reasons to give the preference, for this employment, to metals above every other commodity' (Adam Smith in Dickey 1993, p.18). Smith has, as a result of his writing, been accused of being a 'metallist', defined as someone ideologically wedded to specie as the only viable 'commodity' money (Zarlenga 2002). Yet, this is unfair since it is more likely that he saw no better alternative to specie in his world (Mouatt 2008). Marx had also written about the practical value of specie, since it could transcend the boundaries of the state in terms of its operational quality, yet recognized the existence (and success) of state-sanctioned *fiat* currency issued by law (Marx 1970).[2]

So, in the past money was attached to items of value, such as precious metals like gold and silver indicated by Adam Smith. In the

United Kingdom, for instance, the British 'pound' (£) was the originally the value of a weight of a pound of silver, hence the name pound, and hence the connotation of pound Sterling, with Sterling being used as a standard quality of silver (92.5% silver with 7.5 of other metals – pure silver would be too soft to use as a coin). However, all sorts of things have been used as money, for instance in Glyn Davies' book 'A History of Money' (1994), there is an alphabetical list of some of the more primitive examples of money, including: 'Amber, beads, cowries (shells), drums, eggs, feathers, gongs, hoes, ivory, jade, kettles, leather, mats, nails, oxen, pigs, quartz, rice, salt, thimbles, umiacs, vodka, wampum, yarns, and zappozats' (p.27). Wampums are shells or beads used by North American Indians as money. Zappozats are apparently decorated axes. Using a precious metal, like gold or silver, or a rare and precious item provides a good base for money. The scarcity and preciousness of the items embeds 'value' into those items. People have a tangible basis to trust the *real* value in those items when engaged in exchange transactions.

Each of these different representations of money, of course, required their own system (or systems) to engage in exchange. One of the key parts of any system was the development of a standard. We have already pointed out, in the last chapter, how Governor Kroszner argued that standardization would improve the information needed to support stakeholders in understanding market risks.[3] These measures would also increase money (and thus economic) transaction volumes. Another monetary invention, 'paper money', which probably originated in China where it flourished for several hundred years before it was abandoned, was one such system.[4] Boyle writes that 'China began to abandon paper currency around the year 1455, because it tended to cause inflation, and it didn't reappear until its first tentative and – to the people first presented with it – highly suspicious flowerings in Scotland and Massachusetts in the 1690s' (Boyle 2002, p.139). One of the big challenges for paper money was how to embed similar trust in the value of the paper money item. Most of the earlier paper monies were effectively promissory notes, promising that the person holding the paper money note would actually be paid in 'real' money (i.e. gold, silver or some rare item that constitutes money for the person). The history of this value embedding can be seen on notes today, for instance, in the UK the paper notes still contain the words 'I promise to pay the bearer upon demand the sum of.'

As new payment mechanisms evolve the older ones decline, a current example being the cheque. The growth of credit and debit cards has facilitated the virtual demise of the cheque: In 2008 several retailers, including the likes of Tesco and Marks and Spencer and petrol stations stopped accepting cheques. On 16th December 2009, the UK the Payments Council, an organization set up by the UK government to set strategy for the payments industry, decided to gradually phase out the use of cheques across the UK. By October 2018 cheques will no longer be valid and thus ending over 350 years of banking activity: 'From 1717 Bank of England customers drew on their accounts using special "cheque" paper to prevent fraud, because only customers with a balance at the bank could get the paper. In the early days cheques were used relatively infrequently, mainly by merchants and traders for high-value transactions. They had to be confident that these handwritten pieces of paper could be guaranteed. They were often issued by goldsmiths within a local network of traders who knew and trusted each other, but advances in printing processes meant they began to be used by customers of commercial banks' (Thompson and Bannerman 2009). The number of people writing and accepting cheques grew. In the later part of the 20th century almost all current bank accounts had their own cheque book. There was still the problem of getting people to accept cheques for purchases, which saw the introduction of the 'cheque guarantee card' that guaranteed the value of the cheques to a specific level, say £50. This initiated a substantial increase in the number of cheque transactions particularly for retail items. The cheque backed by a guarantee card helped fuel a consumer spending boom in the 1970s and 1980s as it provided convenience for customers. The widespread use of cheques also saw the widespread use of penalty charges by banks for people that wrote cheques putting their bank accounts overdrawn. Some of these penalty charges were excessive, and banks seemed to be viewing people going overdrawn as a revenue stream. This, of course, is a particularly emotive, and well-publicized, issue for bank customers in more recent times.

One area for innovation in the payments industry is the move towards online transactions. The potential for this in changing user practices and the business environment can be seen by the phenomenal success of PayPal which was originally founded in 1998 and was later acquired by eBay in 2002. In 2008 PayPal's total value of transactions was $60 billion and represented nearly 9% of global e-commerce and 15% of US e-commerce activity (Paypal 2009). Electronic payment systems are at the frontline of innovation and change within the payments industry.

Table 8.1 collates together some of the main forms of money and the corresponding support structure that emerged alongside the money

Table 8.1 Historical perspective on money and corresponding infrastructures

Main Grouping/ Era	Money Instrument	Reason/Background	Structures Needed	Benefit	Problems
'Primitive' Money and Exchange Systems	Bride money Tribute money Barter	Need for tributes and Need to exchange (surplus) goods	Political and social exchanges Market spaces Rules for barter	Social and political interaction provides means of exchanging goods Increased capability for transactions	Exchange (mostly) limited to region Limited store of value Exchanges limited to items available
(Primitive) Commodity Money	Commodity money Common exchange items (Oxen, Arrow Heads)	Need for common forms of exchange	Exchange rates between commodities Intermediaries	Increased capability for transactions and store of value	Limited to commodities (size and availability)
	Precious metals Useful metals	Need for durable common forms of exchanges	Assaying and weighing facilities Smelting facilities Exchange systems Gold/Silver smiths	Common item of exchange Increased capability for transactions	Limited amount of metals Common purity of precious metals

Table 8.1 Historical perspective on money and corresponding infrastructures – *continued*

Main Grouping/ Era	Money Instrument	Reason/Background	Structures Needed	Benefit	Problems
Early Fiat Money	Precious metal coins Non-precious metal coins	Lack of precious metals Lack of money in the economy Need for store of value	Fiat systems – backing of the city or state or ruler Refined metallurgy capabilities (standards in purity of metals, stamps) Gold/Silver smiths	Money backed by something (gold or silver) Increased capability for transactions and store of value	Led to clipping and diluting of coins precious metal content
	Early paper money	Severe lack of (copper) coins (in early China) Convenience (i.e. difficult to carry large amounts of heavy coins)	Fiat systems – backing of the city or state or ruler Paper Printing capabilities Money issuing authorities	Increased capability for transactions and store of value	Lack of acceptance Easy to print Hyper inflation (as in China and Germany (1923)

Table 8.1 Historical perspective on money and corresponding infrastructures – *continued*

Main Grouping/ Era	Money Instrument	Reason/Background	Structures Needed	Benefit	Problems
Industrial Capacity / Industrial Revolution Money	Bills of exchange Early Cheques	Lack of money in the economy Lack of suitable metal money Convenience (i.e. difficult to carry large amounts of heavy coins)	Acceptance of IOUs Gold/Silver smiths, exchange intermediaries Early Banks Early banking laws	Increased capability for transactions	Lack of availability (only to the rich) Acceptance limited to region participating Easy to print
	Paper money	Lack of metal coins and money (in early China or early USA) Convenience (i.e. difficult to carry large amounts of heavy coins)	Banks and other financial institutions (e.g. building societies) Central banks Financial Laws	Increased capability for transactions Increased capability to store value	Easy to print Hyper inflation (as in China and Germany (1923)
	Early Stocks and shares	Need to raise funds for new factories/ corporations	Early Stock market Trading intermediaries Stock laws	New factories and production capability	Crashes – South Sea Bubble
	Company coins and monies	Lack of official money Companies had local communities metal coins and money	Company networks Company local community	Increased local commerce around the company	Acceptance limited to local region Locked in employees to the company money system
	Patents	Protect IPR Stimulate innovation	Patent and IPR laws Lawyers	Stimulated innovation and economic activity	Expensive to get patents Limited to countries

Table 8.1 Historical perspective on money and corresponding infrastructures – *continued*

Main Grouping/ Era	Money Instrument	Reason/Background	Structures Needed	Benefit	Problems
Computer Money	Bank accounts for the masses	General increase	Computing technology Databases Networking technologies	Increased access to banking facilities Company efficiencies (e.g. paying wages by BACS)	Increased fraud potential
	Cheque guarantee cards	Increase acceptance of cheques and convenience (for both retailer and customer)	Wider public acceptance of cheques Banks issuing of guarantee cards Bank charges for going over-drawn	Extra confidence and acceptance of cheques for payment Increased capability for transactions Extra revenue stream for banks (increase in bank charges)	Extra costs to banks (e.g. issuing cards) Increased fraud potential (difficulty in managing system)
	ATM	Efficiency changes	ATM infrastructure User acceptance Security structure	Wider access to cash (time and location) Reduction in banking staff (staffing efficiencies)	Increased fraud potential Reduction in banking staff (less access to banking staff)

Table 8.1 Historical perspective on money and corresponding infrastructures – *continued*

Main Grouping/ Era	Money Instrument	Reason/Background	Structures Needed	Benefit	Problems
Computer Money	Credit and cards	Increase in shopping boom	Credit/Debit card infrastructure Credit laws and infrastructure	Increased commerce based on debt Increased connivance for consumers	Increase debt levels Increased fraud potential
	Modern Stocks and shares Derivatives Money markets	Increased access to stocks and shares The rise of large funds	Stock markets Global systems New electronic markets	Increased commerce	Increased volumes and abstraction of money Increased power of money markets
	Government Bonds	Government need to raise money (for instance to fund wars)	National Banks to issue bonds Bonds market	Government able to raise money	Increase the amount of government debt

Table 8.1 Historical perspective on money and corresponding infrastructures – *continued*

Main Grouping/ Era	Money Instrument	Reason/Background	Structures Needed	Benefit	Problems
Internet Money	Credit/debit cards over the Internet	Need for payment mechanisms over the Internet	Change in credit/debit card infrastructure Chip-and-Pin	Increased economic activity based on debt	Increase debt levels Increased fraud potential
	Online payment innovations (e.g. Paypal and others)	Need for payment mechanisms over the Internet	New electronic payment systems Technological innovations Change in banking laws	Increased economic activity The Internet becoming a full trading place	Increased fraud potential Connection and compatibility Issues (between new and existing (infrastructure)
	New forms of electronic money (e.g. micro-money)	Digital products and services requiring digital payments	New electronic payment systems Innovations to reduce transaction costs Technological innovations Change in banking laws	Increased economic activity and reduced transaction costs The Internet becoming a full trading place	Acceptance and adoption Increased Fraud potential Increased abstraction

forms. It also captures some of the issues related to the different forms of money, including some of the drivers towards new money forms and weaknesses in the money forms.

The political and government needs in driving through innovation in money systems is demonstrated by Ferguson's evaluation: 'After the creation of credit by banks, the birth of the bond was the second great revolution in the ascent of money, Government (and large corporations) issue bonds as a way of borrowing money from a broader range of people and institutions than just banks' (Ferguson 2008, p.65). Money, and the supply of money, is intricately linked to politics and power, such as the ability to fund wars, armies and weaponry. An examination of the evolving nature and supporting structures of money also show that, generally, with each new monetary innovation there is an increase in the *social power* capability of the economy. This usually results in an increase in the volume of transactions of and the net value of the money supply.

The early 'primitive' money systems look very much outmoded when considered against the fast pace of the digital world. However, we may need to reassess what we mean by 'primitive'. The early money systems had strong social dimensions as they were representations of tributes and social interactions, as well as some means of exchange. Similarly, the physical face-to-face interaction of an exchange was an important part of barter systems. In the electronic world by moving towards 'Computer money' and 'Internet money' we may have lost some of the social interactions of money exchanges. ATM machines enable people access to their money in their accounts or overdrafts without physical interaction with a human being. Items can be brought online using a credit card, again with no direct human interaction. However, interaction between people is a large part of defining our culture. We may have lost something by focusing on just the 'means of exchange' attributes dominant in the current modern money perspective. Social interaction in exchanges has been reduced, so from a sociological perspective the earlier 'primitive' forms of money seem less primitive. Modern money (and banking systems) are characterized by increased abstraction, and (at least the appearance of) decoupling, of 'money' from the real items of value such as human labour or the final commodities that people exchange. Modern money has become electronic blips in a bank cyber-account. Arguably, modern money as a consequence has become more remote from society, lacking in 'soul' or the attributes needed to develop deeper social cohesion and interaction within society.

It is interesting to note, however, that some of the newer structures developing around payment (and exchange systems) within the Internet have started to adopt more social structures. The feedback systems on ebay, Amazon and other exchange sites, for instance, allow people to rate and review the transactions they engage in. These rating and interaction systems are starting to take on more of the 'tribute' attributes of the earlier primitive money systems. Whereas within the *Computing money* structures (from Table 8.1) security, trust and fraud protection are predominantly addressed as a technology issue, within the *Internet money* structures social structures are emerging (such as user profiles) to moderate exchanges. Explicit social exchange systems are also emerging on the Internet, such as the Geek Credit peer-to-peer system, that enhances interaction between peoples (GNA 2005).

Conclusion

Money continually evolves in response to the changing needs of society (and the economy), technological innovations or the needs and aspirations of governments and their rulers. Each change in the attributes of money results in corresponding changes in the money support structures and how people actually use money. Some of these changes can be quite significant and impact many aspects of society. One of the most striking changes to how people paid for things in the past was the introduction of paper money. However, it required a significant change in mindset for people to consider paper money as real money, say money based on gold or silver. 'Paper money' is such an integral part today of most countries that it is difficult to consider economic activity without using paper money, at least for most of the members of the population. There may be a time in the future when we consider new forms of electronic money and payment systems in the same way. It is perhaps easy to make comparisons with people's experimentations with the early examples of paper money, with the current early examples and use of e-money. There were clearly teething problems with acceptance and trust of the 'new' paper money systems. There were problems in stopping fraud and with controlling and limiting the money supply. Paper money was (and probably still is) too easy to print if you want some more. This is equally (or more) true with any new forms of electronic money since creating new copies of money would requires just copying the electronic file or electronic representation of the e-money – or just change an entry in a database.

Within the information revolution the new evolving forms of money will face many of the same problems that previous money innovations faced. New e-money (arguably) needs to be supported or backed up with old currencies or items of value. Without 'backing up' the new form of money it is difficult to see how it could be socially accepted and trusted. Yet, with the legitimization of state this could be achieved. This is therefore an exciting time for money and its associated systems. There has been continual innovation over the centuries and, recently, there has been a flurry of significant innovations covering Internet money. We are seeing the emergence of new forms of money and sophisticated ways of using that money. We are also seeing some of the wider (and older) functions of money returning. Internet commerce, for instance, makes use of many feedback systems such as the many peer-to-peer exchange systems of ebay or Amazon, or the individual profiles of social networking sites. These systems are bringing back some of the social dimensions of money that were important part of human exchanges. Interestingly, most economists and their theories do not capture the wider and social functions of money. It is hardly surprising that, as a consequence, the real monetary systems do not fit their models!

Notes

1 This is in direct contrast to the mainstream view of money that sees it as neutral and, therefore, unable to instigate productive activity that would otherwise not occur (Mouatt, S. (2008) 'Evaluating Stephen Zarlenga's Treatment of Historical Monetary Thought', *International Journal of Social Economics*, **35**(11)).

2 The mercantilist Steuart (before Smith) had posited that a currency issued by statesmen would be preferable to commodity money (or symbolic paper monies backed by it) (Itoh, M. L., Costas (1999) *The Political Economy of Money and Finance*. Chippenham: Macmillan).

3 Governor Krozner was discussing some of the innovations and challenges within financial markets in the wake of the sub-prime crisis (Kroszner, R. S. (2007) *Innovation, Information and Regulation in Financial Markets*. P. F. P. Forum. Philadelphia: Federal Reserve).

4 It was a few more hundred years before paper money was used in any serious sense in Europe or elsewhere (Boyle, D., ed. (2002) *The Money Changers*. Ebbw Vale: Earthscan).

References

Adams, C. (2007) 'Can Innovation Survive Virtual Teams and Outsourcing', *Cutter IT Journal*, Executive Updates 01 September 2007, pp.4–8.

Boyle, D. (2003) *The Little Money Book*. Bristol, UK: Alastair Sawday Publishing.

Boyle, D., ed. (2002) *The Money Changers*. Ebbw Vale: Earthscan.

Coutts, R., Coutts, P. and Alport, K. (2005) 'Understanding the User within the Innovation Spiral', in Krogsti, J. and Kautz, K. & Allen, D. (eds) *Mobile Information Systems II*, pp.47–62. New York: Springer.

Damsgaard, J. and Goa, P. (2004) 'A Framework for Analysing Mobile Telecommunications Market Development', in Lawrence, E., Pernici, B. & Krogstie, J. (eds) *Mobile Information Systems*. New York: Springer.

Davies, G. (1994) A History of Money: From Ancient Times to the Present Day. Cardiff, Wales: University of Wales Press.

(Roy) Davies maintains a web site on Electronic Money, or E-Money, and Digital Cash. This is a excellent resource on money, the history of money and electronic money and contains many useful and informative references. The web site draws upon Glyn Davies' book A History of Money (above). Available from http://www.ex.ac.uk/~RDavies/arian/emoney.html

Dickey, L. (1993) Adam Smith 'An Inquiry into the Nature and Causes of the Wealth of Nations'. Abridged, with commentary by Laurence Dickey. Cambridge: Hackett Publishing.

Ferguson, N. (2008) *The Ascent of Money: The Financial History of the World*. London: Allen Lane, Penguin.

GNA (2005) 'Geek Credit, p2p Digital Currency'. Available from http://home.gna.org/geekcredit Accessed July 2005.

Itoh, M. L., Costas (1999) *The Political Economy of Money and Finance*. Chippenham: Macmillan.

Kroszner, R. S. (2007) *Innovation, Information and Regulation in Financial Markets*. P. F. P. Forum. Philadelphia: Federal Reserve.

Marx, K. (1970) *A Contribution to the Critique of Political Economy*. Union of Soviet Socialist Republics: Lawrence & Wishart.

Mouatt, S. (2008) 'Evaluating Stephen Zarlenga's Treatment of Historical Monetary Thought.' *International Journal of Social Economics*, 35(11).

Mouatt, S. and Adams, C. (2010) 'Evolution of Electronic and Mobile Business and Services: Government Support for E/M-payment Systems', *International Journal of E-Services and Mobile Applications*, 2(2), pp.58–73.

Niebyl, K. H. (1946) *Studies in the Classical Theories of Money*. New York: Columbia University Press.

Paypal (2009) Corporate Fast Facts 2009. Available from https://www.paypal-media.com/documentdisplay.cfm?DocumentID=2260, accessed 10/12/09.

Thompson, L. and Bannerman, L. (2009) 'Banks Bounce Cheques into the Recycle Bin of History', *The Times*, Thursday December 17th 2009, p.19.

Zarlenga, S. (2002) *The Lost Science of Money – The Mythology of Money: The Story of Power*. United States: The American Monetary Institute.

9
Ascendant Corporate Monies: Electronic Money in an Electronic World

Carl Adams

Introduction

In this chapter, we examine the development of corporate monies during the information age, which in practice means electronic money. First, we will examine the early development of electronic payment mechanisms and then examine more current examples. Most of these are based on traditional money in the sense that they symbolize legal tender. However, new forms of money are also emerging. In Chapter 1 it was argued that the banking sector was appearing increasingly 'divorced' from the real economy, but also that the real economy has evolved into something new. The examples of some of the significant new structures emerging around the information superhighway are characterized by large numbers of users (tens and hundreds of millions) spread around the global in a very fast changing world. This calls for different business models and the utilization of varying 'quantities of value'. The example of music downloads (in their billions) from Apple (iTunes and Apps) contrast markedly with the rest of the music industry (based on a different infrastructure of CD/DVDs, distributions and larger value transactions), which seems to be struggling to make a profit. The business models of the traditional music industry are increasingly at odds with the reality of user practices within the information superhighway. This chapter will be exploring some of the foundations of these new forms of electronic money, as well as the electronic representations of the existing money exchange systems.

E-payment systems

Some of the first electronic transactions of money date back to the early telegraph period. In the United States this was driven by a need to pay soldiers during and after the civil war and to pay workers, particularly telegraph and rail workers, during the development and expansion into the western parts of the country. 'Following the Civil War, westward expansion created a need to move capital, leading Western Union to introduce its money transfer service in 1871' (Superbrands n.d., p.1). The need to send money continued with the advent of further wars and long-distance commercial activity: 'The service accelerated when the United States entered World War I, when relatives began wiring money to solders throughout the United States and Europe' (Superbrands, p.1). For Western Union, or Western Union Telegraph Company – as it was known then, which was one of the main US telegraph companies of the time, moving into the financial services and money business proved to be a lucrative and business saving activity: 'The telegraph accelerated the speed of business transactions during the late nineteenth century and contributed to the industrialization of the United States. Like most industries, it faced new competition that ultimately proved its downfall. The telephone was easier and faster to use, and the telegraph ultimately lost its cost-advantages. In 1988, Western Union divested itself of its telegraph infrastructure and focused on financial services, such as money orders' (Nonnenmacher 2001). Currently, Western Union continues its role in the financial services arena and keeping up-to-date with some of the latter trends in the payments industry, for instance they own a majority stake in Eposs, a UK-based e-payment provider for the mobile phone market (Superbrands n.d., p.2). It is interesting to note that, in its day, the new technology of the telegraph, with the capability of sending information and enabling funds to be transferred over great distances, made a significant contribution towards industrialization and increasing business activity. Another interesting feature of Western Union's history is that a main player in the 'telecommunication industry' had managed to diversify into the financial services industry (and still maintains a presence today), and had been able to do things that the existing financial institutions could not. Using Porter's five forces model of competitive forces, this is effectively a new entrant (in this case Western Union) moving into a completely different market (Porter 1980). One of the other interesting points is that sending money electronically has a long history, indeed the term wiring money dates from those early telegraph times. The practice of wiring money internationally is still common today, particularly with an international workforce and remittance economy, as migrant workers send money home to relatives.

In more recent times, e-payment schemes based on credit and debit cards are some of the most dominant forms of payment mechanisms (DTI 2005), however these can be considered as effectively providing a secure channel for the existing credit and debit cards. They build on the existing customer practices of using such cards along with the entire infrastructure, retailer expertise and practices and the existing tie into the financial systems. They also build on the existing trust relationships that people have with their card providers. It makes good sense to build on what is already there. Not surprisingly the credit card companies have played a big role in developing such secure channel schemes, such as the Secure Electronic Transaction (SET) (for more full details of each of these see Visa and MasterCard websites).

SET was developed as part of a joint venture between Visa and MasterCard, with the aims of having a secure channel over the Internet for sending peoples' credit card details, and to reduce the potential for fraud by provide mechanisms to validate the credit card users. However, Visa and MasterCard seem to have gone in their separate ways with Visa developing 3D SET (Visa 3-D Secure) and MasterCard developing UCAF. Effectively they both use extra measures to ensure that the person using the credit card for a transaction is who they say they are. This is the classic problem for credit card transactions that of the credit card not being present (e.g. when ordering and paying over the telephone using a credit card).

The take-up of SET and 3D set has been fairly slow and has mostly been limited to retailers and corporate customers, and not the final consumer customers. To use SET, and 3D SET one needs use encryption technologies, such as using encryption keys to set up a secure link between the retailer and customer and between the retailer and the credit card company. What happens with most SET or similar based transactions is that the retailer, or a payment service provider, sets up the secure link with the customer. Most customers do not have their own set of encryption keys, and would probably not know what to do with them if they have them, so the responsibility for setting up a secure link and for 'proving' who the different parties are in an 'e' transaction falls with the retailer.

Credit card companies are a business and need to make a profit to keep operating, so they make a charge for accepting credit card transactions, for both over the Internet as well as traditional transactions in retail outlets. Transaction and associated costs are a crucial area that has to be considered when reviewing e-payment options. Some payment options have registration fees or set-up fees attached to them, whilst others have a flat transaction fee, while others have a variable transaction fee depending on the value of the transaction and other variables (such as how new or risky the company is deemed to be and the number of expected transactions). As the DTI has noted, when discussing the cost considerations: 'you need to explore the cost per transaction [*and*] Does the provider charge a percentage on each transaction (this could be very expensive if you sell high value items) or is it a flat fee? Switch tends to carry a fixed price of around £0.45 per transaction but credit cards can carry percentage charges ranging from a very low 1.79% to a more costly 8 or 9%!' (from http://www.electronic-payments.co.uk/pricing.jsp).

In 2005 the then DTI provided some guidance on identifying other costs associated with running an e-payment system (along with a diagnostic tool to work out costs for a selection of the e-payment options and service providers):

> Main costs are listed below but are not relevant to all products (although the diagnostic tool will work this out for you):
>
> - **Setup Cost**: Ranges between £50 and £250, if applicable £120 is the average.
> - **Annual Cost**: Normally around £150 but often not applicable.
> - **Monthly**: The most standard charge especially from acquiring banks, around £10–25.
> - **PSP**: Can be a commission of as little as 1% but often about £10 per month or 3–4%.
> - **Transaction Charge**: 2.79% for an established business but up to 4–5% otherwise.
> - **Bond**: Dependent on exposure level but is often negotiated down.'
>
> (from http://www.electronic-payments.co.uk/pricing.jsp)

So the range of costs of e-payment options need to be seriously considered: With transaction cost of up to 9% and a range of set-up and running costs, processing e-payments could cut deeply into profit margins. However, the e-payments costs may be more fundamental for companies. Before Visa or MasterCard will let a retailer, or card acquirer for that mater, have access to their online infrastructure they expect the business partners to have fairly secure operating processes and technologies and that these partners follow some fairly stringent rules. As MasterCard describe the rules and need for rules:

> There are over 22 million locations where cardholders can use their MasterCard cards. As you might imagine, a network this large must operate under specific rules and regulations. MasterCard requires

> our members – banks and other financial institutions that issue cards and acquire transactions – to comply with MasterCard rules. Those members, in turn, must ensure that merchants they acquire for also comply with MasterCard rules. Merchants are critical to MasterCard's success, and that success is better assured if merchants are afforded access to and understand MasterCard rules applicable to their businesses. ... Please be aware that these rules establish minimum standards of acceptable conduct; an acquirer may require a merchant to adhere to additional, more stringent standards than MasterCard rules require. ... Please be advised that MasterCard rules and other standards change frequently.
>
> (from http://www.mastercardmerchant.com/accept_mastercard/merchant_ rules.html)

So merchants wishing to use MasterCard systems (and the same for Visa) have to adhere to some fairly stringent standards and rules and that these will change fairly frequently, particularly when new threats arise (e.g. a new virus or technical problem). For a small or even medium-sized retailer/merchant the cost of developing and maintaining sufficiently robust infrastructure (in technology and working practices) to deal with MasterCard and Visa could be very considerable. For instance, it is likely that such a retailer would need to have a dedicated technically competent security person to deal with monitoring the processing of electronic payments and of updating security patches and procedures. So there are the extra staffing, process and expertise costs as well as any extra technology costs that have to be considered.

The high set-up costs and transaction costs have made many retailers and merchants use 3rd party specialist Payment Service Providers (PSPs), such as DebitTech, Worldpay or a host of other providers. PPS's offer expertise, infrastructure and the capability to handle companies' e-payment needs. PPS's also enable a wider range of payment options for customers, not just credit and debit cards. So a PSP can take away much of the e-payments headache for companies, at a price. Just like the credit card companies, PSPs are in business and will charge a fee for handling a company's e-payments and transactions. Again the fees will vary considerably on the type and volume of transactions and the amount of risk involved in the business.

The high setup costs and transaction costs also provide motivation for new entrants to move into this lucrative business arena. The high level of transaction cost emphasis some of the main problems with the existing electronic payments infrastructures coming out of the traditional banking sector. Each time money is moved between different entities within the financial sector then each of the entities want their 'cut' to cover their transaction costs. Banks and the rest of the financial sector are mostly interested in the relatively larger transactions. Small value items are of little interest to most of the banking sector. Indeed, for much of the banking sector handling very large volumes of micro-value items (say less than a few pence or cents) would not be attractive since it would cost them more in transaction costs than the value of the items. Also, as discussed in Chapter 7, banks do not really have the technological expertise to develop system with micro-transaction costs. The traditional banking sector simply has the wrong business and operating model for small value exchanges – even if there is the potential for tens or hundreds of millions of transactions.

However, within the e-payments industry there are other options for e-payments as well as a variety of different forms of e-money or e-cash and new ways of using it. There are many varieties of electronic payment systems – though these are mostly coming from outside of the financial sector. At the local city level some interesting money systems have emerged. For instance, the Oyster smart cards in London and the Octopus smart cards in Hong Kong are used for travelling and purchasing small value items. Another example of a local exchange scheme making use of the electronic world is the 'Geek Credit', described as: 'Geek Credit is a digital complementary currency for internet. It is decentralized, secure, inertest and demurrage free. It is backed by mutual credit (time). There is no central issuing and control authority, so it is a true peer-to-peer currency. It is a digital form of WATT local currency system that is used in Japan. Like any complementary currency it is best fit for paying for services within a community' (GNA).

There is wider encouragement from governments to develop innovative payment solutions for the information age. In Europe, for instance, the EU Electronic Money directive gave member state government's guidelines to develop legislation for corporations in member state to develop their own electronic money. In the UK this has been translated to governance of issuing of electronic money falling to the Financial Services Association (FSA) who issue licences for corporations that wish to issue their own money (as discussed in Chapter 7). The licences are granted under tight rules and monitoring activity. For instance, for small value e-money:

> 'The FSA will only grant a small e-money issuer certificate if any one or more of the criteria set out in article 9C are met. These are:
>
> - e-money issued to consumers is subject to a storage amount of €150 and the total e-money issued is limited to €5m;

- e-money issued to consumers is subject to a storage amount of €150, the total e-money issued is limited to €10m and only issued for use by connected parties; and
- e-money issued to consumers is subject to a storage amount of €150, the total e-money issued is limited to €10m and only issued for use within a limited geographic area.

(FSA 2009 see http://www.fsa. gov.uk/register/eMoney.do)

So it is possible in the UK, much like the rest of the European countries, for a corporation to create their own electronic money provided they follow a set of rules governing the amount that individuals can be issued with and the total amount that corporations can issue. There are also rules governing what the corporations need to do to secure and protect the individuals' monies. These are effectively local money or community money.

At the time of writing, the FSA had issued several e-money issuer certificates to a variety of different types of organizations, including small payment providers, county councils, telecommunication companies and universities (see Table 9.1).

These are local and community electronic money and corresponding e-payment systems. Larger 'e-money' and systems have a similar set of regulatory hurdles to overcome. Under the EU Electronic Money directive telecommunication companies are able to operate, in a limited sense, as a bank, which would open up the mobile payments industry to the telecommunications companies. The aim for such legislation is to support competition, enable new entrants into the developing e-payments arena, but also to protect customers, traders and providers of e-money and e-payment services. There are rules and restrictions, for instance the limited 'banks' cannot lend money in the same way as traditional banks, but it does open the way for other industries such as telecommunications companies to move into the potentially lucrative mobile payments market. Telecommunications companies are ideally placed to provide small value transaction processing solutions; after all they deal with small electronic transaction in the form of phone calls. However, very few telecommunications companies have actually applied for limited banking licences. The challenges facing telecommunications companies to move into this market are considerable. For instance, it would call for a complete change of business model: Banks are good at dealing with financial risk, lending money, and handling transactions between many, many different groups of people, businesses and customers; telecommunications companies are good at connecting

Table 9.1 List of FSA e-money issuer certificates, from FSA (http://www.fsa.gov.uk/register/eMoney.do)

A Capture Limited	Local Secrets Limited	Shimatomo UK Ltd
Allied Wallet Limited	Loughborough University (IMAGO)	Simple Business Worldwide Limited
Bangonet Limited	MGT Plc	Something Mobile Ltd
Bluestone International Ltd	Mothercare UK Limited	Sony United Kingdom Limited
Charge 2 Limited	MPP Global Solutions Limited	Sparta Technologies Limited
Chelsea FC PLC	Naxopay Limited	sQuidcard Limited
Cheshire County Council	netCashis Limited	Teleglobal Limited
Citadel Commerce UK Limited	Opay Ltd	The NoWcard Partnership
Click & Pledge Limited	Opera Telecom Limited	Tikits.com Limited
CNWB (UK) Ltd	Orange Home UK Plc	Toni & Guy International Limited
Cobalt Telephone Technologies Limited	Orionpay.com Limited	Tranzcash Limited
Concessionary Solutions Limited	PAL Telecom Limited	U-B Energy & Finance Ltd
Credecard Plc	PayHound Ltd	Universal Money Ltd
Earthport plc	PayLane UK Limited	University of Wales Institute Cardiff (UWIC)
Easy Debit Card Limited	Payment Solution Services Limited	Voicepay Ltd
EB Payments Limited	Pixpay Limited	Wallie Limited
Epayment Ltd	Pizza Hut (UK) Limited	Yorcard Limited
Evening Standard Limited	PPPay Ltd	
G11 Bill Limited	Press-Pay World Wide Limited	
Globaldosh Limited	Probability Games Corporation Limited	
Golden Management LLC, Limited	Queen Margaret University, Edinburgh	
Instant Pay Limited	Queen's University Belfast	
Internetwith Limited	Roqipay System Ltd	
ISpire Financial Services Limited	SecureAccountnet Limited	
Ixaris Systems Ltd	Seed Capital Limited	

up people and getting them to pay, usually at the end of the month for communication services. Telecommunications companies are already facing a real upheaval in their core business models as they move into providing digital services, such as 3G/4G, and are already facing high levels of risk and uncertainty in their market place. Adding widespread m-money and m-payments may be too much change and uncertainty for the mobile telecommunication operators. Interestingly, Paypal, owned by giant peer-to-peer auction company e-bay, was one of the few early companies that applied for and received such a limited bank licence.

The e-payments industry: Too much variety?

The e-payments 'industry' isn't really one industry; it is very much a set of evolving different industries all converging around something to do with e-payments. Porter's five competitive forces covered: (a) Threats from potential new entrants, (b) Buyers' bargaining power, (c) Supplier bargaining power, (d) Threats from substitutes and, (e) the Competitive rivalries within the industry. Within the e-payments industries most of the players are effectively new entrants having being around in 'e-payments' for a relatively short period of time. Even comparatively long-standing players in the payments industry, say credit card companies like Visa and MasterCard, have relatively few years experience in dealing with the online payments. And online business and activity with corresponding e-payments are continually changing and evolving: after only a few years we are dealing with a new business arena. This also means that the main corporate players in e-payments have come from different industries, including from the payments services sectors (e.g. credit cards companies, payment service providers), the banking sector (banks and building societies), the telecommunications sectors (e.g. mobile and fixed telecommunication operators), technology sectors (e.g. Software and hardware companies) and other places. So the e-payments industries are fiercely competitive places with competition within the evolving sectors (e.g. within the telecommunications industry) and within the final e-payments market places (e.g. competitive clashes between credit card e-payment schemes and between mobile telecommunications-based schemes and between banking-based schemes, etc). One might describe the e-payments industries as a hyper-competitive market place, and it is not clear which sectors or companies within those sectors are likely to be successful. So banks have alliances with other banks along with alliances with technology companies and telecommunication companies. Often companies are involved in different alliances that are effectively in competition with each other.

The mobile payments arena shows some of the problems with this hyper-competition. Effectively the mobile payments offerings are originating from two very different industries: the financial services and banking industries on one hand and the telecommunications and technology industries on the other, each with different business models and different relationships with their customers. This fierce hyper-competition is not very good for customers and retailers, as they don't know which system to choose themselves. For instance, currently there are well over 100 electronic payment systems in operation in Europe, the US and elsewhere. However, not all the e-payment systems will be successful. Indeed many of the earlier e-payment systems have already collapsed and being consigned to the e-payments graveyard. The lack of success for e-payment systems is not just limited to the older and first-to-market systems, or even small e-payment operations. Take for instance Simpay which was set up by four of the largest mobile operators in Europe, as the technology news site Cellular.co.za reported it in May 2004: 'Simpay, the consumer m-payment brand formed by Orange, Telefónica Móviles, T-Mobile and Vodafone in 2003, along with Encorus' processing capabilities will make large-scale m-commerce a reality. The Founding members of Simpay represent more than 280 million wireless subscribers worldwide. Simpay's commercial launch is scheduled for the first quarter of 2005' (Simpay 2004). So Simpay, set up and backed by some major players in the telecommunications industry, and with a very impressive and growing user base, seemed set to be a big and successful player in the e-payments marketplace, particularly the mobile payment (m-payments) arena. However, in June 2005 one of the founding members of Simpay, T-Mobile, pulled out of Simpay and the rest of Simpay collapsed. So even the big and powerful players in the e-payments market are not immune to failure.

New forms of money

There are a variety of new forms of electronic money emerging that operate in a global operating space. Here are a few examples that bring out some new aspects that are suited to operating in the information superhighway. They mostly have some link (even if it is nominal) to the 'real money' of the traditional currencies, however they show the potential of operating in a new dimension separated from the traditional currency system. Indeed, it would only take a small level of abstraction to separate from the traditional currency system.

e-Gold (see http://www.e-gold.com/) is an electronic currency that is issued by e-gold Ltd and (supposedly) 100% backed at by gold bullion. It also allows other e-metals to be issued (i.e. e-silver backed by silver, e-platinum backed by platinum, and e-palladium backed by palladium), but e-gold is the most popular. It is really an account-based system where people effectively transfer the ownership of gold between e-gold accounts. Once users are operating within the e-gold system then the transaction costs should be relatively low as it is just moving entries within an account database. Also it is interesting to note that exchanges can be made between countries using a common unit of value without the need to resort to expensive exchange rate conversions.

FarmVille coins and cash is a set of electronic currency that is used to exchange farm items within the FarmVille game produced by Zynga (they produce other games such as FishVille) which run on social networking sites like Facebook. There is a virtual marketplace where game players can exchange their items. Players can also buy FarmVille coins and cash from Zynga to help players develop their farm game. However, the majority of farm coins are generated by the users 'working' on their virtual farms, which demonstrate the potential operating a transaction system completely within a virtual environment. Also that the number of players transacting within the virtual environment can be quite significant – as of 7th March 2010, there were over 83 million players of FarmVille on Facebook.

Second Life Linden dollars is another example of transacting exclusively within the virtual environment. Linden dollars can be converted into United States dollars (and vice-versa at rates of about 250 Linden dollars to each US dollar), however the main transactions take place within Second Life system. Second Life is a sophisticated 3D virtual world where people can generate their own avatar which can interact with each other people's avatars within different created virtual environments. It has a variety of users from the general public, education (including several Universities) and even businesses. One can generate virtual objects within Second Life and exchange these for Linden dollars. Consequently it can operate as a completely separate market place to the traditional 'real' economy.

Conclusion

A substantial part of the global economy operates in an electronic world, using the new structures emerging around the information superhighway. The electronic part of the real economy is also characterized by large numbers of users that are spread around the global in a fast changing world. This means that the business models of traditional industry are increasingly at odds with the reality of user practices within the cyber-world. There seems to be a growing need for new forms of money and payment systems, specifically designed for the virtual operating environment, that are able to evolve in tandem with the evolution of the information revolution itself. In addition to challenging the traditional banking infrastructure, these developments are likely to contribute towards a competitive monetary diversity that is likely to provide more stability and resilience for a future capitalist order.

References

DTI (Department of Trade and Industry) (2005) *Transaction Costs – Electronic Payments,* available from http://www.electronic-payments.co.uk/pricing.jsp

FSA (Financial Services Authority) (2009) *Small E-Money Issuer Certificates,* available from http://www.fsa.gov.uk/register/emoney.do

Nonnenmacher, T. (2001) 'State Promotion and Regulation of the Telegraph Industry, 1845–1860', *The Journal of Economic History*, Cambridge University Press, 61(1), pp.14–36.

Porter, M. (1980) *Competitive Strategy*. New York: Free Press.

Simpay (2004) available from http://www.cellular.co.za

Superbrands (n.d.) Western Union, available from http://www.superbrands.org/files/westernunion_1125.pdf

10 Complementary Currencies at Work

Bernard Lietaer

This chapter regroups some examples of complementary currencies that are fully operational today somewhere in the world. They are classified in two categories: first some business initiatives, and later a sampling of some social purpose projects.

Their relevance is that they are part of what we claim is necessary for creating better financial and social stability: a monetary ecology, which by definition should include systems that can operate at very different scales, and can involve institutions of different types than banks. To be clear, we should stop believing that the 'financial system' is one and the same with the 'banking system'. In our language, the banking system is only a subset of the financial system, a most important subset, but not identical with it.

The two business examples provided next operate on a scale up to a national level, and involve small and medium-sized businesses as their core protagonists. All the other systems that will be mentioned here are operating on a scale smaller than a nation state, and are typically run by on a local level by a NGO. None of them are destined to replace the conventional monetary system, which would remain in operation, and be run by the banking system as today. That is why we call all these other systems *'complementary'* currencies. Together with the conventional money system, they form the beginning of a monetary ecology.

A. Business complementary currencies

The WIR

Once upon a time, 16 businessmen inspired by the work of Silvio Gesell got together to decide what they could do among themselves to deal with a systemic financial crisis. They or their clients had each received a notice from their respective banks that their credit line was going to be reduced or eliminated; hence bankruptcy was only a question of time. They realized that business A had needed the bank loan to buy goods from business B, which in turn needed money to buy stuff from its own suppliers. So they decided to create a mutual credit system among themselves, inviting their clients and suppliers to join. When business A buys something from B, A gets a debit and B the corresponding credit. In this simple way, they created their own currency, whose value was identical to the national money, but with the interesting feature that it didn't bear interest.

The country's banks mounted a massive press campaign to try to squelch this revolutionary idea. Miraculously, that campaign failed, and this little system saved the businesses involved at the time. A cooperative was set up among the users to keep the accounts dealing with that currency. Soon participants could also borrow from that cooperative in that currency at the remarkably low interest rate of 1% to 1.5%. All such loans need to be backed by inventory or other collateral. Over time, the system grew to include up to one quarter of all the businesses of the entire country.

Sixty-five years later, an American professor performed an econometric study proving that the secret for the country's legendary economic stability was that strange little unofficial currency, circulating among businesses in parallel with the national money. That country's well-known economic resilience was usually credited to some mysterious and unknown national characteristic. Whenever there was a recession, the volume of activity in this unofficial currency would expand significantly, thereby reducing the recession's impact on sales and unemployment. Whenever there was a boom, business in national currency expanded, while activity in the unofficial currency proportionally dropped back again. The surprising implication of this study is that the spontaneous counter-cyclical behaviour of this little 'unorthodox' system actually helped the national bank in its efforts to stabilize the economy.

This story is not an urban legend, but the true story of the WIR system. The country is Switzerland and the sixteen founders met in Zurich in the year 1934. And the system is still operating today. The annual volume of business in the WIR currency is now about $2 billion per year. The American professor is James Stodder from Rensselaer University. His remarkable quantitative study uses more than 60 years of high quality data to prove the points made in this story (Stodder

1998, 2000). The WIR system has evolved into a fully fledged cooperative bank, which operates in two currencies: it is accepting deposits and making loans in Swiss Francs, as well as in WIR (Studer 1998).

It would make sense that businesses take the initiative of creating such Business-to-Business (B2B) systems with their supplier and client networks. The big advantage, compared to what happened in Switzerland, is that with what is available with today's information technology tools, setting up such a system can be achieved in a fraction of the time and costs of what it took in the 1930s.

The C3

Cash flow presents many problems for modern businesses, particularly for Small and Medium-sized Enterprises (SMEs). Indeed, SMEs are being pressured by suppliers for prompt payments, say within 30 days; while their larger customers pay them only in 90 or more days. This becomes a deadly cash flow trap whenever banks refuse to provide bridge financing, or do so at steep conditions. This problem has become more critical recently in developed countries under the impact of the financial crisis, but it has long been an endemic issue in developing countries.

The 'Social Trade Organisation' (STRO), a Dutch Research and Development NGO, has successfully developed business-models over the past decade in several Latin American countries which culminated with a financial innovation that structurally addresses this precise challenge. The process uses insured invoices or other payment claims as liquid payment instruments within a business to business (B2B) clearing-network. Each recipient of such an instrument has the choice to either cash it in national money (at a cost), or directly pay its own suppliers with the proceeds of the insured invoice. Information on the C3 is available on their website c3@socialtrade.org.

C3 step by step

The C3 mechanism involves the following six steps:

1. Participating businesses start by securing invoice insurance up to a predetermined amount, based on the specific creditworthiness of the claims they obtain on third parties.
2. The business that has obtained such an insurance (hereafter referred to as business A) opens a checking account in the clearing-network, electronically exchanges the insured invoice for clearing funds, and pays its supplier (business B) immediately and fully with those clearing funds via the clearing network.

3. To receive its payment, business B only needs to open its own checking account in the network. Business B has now two options: either cashing it in for conventional national money (at the cost of paying the interest for the outstanding period, for example 90 days; plus banking fees); or pay its own suppliers with the corresponding clearing funds (at no cost).
4. Whatever the timing of the payment is to business A, business B is in a position to use the positive balance on its account in the network, for instance to pay its supplier business C.
5. Business C only needs to open an account in the network. It has then the same two options as business B: cash it in for national money, or spend it in the network. And so on...
6. At maturity of the invoice, the network gets paid the amount of the invoice in national money, either by business A or by the insurance company (in case of default of business A). Whoever owns at that point the proceeds of the insured invoice can cash them in for national money without incurring any interest costs. The flows of transactions in the C3 system are represented in Figure 10.1.

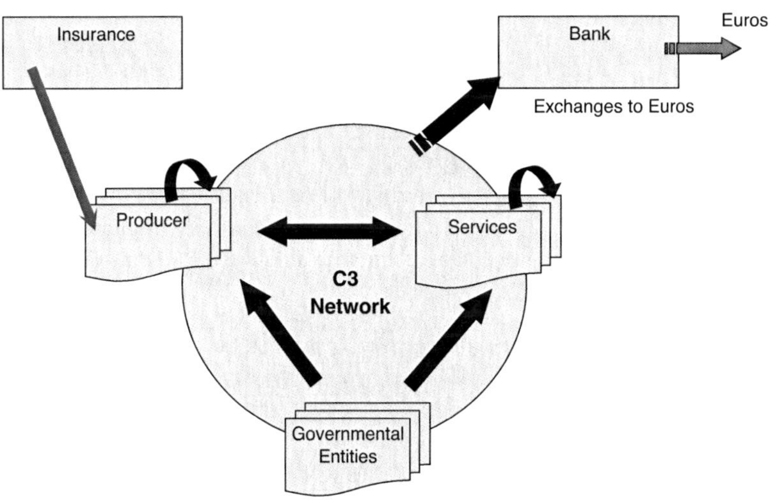

Figure 10.1 The Flows of Transactions in the C3 System

This proposal is beneficial for all parties involved, and also has implications across a broad range of policy issues, which will be summarized next.

Benefits

For *businesses*:

- Businesses increase their access to short-term credit as needed to improve their working capital and the use of their productive capacity. The size of this credit can be built up to a stable level between a quarter (covering therefore up to an average of 90 days of invoices) and half of annual sales; at a cost substantially lower than what is otherwise possible.
- Suppliers are paid immediately, regardless of the payment schedule of the original buyer, injecting substantial liquidity at very low cost in the entire C3 network. The approach provides a viral spreading of participation in the process from clients to suppliers.
- The technology is a proven one, doesn't require any new legislation or government approvals, and the necessary software is available in open source.[1] It is also compliant with existing regulations (in the EU for instance) on digital currencies. Only invoices and other claims that are 100% guaranteed, and 100% computerized, are acceptable in a C3 system. C3 thereby encourages the generalization and more efficient use of IT infrastructure among SMEs, including the opening of new markets and marketing channels through e-commerce.

For *governments*, particularly *regional governments*:

- The C3 approach is a dependable way to systemically reduce unemployment. Governments at different levels (EU, national, regional) could contribute to a joint guarantee mechanism. Such a guarantee mechanism is considerably cheaper to fund than subsidies or other traditional approaches to reduce unemployment.
- C3 systems are best organized at a regional level, so that each network remains at a manageable scale. Businesses with an account in the same regional network have an incentive to spend their balances with each other, and thus further stimulate the regional economy. C3 provides a win-win environment for all participants, and therefore promotes other collaborative activities among regional businesses.
- Each C3 network should use the same insurance standards and compatible software so that they can interconnect as a network of networks to facilitate exchanges internationally, so that the principle is respected of the integrity of the jurisdiction and competitive markets across regions.

For *banks and the financial system*:

- The win-win approach of C3 includes also the financial system. As the entire C3 process is computerized, it significantly streamlines the lending and management for the insurance and loan providers. SMEs can therefore become a more profitable sector for banks than is currently the case, because the credit lines are negotiated with the entire clearing network, providing the financial sector with automatic risk diversification among the participants in the network. In the upcoming surge of new competitors in the market – such as Facebook, Google or Tesco, which all plan to introduce their own currencies and payment systems – the C3 innovation provides an additional window for banks to sell their core activities. Specifically, C3 is only providing short-term working capital to businesses that are successful in selling their goods and services in the market. It isn't a long-term financing tool, and therefore doesn't compete with bond, mortgages or other long-term credit instruments. The one market segment where it competes with existing banking practice is in the bridge financing loans for SMEs. This is currently a highly fragmented and particularly expense market to service by the financial services industry.
- Most banks are also involved in providing insurance services. C3 opens for them a whole new market for insurances and credit, all the way down to services for microfinance enterprises. As C3 is completely computerized, even such individually small-scale entities can now be serviced at a very low cost.
- The C3 mechanism systemically contributes to the stability of employment and of the entire economy, which is helpful for the overall solidity of the banks' portfolios.

We emphasize that such a C3 system is one of the most powerful ways to reduce unemployment in a country or region. Furthermore, the most effective way for governments at any level to encourage the implementation of the C3 strategy is for them to accept payment of taxes and fees in the C3 currency.

This is, after all, the mechanism by which the demand for conventional bank-debt money is made compulsory by governments (Wray 1998).

It encourages everybody to accept the C3 currency in payment, and provides additional income to the government from transactions that otherwise wouldn't take place. Finally, that additional income becomes automatically available in conventional national currency at the latest 90 days after the payment, thereby not upsetting any existing procurement policies. The first country that has followed this strategy is Uruguay.

B. Some existing social purpose complementary currencies

Currencies that build community

It is a general rule that whenever money gets involved, community breaks down. However, this turns out to be true only when scarce, competition-inducing currencies are involved, such as our official national currencies. In fact, the use of some other types of currencies can have exactly the opposite effect of *building* community. Economic theory claims there is no reason why people should accept the inconveniences of dealing with complementary currencies and the national currency in parallel. However, nobody has forced anyone to do so in the examples that will be listed in this and the previous chapter. The fact is that people around the world create their own currencies and continue using them in parallel with the normal national currencies. 'A fact is more respectable than the Lord Mayor of London,' goes one English saying. Some conventional economic theorists have tried to explain away the whole non-traditional currency phenomenon on the basis of tax dodging. However, the complementary currency phenomenon cannot be explained away on such a simple basis.

The proof is that the most prevailing type of complementary currency is the Local Exchange Trading System (LETS), in which all transactions are stored in a computer. It is very easy for a tax authority to find out and tax what is going on in such a system. In fact, a lot easier than when the normal national currency bills are used. Participants themselves justify the inconvenience of using two currencies in parallel because they have experienced a re-birth of community whenever well-designed complementary currencies are used for social purpose.

There are indeed many currencies which have reciprocity built in, that are more compatible with a gift economy than our national currencies. Practice has demonstrated that such currencies *build* community instead of destroying it.

What kind of money could that be?

Some real-life examples

The balance of this chapter will, therefore, provide five case studies:

1. Time Dollars, invented by a prominent Washington lawyer, and applied now in several hundred communities in the US. Thirty different states have recently started promoting this approach to pragmatically solve local issues.
2. Ithaca Hours, a paper currency launched by a community activist in the small university town of Ithaca, New York. Ithaca is a relatively low-income community of about 27,000 inhabitants. Similar types of paper currency systems are now operational in 39 different communities in the US.
3. The PEN Exchange, illustrating how a complementary paper currency helped build community relations in Takoma Park, Maryland, a suburb of Washington D.C.
4. Curitiba, a provincial capital of 2.3 million inhabitants in Brazil, where a mayor has used complementary currencies for 25 years, propelling this 'third world' city to 'first world' standards in less than one generation. In 1992, Curitiba was awarded the title of 'the most ecological city in the world' by the United Nations. Its mayor has become a nationally recognized political (and economic) hero.
5. A remarkably successful application of a specialized 'Health Care Currency' operating at the national level in Japan which provides an innovative way to improve the quality of health care at no cost to the government.

1. Time Dollars

Edgar S. Cahn, Professor at the District of Columbia Law School, developed his Time Dollar concept in 1986, initially for retirement homes in Florida, a school district in Chicago, and a social project in Washington, D.C. Now it has spread into hundreds of applications. One incentive is that the Internal Revenue Service (IRS, the US tax authority) has ruled that Time Dollar transactions are tax free. Time Dollars has an elegant simplicity. Here is how it works. Joe doesn't have good eyesight and can't drive a car anymore. But he needs a special pair of new slippers from the other side of town. Julia agrees to make the one-hour drive to get the slippers. Julia gets a credit for one hour, while Joe gets a one hour debit, which they can mark on the blackboard near the superintendent's office. Julia can then spend her credit on the cookies baked by another neighbour, while Joe will offset his debit by tending the community garden, or something else that his bad eyesight allows him to do. If Joe was going to spend one hour working in Julia's garden, that would be simple barter. However, the fact that Joe can work for an hour in the garden of someone else in the community to cancel his Time-Dollar debit, and that Julia can use her credit to buy Jane's cookies, makes Time-Dollar exchanges much easier to complete than barter with their necessary double coincidence of wants. Joe and Julia do not need to have to complete the transaction. Time Dollars are, therefore, real money: an agreement within a community to use an entity as a means of payment.

The goods and services exchanged are only the start. A comparative survey was made of retirement homes: those using the Time Dollar approach compared with those that didn't.[2] In the retirement homes using the Time Dollar approach, they found that using this money knits the group together. In short, *community had been created.* In Brooklyn, New York, a health insurance company called Elderplan has decided to accept 25% of the premiums for its senior health programs in Time Dollars. Elderplan has even created its own 'Care Bank' where 125 participants log in an average of 800 hours of service per month. It started as a home repair service by which potential problems are fixed *before* they cause accidents. The Care Bank has as motto: A broken towel bar is a broken hip waiting to happen.[3] For the insurance company, this is clever marketing. But Elderplan also took these unusual initiatives because it had noticed that seniors participating in Time Dollar systems were experiencing fewer health problems. The bottom line was that their health care is less expensive for the insurance company. The Elderplan system expanded during the year 2000 to include various boroughs of New York. A special new program focusing on diabetics and which includes a major component of self-help is being launched by the same time bank. The time credits are now also redeemable against cinema and theatre tickets, healthcare products, transport vouchers, supermarket and luncheon vouchers throughout Brooklyn. Research has also proven the value of this model. Time Dollars systems have proven effective not only in boosting health care systems, but on other social problems such as youth crime, and lawlessness in run-down neighbourhoods. Research by the University of Maryland's Centre of Ageing has shown that about a third of the people taking part in time dollars had never volunteered for anything before. They also showed that the 'burn-out' or 'drop-out' rate which for volunteers reaches 40% per year, drops down to 3%.[4]

More than 80 townships and social service programs have started Time Dollar systems in the US. One of the pioneering states was Missouri, which has officially included Time Dollars as a key ingredient in its social policy. Maine was the first state to have officially created a position of 'Time Dollar Coordinator' as a full time state employee responsible to start dozens of Time Dollar networks and link them up among each other (George 1997).

The Time Dollar concept is definitely ready to spread outside of the traditional US circles. For example, Pat McMaster has started three projects within the Cambodian immigrant society in the US. These are Long Beach, CA (50,000 Cambodian population); Lowell, Chelsea, MA (where 25% of the city is Cambodian); and Riviera, MA. They are using 'TimeKeeper' software which they downloaded free from the Internet to keep track of the hours for the participants. The Cambodians themselves call the system 'Community Building' money, which makes clear what they believe to be its most interesting feature. Time Dollar systems, or Time Banks have now blossomed in several dozen countries around the world.

2. Ithaca HOURS

Ithaca is a small university town with a population of about 27,000 in up-State New York. It is not a rich town. It has, for example, the highest percentage of 'working poor' in the state of New York (people who are fully employed, but whose income is so low that they still remain eligible for food stamps). Paul Glover, a local community activist, felt that the proximity of New York City kept diverting the community energy into the vastness of the big city and decided to do something about this problem. In November of 1991, he launched a complementary currency designed to encourage people to spend their money and time in the community. Although it requires a little more infrastructure than Time Dollars, it still remains remarkably simple.

The community in which Ithaca *hours* can be spent is voluntarily limited to a geographical radius of 20 miles around the center of town and is organized around a local newspaper. This bimonthly tabloid typically contains well over a thousand listings. These include a local supermarket, three movie houses, the farmer's market, medical care, lawyers, business consulting, and the best restaurant in town. The local bank also accepts accounts in the complementary currency, and has been able to attract a very loyal local customer base as a consequence.

One of the keys here is that the advertisers provide their quote in a combination of the two currencies. For example, a house painter advertises that he wants US$ 10 per hour, 60–40 (meaning 60% is payable in Ithaca HOURS, and 40% in regular US dollar currency for the paint, brushes, gasoline, taxes, and so on) Another painter may advertise at $11 per hour, 90–10 (meaning that he is willing to accept up to 90% in Ithaca HOURS). So, if you happen to have more Ithaca HOURS available than dollars, you may prefer to go to the latter painter, even if his nominal rate is a bit higher.

Ithaca's movie houses, for example, accept up to 100% in Ithaca HOURS in the afternoon because the cost of projecting a movie is a fixed cost, independent of how many people are present (that is, the marginal cost of one more viewer as long as seats are empty is, in fact, zero). Over one thousand people use the complementary currency regularly, and many pay rent or other services with it.

Finally, 9.5% of all Ithaca HOURS issued are being given to local non profit organizations who perform various tasks for the community at large.

Here are some real-life testimonials of participants:

- Ed provides ophthalmology (eye doctor) services for HOURS, most of which he spends on food. 'No one should lack medical care because they lack dollars,' he says. 'HOURS and barter are a solution to health care needs. HOURS say that everyone's time is important, and I like that.'
- Richie earns HOURS in his video rental business. He has used them for shoe repairs, books, house-sitting, lawn-mowing, hauling, and so on. 'HOURS have become the driving force behind who I patronise at the Farmer's Market. I look for the telltale yellow sign that says, "we accept Ithaca HOURS." This keeps the money in the community and that means economic prosperity for all.'
- Neal is one of Richies' suppliers. He sells organic food at the Farmer's Market. He spends his HOURS on movies, bread, and farm help during crop season. 'Every community needs to grow as much local food as possible. It's absurd when more calories are used to transport food than the food contains. Our money logo says "In Ithaca We Trust." That's the bottom line, right?'

Paul Glover summarizes the benefits. 'Thousands of purchases and many new friendships have been made with our own money, and hundreds of thousands of local trading has been added to what we call our Grassroots National Product.' The big decisions concerning the system as a whole (printing, denominations, manner of issue, grants) are made during twice-monthly dinners, which act as the 'Ithaca Reserve Board.'

The system has been featured on national TV, first in Japan, and more recently in the United States. The participants are happy with the results, and the businesses have seen more locals stay around to spend both their regular dollars and their Ithaca HOURS. Even the people who don't like Paul Glover's activist style or politics have come to like his system. This system has also started spreading around the country. Paul Glover sells a kit describing how to set up such a system for $25 or two and a half Ithaca HOURS. By now, there are over fifty similar systems that have sprouted in a variety of cities.

In short, it is a successful model with very low start-up costs that works. However, it has one drawback that is common to all fiat currencies: Ithaca HOURS require someone centrally to decide how much currency to issue. Whilst this is done in a democratic way by the 'Ithaca Reserve Board', all Central Bankers will confirm that managing a fiat currency supply remains a tricky decision. The biggest risk is that if more currency is issued than people want to use, there will be inflation and a *de facto* devaluation of the complementary currency. This will not happen, of course, as long as Ithaca HOUR managers follow Paul Glover and his colleagues lead in remaining conservative in their money supply decisions.

3. The PEN Exchange

Olaf Egeberg lives in Takoma Park, Maryland, on the border of Washington, D.C., where the US Treasury and the Federal Reserve headquarters are located. After he retired, he wanted to give something back to his community. 'In this day and age, we lose sight of the most valuable resources: each other. We can have a walking-distance society right here, where we already are. I think neighbourhoods are the most important society for us to build now' he reasoned.

In contrast with Ithaca, this is a decidedly middle-class community with a very low unemployment level (about 1%). Olaf decided to define his neighbourhood as all of the families within five minutes walking distance from the centre of town, roughly 450 families in total, hence the name 'Philadelphia-Eastern Neighbourhood' (PEN for short).

He began by sending out fifty letters, describing how the PEN Exchange would contribute to 'building a more supportive society for us here...

with [my emphasis] more human contact, more communication, more getting to know each other than before.' Unfortunately, he received no replies. Puzzled by this lack of response, he decided to make the tour of the houses in person where it transpired no one thought they had anything to offer and had perceived the exchanges would be just like normal commercial transactions. An accountant, who loved to forage for mushrooms at the weekend, for instance, had not thought that other people might be interested in learning about mushrooms. A retired person who had lived in Europe for ten years had never thought to exchange her knowledge of the area for something she might need in return. As a consequence, it turned out that the *pen exchange* complementary currency, and its goods/services directory, was just what had been needed.

The Washington Post[5] covered the story. It quoted Mary Rodriguez, 89, who has lived in Takoma Park for over 40 years, and has never seen anything like it. 'There are so many neighbourhoods where you never get to know the people next to you. Here the neighbours do things for one another. It gives a small-town feel.' After only three years, the community fabric already runs deep and goes way beyond what an economic analysis may show about people exchanging goods or services in another way. Neighbours keep abreast of local issues by e-mail, and computer-literate residents offer free Internet lessons to any neighbour wishing to join. Nikolai Vishnesky, 40, who started the e-mail system, says in *The Washington Post* article 'Now folks can take technology that is usually used for global interaction and make it available as a local resource.'

Neighbours deter crime by patrolling the streets at night, publish a newsletter, take turns watching each other's children at play groups, help housebound seniors, grow food on a community farm in Upper Marlboro, and greet new neighbours. Martha Monroe, 38, believes, 'We are unique because in most Washington suburban neighbourhoods, people get home from their job in the city, watch television and go to bed.'

4. Curitiba: The Brazilian city which left the Third World[6]

In 1971, Jaime Lerner (an architect) became mayor of Curitiba, the capital of the southeastern state of Paraná, Brazil. Quite typical for the region, the urban population had mushroomed from 120,000 people in 1942 to over a million when Jaime became mayor. By 1997, the population had reached 2.3 million. Again, quite typically, the majority of these people lived in '*favelas*,' the shanty towns made out of cardboard and corrugated metal. One of Jaime Lerner's first big headaches was garbage. The town garbage collection trucks could not even get into the favelas because there were no streets wide enough for them. As a consequence, the garbage just piled up, rodents got into it, and all kinds of diseases broke out. A mountain-sized mess (Rabinovitch 1992).

Since they didn't have the money to apply 'normal' solutions, such as bulldozing the area and building streets, Lerner's team invented another way. Large metallic bins were placed on the streets at the edge of the *favelas*. The bins had big labels on them which said: glass, paper, plastics, biodegradable material, and so on. They were also colour-coded for those who couldn't read. Anyone who brought down a garbage bag full of presorted garbage was given a bus token. A school-based garbage collection program also supplied the poorer students with notebooks. Soon the neighbourhoods were picked clean by tens of thousands of kids, who learned quickly to distinguish even different types of plastic. The parents use the tokens to take the bus downtown, where the jobs are.

What Jaime Lerner did, from my perspective, is invent Curitiba money. His bus tokens are a form of complementary currency. His program, 'Garbage which is Not Garbage,' could just as well have been named, 'Garbage which *is* your Money'.[7]

Today, 70% of all Curitiba households participate in this process. The 62 poorer neighborhoods alone exchanged 11,000 tons of garbage for nearly a million bus tokens and 1,200 tons of food. Over a three year period, more than 100 schools have traded 200 tons of garbage for 1.9 million notebooks. The paper recycling component alone saves the equivalent of 1,200 trees each *day*. Lerner's team did not begin with the idea to create a complementary currency. What happened instead is that they used an *integrated systems* analysis for all the major issues at hand and spontaneously ended up creating a complementary currency to solve them (Rabinovitch and Leitman 1996).

Nor is the garbage cycle the only form of local money in Curitiba which has resulted from this approach. For instance, another system has been designed specifically to finance the restoration of historical buildings, create green areas, and social housing in a way that would not financially burden the municipality. It is called '*sol criado*' (literally, '*created surface*') and works as follows:

Like most cities, Curitiba has a detailed zoning plan which specifies the number of floors that can be built in each zone. In Curitiba, however, there are two standards: the normal allowable standard and the maximum level. For instance, a hotel with a ground plan of 10,000 square meters is being built in an area where the normal allowable level is ten floors and the maximum 15. If the hotel owner wants to build 15 floors he has to *buy* 50,000 square meters (5 × 10,000 square meters) in the *sol criado* market. The city itself only plays the role of an intermediary matching demand with supply in that market.

But where is the supply for these *sol criado* surfaces generated? One source is historical buildings. For instance the *Club Italiano* owns a beautiful historic landmark building called the Garibaldi House. The property has a total ground surface of 25,000 square meters, but the place needed a serious restoration job. The Club did not have the money to restore the building. But because it is located in an area where up to two floors could theoretically be built, it sold 50,000 square meters (2 floors × 25,000 square meters) to the highest bidder, for instance, the hotel owner mentioned above. The proceeds belong to the Club to administer, but have to be used to restore the property. Therefore, the hotel owner ends up paying for restoring of the historic edifice to obtain the right to build the extra floors of the hotel, without financial intervention from the city.

Several of the more recent 16 extensive nature parks, open to the public, have been completely financed in a similar way. The owner of a large plot of land obtained the right to develop one side of the street on the condition that the other side becomes a public park. The new housing has an extra value because it is located at walking distance from the park, the people of Curitiba have another park for their weekend strolls, and the township does not have to go into debt or raise taxes to obtain all of that.

What is most interesting is that this market for 'created surfaces' is another type of specialized complementary currency, which enables Curitiba to obtain public goods for which other cities have to obtain traditional financing. Whenever a well-designed new currency system is implemented, something much bigger than the money and the economic activities it generates starts happening. The original garbage and public health problem has become a way to solve public transportation and unemployment difficulties in a uniquely innovative way. By creating the *sol criado* market system, significant public advantages are obtained at no cost to the city itself.

Another example: public transportation is encouraged over individual car usage and a very successful infrastructure has been established. Conventional city planners normally claim that any city with more than one million inhabitants must have a subway system to avoid traffic congestion. Similarly, cities that generate more than 1,000 tons of solid waste per day need expensive mechanical garbage-separation plants. Curitiba has neither. In addition, the investment needed for their public transport system costs only 5% of an equivalent underground system. The savings has allowed Curitiba to keep its fleet of buses among the newest in the world. The town also boasts a free 'University for the Environment' that offers practical short courses for many diverse groups of people. They are taught, amongst other things, the environmental implications of their daily activities. The building is a breathtaking architectural landmark made mostly out of recycled telephone poles, in what is now an idyllic setting near a lake. The location used to be an abandoned industrial stone mine.

Curitiba is the only town in Brazil that now has a significantly lower pollution level than in the 1950s; it also has a lower crime rate and a higher educational level than comparative Brazilian cities. It is the only city in Brazil that has actually turned down grants from the federal government, because they have solutions which involve less red tape. A botanical garden has also been planted on what was once the inner city dump, which now serves as a recreation and research centre. In addition, there are currently 16 different nature parks around the city, based on different themes. As a consequence, Curitiba has 52 square meters of nature per inhabitant. The UN ideal standard is 48 square meters of green surface per city inhabitant, a level rarely, if ever, reached by cities in either the developed or developing world. Furthermore, all these nature parks are easily accessible from the transportation network, so that the ordinary people can – and do – take full advantage of them. Perhaps the clearest political signal that these complementary currencies work is that every time Jaime Lerner has presented himself for election, he has been re-elected by a landslide. Next, he became Governor of the State of Paraná.

Finally, the impact of complementary systems is identifiable in economic terms. The average Curitibano makes about 3.3 times the country's minimum salary, but its real total income is at least 30% higher than that (that is, about five times the minimum salary). This 30% difference is income directly derived in non-traditional monetary forms, such as the food for garbage schemes. Another indication is that Curitiba has by far the most developed social support system in Brazil, and one of its most vibrant cultural and educational programs, and still doesn't have a higher tax rate than the rest of the country.

Curitiba is a practical case study where 25 years of experience show that a whole system approach using *both* the traditional national currency and well-designed complementary currencies is beneficial to everybody, including people who are focused exclusively on the traditional economy denominated in national currencies. It has enabled one fortunate 'third world' city to join 'first world' living standards in just one generation.

5. Japanese health-care currency

The Japanese population is the second fastest ageing one in the world. There are already 800,000 retired people needing periodic help (and one million handicapped people) and the Japanese Ministry of Health forecasts a vast increase in these numbers for the foreseeable future. In order to face this rapidly rising problem, the Japanese have implemented a new type of Health-Care Currency. In this system, the hours that a volunteer spends helping older or handicapped persons in their daily routines is credited to that volunteer's 'Time Account' instead of being paid in Yen. The currency is managed exactly as a savings account, except that the unit of account is hours. The credits are then available to complement normal health insurance programs (EU 1995).

Different values apply to different kinds of tasks. A meal served between 9 a.m. and 5 p.m. for instance, has a lower credit value than those served outside of that time slot; household chores and shopping also have lower values than say personal body care.

These Health-Care Credits are guaranteed to be available to the volunteers themselves, or to someone else of their choice, within or outside of the family, whenever they may need similar help. Some private services ensure that if someone can provide help in Tokyo, the time credits become available to his or her parents anywhere else in the country. Many people just volunteer the work and hope they will never need it. Others not only volunteer, but also give their Time-credits away to people who they think need them. To them, it amounts to doubling their time. It works like a matching grant: for every credit hour of service, the amount of care provided to society is two hours (EU 1995).

Most significantly, this type of service is also preferred by the elderly themselves, because the caring quality of the service often turns out to be higher than those obtained from Yen-paid social service workers. One of the names of this currency *'Fureai Kippu' ('Caring Relationship Ticket')* illustrates the reasoning for this. Another advantage of the scheme is that it also provides a more comfortable emotional space for the elderly, who would otherwise be too embarrassed to ask for free services.

The Japanese also report a significant increase in volunteer help, even by people who do not bother to open their own Fureai Kippu Accounts. The reason may be that with this system, all volunteers feel more acknowledged in the community. This precedent should put to rest concerns that paying volunteers with complementary currency might inhibit those who do not get paid from volunteering (EU 1995).

As of the end 2005 there were over 487 municipal level health care time credit systems in Japan, mostly run by private initiatives such as the Sawayaka Welfare Institute, or the 'Wac Ac' (Wonderful Aging Club, Active Club) and the Japan Care System (a non-profit organization with some governmental funding). In summary, the Japanese Health-Care Currency has proven both more cost effective and compassionate than the system which prevails in the West. As the United States and Europe embark on an identical trend of an ageing population, why not learn from the Japanese experience?

In conclusion, these examples give an idea of the range of non-conventional media of exchange that are already available and operational today. Most of them are small scale, have emerged as grass-root initiatives, without any governmental support. What matters is that they show what we mean with the emergence of a 'monetary ecosystem'. They illustrate the possibilities for a variety of systems that can operate in parallel with, and at different scales, than the conventional system, while providing a tighter interconnectivity and diversity that a sustainable ecosystem requires.

Notes

1 *Open Source* means that the source code of the software is publicly available, making it possible for users to adapt the system to their own requirements. Specific parts of the C3 methodology are protected by a patent and there are conditions that users have to meet, in order to obtain a user licence, including maintaining transparency. Monitoring procedures guarantee fair treatment for the network participants, who also make a small contribution to fund the spreading of the system. This generates the benefit of additional spending opportunities for the existing network. More information is available on their website c3@socialtrade.org.

2 *The Multinational Monitor* April '89.

3 *US News and World Report* December 30, 1996 p.72.

4 Robert Wood Johnson Foundation: *Service Credit Banking Project Site Summaries* (University of Maryland Centre of Aging, 1990).

5 Article by Lina Fina in *The Washington Post* (Thursday, February 1, 1996).
6 Information on the development of Curitiba has been obtained from several sources, including a dozen first-hand interviews with local officials during a field trip to Curitiba in 1996–97. Other information about Curitiba's development strategy has also been published in English; see Rabinovitch (1992) and Rabinovitch and Leitman (1996).
7 Over the more recent years a good part of the token distribution has been taken over by the private sector. 50 tokens, for instance, are given per month by the corporations to their employees. In parallel, the component of fresh fruits and vegetables in exchange for garbage has increased. Also for the holiday seasons Panetone's, and other festive ethnic foods, are supplied in exchange of 'garbage money'.

References

EU (1995) *A l'ecoute du Japon*, Information Bulletin of the Japanese Mission to the European Union, European Union, Brussels, July 3, 1995 pp.7–8.

George, R. (1997) 'Barter Network Affords Welfare Recipients Some Purchasing Power', *The Boston Globe* (July 20).

Rabinovitch, J. (1992) 'Curitiba: Toward Sustainable Urban Development', *Environment and Urbanization,* 4(2), pp.62–73; October.

Rabinovitch, J. and Leitman, J. (1996) 'Urban Planning in Curitiba', in *Scientific American*, March, pp.46–53.

Stodder, J. (2000) 'Reciprocal Exchange Networks: Implications for Macroeconomic Stability'. Albuquerque, New Mexico: Paper presented at the *International Electronic and Electrical Engineering* (IEEE) Engineering Management Society (EMS) August, 2000.

Stodder, J. (1998) 'Corporate Barter and Economic Stabilization', *International Journal of Community Currency Research,* Vol. 2, http://www.bendigo.latrobe.edu. au/a/.

Studer, T. (1998) *WIR in unsere Volkswirtschaft*. English translation by P. H. Beard, PhD, *WIR and the Swiss National Economy,* available at http://www.lulu.com/content/268895.

Wray, R. L. (1998) *Understanding Modern Money: The Key to Full Employment and Price Stability*. Northampton, MA: Edward Elgar.

Part III

The Future

11
Towards a Monetary Ecology

Bernard Lietaer

In this chapter we explore some new proposals that are not yet operational at this point, to get an idea of what a complete range of systems would look like if and when we have a fuller 'monetary ecology'. In the previous chapter we dealt with complementary currencies systems that have two characteristics: they are already operational somewhere in the world and, where they function on a scale smaller than or equal to the nation state.

In contrast, this chapter will describe the Terra, a complementary currency designed as a global currency, while not being any country's national currency. Such a currency would complete the spectrum of different scales at which currency systems should operate. The Terra would specialize in global trade. One of its objectives is to make it profitable for corporations to think long-term, something which we are convinced will be needed if we want to shift the global economy towards a sustainable path.

The necessary diversity of currency types, and of agents that create them, can express itself in other ways than the geographical scale on which they operate. That is why we will give some examples of what we will call 'functional' complementary currencies, i.e. systems that are designed to deal with only a specific domain of human endeavors and behavior patterns.

We could choose various fields as focus for such functional systems. For instance, complementary currencies have been designed to answer questions such as: even when budgets in conventional money are not available, how can we empower a learning society, or how can more generalized health awareness and physical wellness be encouraged in the general population. Such examples are provided in other publications (see www.lietaer.com).

Here we will choose a domain about which there is today a growing consensus: the need to rapidly shift to a worldwide post-carbon economy. In this chapter we will use the shorthand expression of 'carbon reductions' to refer to all Greenhouse Gas Emissions.

A. Examples of environmental complementary currencies

Until now, the favoured policy instrument to achieve such reductions is a market in carbon emission rights, traded in US$ or Euros, involving only governments and corporations. However, such an approach works only indirectly, is very vulnerable to lobbying at every stage (rules and exceptions, fixation of emission caps, permissions for projects, etc.) hence turns out to be somewhat blunt and unreliable. We claim that some specialized complementary currencies can function more directly and in a more reliable way. More importantly, they can mobilize not only corporations and governments, but the population at large, in the battle to reduce the risks of climate change.

Role of governments

There is no reason to believe that carbon reductions are going to occur spontaneously in a market economy at the speed that climate change scientists claim that will be required, unless governments intervene seriously in one way or the other. There are five main policy options available for governments to reduce carbon emissions:

1. Subsidies to promote specific types of investments either by businesses or by citizens that result in carbon reductions (e.g. subsidies for smoke stack scrubbers in power stations; or consumer subsidies to buy hybrid cars or solar panels).
2. Regulations that impose given minimum standards of energy efficiency, or maxima on emissions of carbon (e.g. minimum car efficiencies; or maxima on smoke stack emissions).
3. 'Green taxes' on carbon emissions, payable in conventional money (e.g. a carbon tax).
4. Rationing of carbon emissions, which can be achieved effectively through a complementary currency (e.g. the TEQ system described below).
5. Taxes payable only in a special purpose complementary currency. (e.g. the Green currency system below).

Of those five, only the first – subsidies – is politically popular, but it predictably quickly hits the wall of governmental budget deficits. All the other policies will be unpopular among at least some segments of society. Until now, practically all governmental initiatives to reduce carbon emissions have been based mainly on the subsidy approach. Realistically, however, after the governments have indebted themselves deeply in 2008 and 2009, to save the banking system and provide a stimulus to save the world from a repeat of the Depression, another way than generous subsidies is going to have to be used.

There exists a vast amount of policy literature about the next two policy approaches: regulations and 'green taxes'. This chapter will focus on the last two: the lesser known complementary currency approaches. Their strongest suit is that they can generate very specific behaviour changes. They can also be combined with whatever subsidies will remain available to motivate specific investments, although they operate successfully without any subsidies. Finally, carbon reducing complementary currencies can be implemented at different scales: from the scale of a city to a multinational zone like the European Union, and any level in between, are voluntary, many are subsidy driven; others are compulsory.

The NU-Kaart

The first example, the NU-Kaart is a system worth mentioning because it was one of the first attempts at an ecological currency system in Europe. It was funded by the European Union, and was tested at the size of a large city, specifically in Rotterdam, in the Netherlands. It can be seen as a simple loyalty currency for rewarding green behaviour. Credits are earned when an ecological activity is performed by a consumer, such as bringing pre-sorted garbage to a depot, or purchasing low energy appliances. These credits can then be spent to purchase other carbon-reducing services or products (e.g. paying for public transport), thereby creating an economy with a virtuous loop of carbon reductions (see details in www.nu-kaart.nl). This system operated only for less than two years, because it was stopped after the dramatic political shift in the Netherlands due to the murder of the political figure Pim Fortuyn. In this political shift, most programs that had been launched by the previous administration were stopped in their track, including the NU-kaart.

The ECO_2 system

The ECO_2 system is another voluntary carbon reduction program whereby consumers receive electronic credits for purchases or investments that contribute to carbon emissions reductions. It was initially designed in 2007 by David Johnston and the author for implementation in California, as a way to maximize the effects of a budget proposal to reduce

California's carbon emissions of US$1 billion proposed by the Republican Governor Schwarzenegger. The program did not pass political tussles with the Democratic majority in the California legislature.

The aim of the ECO_2 system was to mobilize not only those people already converted to ecologically responsible behavior (e.g. current owners of a fuel efficient car or solar power generator), but also the much larger group of consumers who have adopted a 'wait and see' attitude. Furthermore, it would have provided individuals and communities with a reliable way to track and compare their carbon emission reductions, as all transactions are recorded in real-time and independently verifiable.

With the ECO_2 system, *businesses* providing goods and services that reduce carbon emissions or have formally engaged in sustainability activities (qualifying for the '*green business*' label) would accept ECO_2s as a loyalty currency in partial payment for additional carbon-reducing goods and services. Each business decides what percentage of an invoice or bill they are willing to accept in ECO_2s. An electric or hybrid car dealer, for example, could decide to accept 10% of the purchase of a new car in ECO_2s, whereas a shop selling energy efficient light bulbs or solar panels might accept 20% of their payment in this currency. It's their choice.

The participating businesses that sell the carbon-reducing goods or services to the customer provide the data relevant to the transaction, which automatically generates an electronic certificate. If this is a first carbon-reducing purchase by the customer, the retailer gives the customer an ECO_2 debit card, and the corresponding account is credited with their carbon savings in ECO_2 units. Subsequent transactions are performed with this card as any normal debit card transaction.

In turn, these businesses – the car dealership, hardware store, solar panel distributor – have two options for the use of the ECO_2s they receive. They can make purchases with other businesses participating in the program (B2B transactions); or sell the ECO_2s through the program's administrator to the funder of last resort (in the California case that would have been the California State's Carbon Reduction Fund).

Final redemption of ECO_2 units would be at a fixed price previously agreed upon between the funder of last resort and the businesses. This funder of last resort could be any organization willing to pay for carbon reducing emissions. Given the additional sales tax generated by this program, it would be ideal that the tax authority of the particular municipality, county, state, or local government that has a mandatory reduction in carbon emissions, would play this role. With each transaction sales tax is generated.

For example, if sales tax is 8% in a given municipality with a business accepting ECO_2 for 20% of their sales price, and an ECO_2 is worth \$20, the government would need 2.5 sales tax incomes to earn the \$20 cost of redemption. So, by the third exchange (first a Consumer to Business (C2B) followed by one or more Business to Business (B2B) transactions), the sales tax accrued is greater than the cost of redeeming the ECO_2 units. They can then be counted as carbon reductions towards that area's Kyoto goal.

For *homes*, an evaluation would have been made of the carbon credit consumption of different types of dwellings by professional raters. In the U.S., many have already been trained and certified by the trade association called *Build it Green* (www.builditgreen.org). Residential homes are then rated on performing beyond their city/county's energy code minimum standards. Adding better insulation or double-paned windows, for example, is one way to reduce heating bills and carbon consumption. If a house scores, for instance, 25% better than code that fact is logged, certified, and corresponding carbon savings are computed.

For *transportation*, the type of car used, and any reduction in mileage driven compared to the State's average mileage driven, would similarly provide ECO_2s to the consumer. These would be credited to his or her ECO_2 account following a smog test or compared through the driver's previous annual mileage.

Tradable energy quotas (TEQ)

A third example of a carbon reducing complementary currency is a UK proposal called a Tradable Energy Quota (TEQs). It is also known as Domestic Tradable Quotas (DTQs), Personal Carbon Allowances (PCAs), Carbon Quotas, Personal Carbon Rationing and Tradable Permits.

The TEQ system is a compulsory system amounting to a rationing of carbon emissions in all parts of society. A given quantity of TEQs is created, corresponding to the maximum emissions allowed for that year, in a particular country, or region. Whenever an individual, business or government entity buys any form of carbon-based energy, such as petrol for a car, fuel for heating, gas for cooking, or electricity for a business, payments occur in two currencies: its cost payable in conventional money (as today) and the quantity of TEQs corresponding to the carbon content. Those who spend more than their quota have to obtain extra TEQs from other people's who have a surplus through an electronic auction system. Such dual currency payments would be completely electronic and automatic, typically using direct-debit technology (see details on www.teqs.net).

One of the main advantages of this approach is that it mobilizes all segments of society to achieve carbon reductions, and that it guarantees that a commitment of a given carbon reduction will be obtained by a given year. This is something which neither a voluntary nor a subsidy-based approach can achieve. It also doesn't burden governmental budgets, or requires a funder of last resort.

A Green contribution system

An alternative to rationing, regulation and subsidies, is to raise a tax that is payable only in a specially designed carbon reducing currency. This act is the most effective way to encourage the generalization of the acceptability of any particular currency.

The choice of a currency acceptable for payment of taxes is, after all, the key mechanism by which the demand for conventional bank-debt money is made compulsory by governments (Wray 1998). Indeed, the hard-nosed mechanism by which the monopoly of bank-debt money is enforced is that governments accept only that particular kind of currency in payment of all taxes. As Keynes quipped, the only certainty in life is death and taxes. As everybody needs to pay taxes, everybody will need to accept that currency in his or her exchanges.

For instance, let us define a unit which we could call a 'Green' as the reduction of one kilo of carbon emission compared to a moving average of the past three years. For instance, a reduction of 3KWh of electricity use at the consumer level, corresponds to a reduction of 1kg of Carbon emissions at the primary electricity producer level using conventional technology.

The government can then require payment of, say 100 Greens per year from all users, payable only in Greens. And, similarly as with the TEQ system, those users that don't have enough of them can obtain them from users that have obtained more than needed in an e-Bay type auction market. The exchange rate of that particular currency in terms of bank-debt money can then be left to freely fluctuate in an e-Bay type free market.

Smart electrical metering would make the necessary measurements available, and take into account the different carbon emissions due to different sources of electrical energy production, thereby track the generation of the Green currencies. Furthermore, mobile phone technologies could facilitate the trading among end users of those units.

B. The Terra: A global currency that is nobody's national currency

The Terra Trade Reference Currency (Terra TRC, hereafter referred to in shorthand as Terra) – is a supra-national complementary currency initiative. Because it is probably not a familiar complementary currency design, and because of its considerable potential to systemically shift the global economy towards large-scale more sustainable patterns, more details will be provided than in the other examples. The Terra's benefits include:

- It is designed to resolve the conflict between short-term financial interests and long-term sustainability. It makes it profitable to think and act on long-term considerations, particularly for multinational corporations that are influential on the future evolution of technologies and social patterns.
- It would provide more stability and predictability in the financial and business sectors by providing a stable international currency for planning, global contracting and payment purposes worldwide. It would actually be the first time since the gold-standard days that a robust, inflation-resistant standard of value would be available globally.
- It would also counteract the booms and busts of the business cycle and stabilize the global economy. Such a tool could be particularly useful in a period of a simultaneous recession of the three major world economies as we are currently engaged in.
- Finally, it would not require any new legislation or international agreements to become operational.

The Terra characteristics

The Terra is a complementary, privately issued, demurrage-charged, Trade Reference Currency, that is backed by an inflation-resistant, standardized basket of the dozen most important commodities and services in the global market. Each of these characteristics deserve a few words of explanation.

Complementary currency. The Terra is designed as a complementary currency, which by definition are operating in parallel with conventional national currencies. Therefore, everything that exists today as monetary and financial products continues to exist. The Terra mechanism is only one additional option available for those international economic actors who voluntarily choose to use it.

Private issue. The Terra will be issued as an inventory receipt by the Terra Alliance. The Terra Alliance could be part of a reformed IMF, or a private, non-governmental initiative. What matters is that its organizational structure should be open to all newcomers meeting certain pre-established criteria (organizationally similar to that of the Visa credit card system). Such inventory receipts are issued for the value of the commodities sold to the Terra Alliance by producers of those commodities that are components of the Terra Basket. As a private initiative this does not require governmental negotiations or international agreements. From a legal and taxation viewpoint the Terra is simply a standardization of countertrade. And legislation for countertrade exists already in practically all nations around the world.

Trade reference currency. The Terra is backed by a standardized basket of the most important internationally traded commodities, as well as some standardizable services. Though conceptually similar to a fully backed gold standard, the Terra backing would consist not of one single commodity, but a dozen of the main international commodities, including gold. Since it is fully backed by a physical inventory of commodities, it would be a secure, very robust, and stable mechanism for international contractual and payment purposes.

Demurrage-charged. The Terra is a demurrage-charged currency. A demurrage charge acts like a parking fee, incurring a cost over time to its holder. The cost for holding onto the Terra currency is estimated at 3.5%–4% per annum and corresponds to the costs incurred for storing the physical commodities included in the Terra basket. This demurrage charge insures the currency's use mainly as a planning, contractual and trading device: it would not be hoarded but always tend to remain in circulation. It would thereby strongly activate commercial exchanges and investments wherever it circulates. In short, the Terra purposely fulfills only two of the three traditional monetary functions. It is designed to serve only as unit of account and medium of exchange, and not as a store of value.

Inflation-resistant. The Terra is designed as an inflation-resistant currency by its very composition. Inflation is always defined as 'the changes in value of a standardized basket of goods and services.' By selecting the appropriate ingredients to be placed in the basket, the Terra can be protected against inflation. For example, the composition of 100 Terras could include 1 barrel of oil, 5 bushels of wheat, 10 pounds of copper, 3 pounds of tin plus...1/10th ounce of gold, 1 Carbon Emissions Right, etc.

Practical operations of the Terra

The following scenario and accompanying diagram walks through the key elements that are involved in the Terra mechanism – from the creation of Terras to their final cash-in. The numbers listed in parenthesis in the description below corresponds to the steps illustrated in the accompanying diagram (Figure 11.1).

(1). The Terra creation process

(1a). Excess inventory sale. The process whereby the Terra Trade Reference Currency is created begins with the sale of some excess commodity inventory to the Terra Alliance by one of its backer/members (e.g., 1 million barrels of crude oil by an oil producer).[1]

(1b). Commodity valuation in Terras. The value of this sale of oil to the Terra Alliance (i.e., how many Terras the one million barrels of oil will be worth) is calculated at market prices. This is accomplished by determining the commodity prices at the time of the sale for both the inventory in question (in this case oil) and the sum of each of the commodities in the Terra basket using a pre-agreed-upon procedure.

The formula used to calculate the commodity valuation in Terras is:

$$\frac{\textit{Commodity value per unit} \times \textit{number of units}}{\textit{Terra Unit Value}} = \textit{Terras}$$

Let us assume that in our example that the commodity price for a barrel of oil at the time of the sale is \$20. The commodity prices for each of the items in the Terra Basket at the time of the sale (i.e., copper, grains, lead, one unit of Carbon emissions rights, etc, including oil,) totals \$200. Let us further assume that one million barrels of oil are sold. Therefore, 100,000 Terras are created

$$\frac{\textit{\$20 per barrel of crude oil} \times \textit{one million barrels}}{(200)} = \textit{100,000 Terras}$$

(1c). Inventory balance. The Terra Alliance rebalances its portfolio to take into account the inclusion of the 1 million barrels of oil. This may

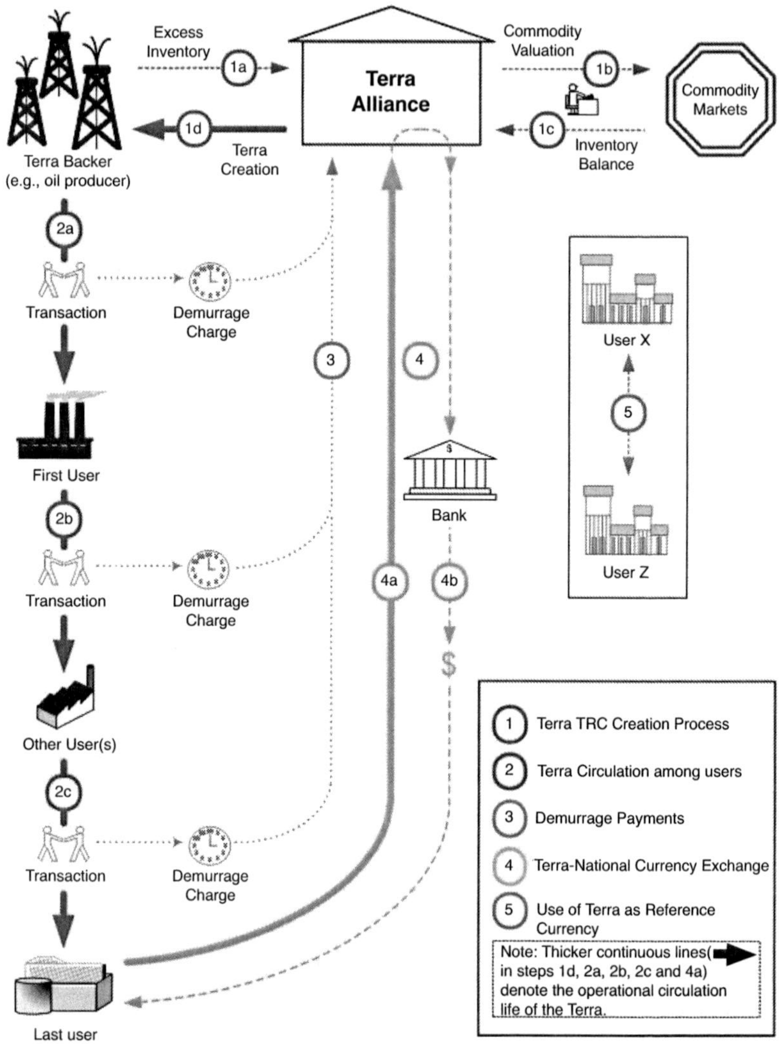

Figure 11.1 Terra Trade Reference Currency Mechanism

be accomplished through future market transactions or through spot transactions.[2]

(1d). Terra creation. The Terra Alliance credits the oil producers' account with 100,000 Terras (note that all Terra currency movements in the diagram are denoted by the thicker continuous arrowed lines).

(2). Terra circulation among users

Once the Terra is created, it enters into and may remain in circulation for a period determined entirely by users.[3] For example:

(2a). First user – The oil producer may decide to pay one of its suppliers (e.g., a German engineering company for the construction of an off-shore rig). It may pay partially or completely in Terras for this project.[4]

(2b). Other user(s) – The German engineering firm in turn decides, to purchase specialty steels from a Korean steel mill, and may decide to pay partially or completely in Terras. The Korean steel mill in turn uses the Terras to pay a mining company in Australia, etc.

(2c). Last user – Each Terra remains in circulation for as little or as long as its various Users continue to use this currency (from one to an infinite number of transactions and without any particular date of expiration). The process comes to an end only when a particular User determines to cash in the Terra(s), in effect, becoming the Last User.

(3). Demurrage

Throughout the circulation life of each Terra(s), from its creation to its final cash-in, a demurrage fee of 3.5–4% per year is in effect. Demurrage is a time-related charge on money. This demurrage fee acts in a similar manner to a rental fee, the charge increasing the longer the rental is held onto. Anybody holding the Terra would be charged the demurrage fee in proportion to the time it is held. The demurrage is estimated at 3.5% to 4%, so the cost of holding it for a few days, or even a few months is still low compared to today's normal international transactions costs. Because the Terra exists only in electronic form, it is easy to know exactly how much time has elapsed between the moment a user receives the Terras and when it is transferred to someone else.

The demurrage charge serves two key functions: it serves as a circulation incentive; and covers all operational costs for the Terra system:

- Terra Circulation Incentive. The demurrage charge is designed as an incentive to keep the Terras circulating in a timely fashion from one user to another. As the Terra demurrage charge increases the longer it is held onto as calculated below. Thus, the demurrage charge insures the Terras' usage as a mechanism of exchange and not as a mechanism of storage.

- Terra Operational Cost Coverage-The Terra demurrage charge(s) is calculated to cover the costs of the entire operation of the Terra mechanism (e.g., storage costs of the basket, administrative overhead, transaction costs in the futures markets).

The demurrage fees for a particular Terra transaction may be calculated by the following formula:

(Terra Operation Costs/time unit) × (Terra holding period) × (Terras on account) = Demurrage Charge

Let us assume that the Terra operation costs are evaluated at 3.65% per year, or 0.01% per day. Let us further assume that the German engineering firm (First User in our diagram) received all 100,000 Terras from the oil producer and has kept these on account for a period of 10 days (prior to paying the Korean steel mill in transaction 2b in our diagram). Thus, the demurrage charge (represented by the dotted blue line) in Transaction 2b would be calculated as follows:

0.01%/per day × 10 days × 100,000 Terras = 100 Terras

4. Terra cash-in

The circulation (and existence) of a particular Terra comes to an end when one entity (designated the Last User in our diagram) decides to cash in part or all of its Terras (for example, to pay its taxes and/or payroll and requiring national currency to do so.

A transaction fee (proposed at 2% of the amount of Terras cashed in) is charged. This transaction fee serves two purposes:

- Terra Circulation Incentive The transaction fee is designed as an incentive to keep the Terras in circulation and to not cash in its Terras too readily, thus continuing the beneficial effects of the circulating Terras. In effect, the 2% transaction fee motivates anybody in possession of Terras to make the following consideration: 'Cashing in the Terras now will cost me the same as paying the demurrage fee for more than six months (assuming a demurrage of 3.65% per year). It is likely that I will be able to pay someone at least partially in Terras over the next six months. After all, most suppliers would rather be paid earlier than later....'
- Cash-In Operational Costs. When the Last User decides to cash in its Terras, the Terra Alliance sells the necessary volume of commodities

from its basket to the commodity markets in order to obtain the necessary funds in conventional currency.

The Terras are thus handed into the Terra Alliance (4a) and converted to either national currency[5] or a volume of Terra commodities (as determined by the Last User) to the amount equal to the value of the Terras cashed in minus the transaction fee (e.g., 2%). The cash-in may take place directly with the Terra Alliance itself or by means of an intermediary bank for example as any foreign exchange transaction today. (4b)

5. Reference currency

Once the Terra mechanism is operational and the advantages of using an inflation-resistant international standard is known, there is nothing to impede two entities (User X and User Z in the diagram) that may have no direct involvement in the Terra mechanism to denominate contracts in Terras, even if the final settlement may happen in the corresponding value in conventional currency. The Terra, in this instance, functions purely as a Trade Reference Currency, a reliable standard of value. This is similar to the gold standard days when two parties agreed on contracts denominated in gold, even if neither party owned gold or had any involvement in gold mining or processing. The only significant difference with the Terra is that, again, it is backed not by one commodity (i.e., gold) but by a dozen or so commodities and services (i.e., the Terra basket) making it more stable a reference than the gold standard.

Benefits of the Terra

General and specific benefits will be examined next, followed by an analysis differentiating the Terra from other proposals and initiatives aimed at redressing present monetary concerns.

General benefits of the Terra

The Terra mechanism, by virtue of its demurrage charge and being inflationary-resistant, endows this trading instrument with three unique economic advantages. These are:

- It provides a robust international standard of value.
- It counteracts the boom/bust fluctuations of the business cycle, thereby improving the overall stability and predictability of the world's economic system.
- It realigns financial interests with long-term concerns.

Robust international standard of value

The Terra would provide a robust international standard of value, something that has been missing since the end of the Bretton Woods system in 1971. Since it is fully backed by a physical inventory of not one, but a dozen or so of the world's most important commodities, including gold, the Terra would be a very robust and credible payment unit that offsets volatility and currency risks.

This robust standard of value benefits commerce as follows:

- Lowers costs by reducing the need for expensive hedging countermeasures;
- Enables greater opportunities (including investments in developing countries) by providing stable alternative mechanisms by which to conduct commerce;
- Offers a dependable, cost-effective reference mechanism for global trade.

Cycle-stabilization

The Terra automatically tends to counteract the fluctuations of the business cycle, thereby improving the overall stability and predictability of the world's economic system.

When the business cycle is weakening, corporations customarily have an excess of inventory and a need for credit. The excess inventories can now be sold to the TRC Alliance (who would place these inventories into storage). The TRC Alliance would pay for these inventories in Terras, thus providing corporations with a means of payment (typically, less readily available in this part of a business cycle). These corporations would immediately spend the Terra's, to pay their suppliers, for example, so as to avoid the demurrage charges (whose holding costs accumulate over time). Suppliers, in turn, would have a similar incentive to pass on the demurrage-charged Terras as a medium of payment. The spread of this currency (with its built-in incentive to trade) would automatically activate the economy at this point in the cycle.

On the contrary, when the business cycle is in a boom period, demand for goods and services go up and both suppliers and corporations have an increased need for inventory. The Terras would now be cashed in with the TRC Alliance (even at the cost of the 2% transaction fee), and the now needed inventories would be taken out of storage and delivered to the respective commodity markets to obtain the conventional currency required. This would also reduce the amount of

Terras in circulation when the business cycle is at its maximum, counteracting an inflationary boom phase.

None of this is theory. There is now quantitative proof that the availability of a complementary currency designed for business use spontaneously tends to stabilize the business cycle and the overall economy. Detailed analysis on the WIR system, described in Chapter 10, is a complementary currency program that has been in use for more than 50 years in Switzerland, provides strong evidence that significant complementary currencies can flourish.

In case one might think that such effects are valid only for Switzerland, Prof. Stodder also evaluated the effects of commercial barter by members of the International Reciprocal Trade Association (IRTA) upon the U.S. economy (Stodder 1998). Though the data here covers only 21 years (instead of WIR's 50 plus), exactly the same type of impact occurs. But with IRTA exchanges proportionally smaller in the U.S. economy than the WIR for the Swiss economy, the overall effect is also proportionally less powerful.

In summary, the Terra-denominated exchanges would stabilize the business cycle by providing additional monetary liquidity that counterbalances the pattern observed in the money-creation process of conventional national currencies.

Realignment of financial interests with long-term concerns

The demurrage feature of the Terra would provide a systematic financial motivation that realigns financial interests with long-term concerns. This is in direct contrast with what happens today with conventional national currencies. The discounted cash flow of conventional national currencies with positive interest rates systematically emphasizes the immediate future at the expense of the long-term. The same discounted cash flow with a demurrage charged currency produces the exact opposite effects. The use of the Terra for planning and contractual purposes will therefore reduce the conflict that currently prevails between the stockholder's financial priorities and the long-term priorities of humanity as a whole.

Specific group benefits

Virtually everyone stands to benefit from the Terra. A partial list of the specific advantages applying to humanity at-large, multinational corporations, the banking sector and financial services, Less Developed Countries and developed nations are offered in following.

Humanity as a whole

- As long as business is focused on short-term profits, chances are minimal that any long-term sustainability is possible. Inevitably, it will be the humanity as a whole that will end up paying for a failure in sustainable development. In contrast, the introduction of the Terra with its demurrage functionality makes long-term thinking profitable, and therefore, long-term sustainability much more likely.
- The typical booms/bust of the business cycle will automatically decrease, creating a more dependable economic environment, which will translate into more reliable job employment opportunities and less job instability.

Multinational corporations

The Terra offers corporations the following advantages:

- Makes it possible to convert inventories of illiquid assets, such as major raw materials, into liquid ones. This is a significant advantage, given that inventories are otherwise a cost item to businesses. Over time, such storage costs can become substantial.
- Provides working capital at a lower cost than with conventional national currencies, as the Terra demurrage fees only kick in for a particular user if the Terras are not spent.
- Makes available to businesses a robust international standard of value, with a consistent value in real terms for international contracts. No party would lose out because of monetary instability or currency fluctuations.
- Lowers the cost of doing business, by reducing the need for expensive currency hedging counter-measures and providing a dependable, low-cost insurance against uncertainties deriving from international currency markets.
- Offers a dependable, more cost-effective reference mechanism than conventional corporate barter.
- Develops new markets and enables greater opportunities by which to conduct global commerce, including investing in developing countries, by providing a stable international currency. This situation has limited the creation of new markets, because entire continents remain too poor to participate in the global market-place.
- Saves money and vital resources. Corporations, as a result of the boom and bust business cycle phenomenon, are often under-equipped and

looking for qualified staff, or over-equipped and over-staffed. The costs of training people, for example, are considerable (only to then fire them afterwards). Expenses incurred in plant and equipment over-investments or under-investments are also considerable.

- And, it is well known that political instabilities often occur during, and result from, economic downturns. Such instability is not contributing to a healthy climate for businesses either. The Terra counteracts such downturns.

Benefits to financial services and the banking sector

There are three main advantages of the Terra mechanism for the banking system:

- It introduces standardization in countertrade, thus making the countertrade mechanism bankable. Currently, the banking system has no role at all in the fast-growing countertrade field (countertrade grows at a rate of 15% per year,[6] three times faster than trade facilitated in conventional currencies). Banks will be able to provide traditional foreign exchange services utilizing the Terras, which can then be converted into any and all other national currencies. They can, as well, provide their customers services such as Terra account management, as they do today with any foreign exchange.
- The counter-cyclical impact of the Terra mechanism will stabilize the value of banking loan portfolios. There have been numerous major banking-related crises around the world over the past two decades, in which borrowers can't repay their loans, while the collateral upon which the loans were based depreciates. These conditions are aggravated by the boom/bust cycle and currency fluctuations. Therefore, as the Terra mechanism helps to stabilize economic cycles, the number and severity of crises in bank portfolios would also be reduced.
- Finally, the task of central banks would also be made a bit easier with the Terra mechanism in play. Not only would there be fewer banking crises to manage, but also their routine job of trying to counteract the business cycle would be eased as already demonstrated in practice by the WIR.

Less developed countries (LDCs)

Currently, as a direct result of currency instability, LDCs suffer from a lack of investments. Furthermore, the degradation of terms of trade with developed nations, and the scarcity of hard currencies create debt traps resulting in the inability to repay foreign loans.

This is illustrated by the comment on his country's debt made after the G8 summit in Okinawa in 2000 by President Obasanjo of Nigeria: 'All that we had borrowed up to 1985 or 1986 was around $5 billion. So far we have paid back about $16 billion. Yet we are being told that we still owe about $28 billion. That $28 billion came about because of the foreign creditors' interest rates. If you ask me what is the worst thing in the world, I will say it is compound interest.' When President Obasanjo spoke out, the developing world was spending $13 on debt repayment for every one dollar it received in foreign aid and grants.

The Terra mechanism helps to address these problems and offers two distinct and important benefits to LDCs.

- A stable international currency enables greater opportunities by which to conduct commerce and make investments in developing countries. As noted earlier, because of the instability created by floating exchanges, there has been approximately a 33% decrease in investments to Less Developed Countries.
- LDCs that produce commodities (i.e., raw materials such as copper that are components in the basket of the Terra) would be in a similar position as any producer member of the TRC Alliance. By virtue of the fact that the Terra is a commodity-backed currency, LDCs would find themselves in a position similar to gold-producing countries during the gold standard days: What they extracted – gold – was in fact directly an internationally convertible currency.

Developed countries

- As stated earlier, the developed world is facing its first simultaneous economic downturn since the 1930s. (At that time, only a World War got us out that economic stranglehold. A better way is available). If the Terra were implemented now on a sufficient scale, it would help re-launch the world economy by injecting international liquidity that would reactivate the global economy.
- By helping LDCs, new markets are created.
- By stabilizing the business cycle, greater job stability and opportunities would become available as well.

Differences with earlier proposals

The Terra is a commodity-basket currency. For more than a century, there have been several proposals for commodity-basket currencies by a series of well-known economists.[7] The main reason why they have not been implemented is not due to a technical fault of the concept, but rather because they were aiming at replacing the conventional money system. Such replacement would have put in jeopardy powerful vested interests. This is not the case with the Terra proposal.

On the contrary, the win-win strategy underlying the Terra mechanism includes the financial sector as well. Anything that exists under the current monetary modus operandi would remain in operation after the introduction of the Terra, as it is a complementary currency designed to operate in parallel with the existing system.

Finally, as stated earlier, the political context for an international monetary treaty has not been available. From a legal or tax standpoint, it would fit within the existing official framework of countertrade, and not require any formal governmental agreements to make it operational.

The other conceptual difference between the Terra proposal and all previous proposals, perhaps the most important one, is the introduction of the demurrage concept. The fact that the storage costs of the basket would be covered by the bearer of the Terra, resolves the inherent problem that previous commodity proposals were facing, namely: Who will pay for it all?

The Terra mechanism is a win-win approach for all major participants in the global economy, and that is why it may have a better chance to succeed where other proposals for monetary innovations have failed in the past.

C. Beyond 2025?

This section provides a personal view of how the world of money may unfold in the longer term. In the long run – some time after 2025 – I expect that new economic and governance structures will emerge at the next order of complexity, and that after a period of highly unpredictable instabilities, a new era of predictable patterns will return Other monetary systems than the ones described in this book will be necessary at that point. Maybe at some point in the future we will not need money at all. If we have to believe Jean Luc Godard of Star Trek fame, 'money does not exist in the twenty-fourth century.' Meanwhile,

I think we will need transitional money systems, which can be used as crutches to re-educate atrophied collective behavior patterns.

Meanwhile, during the current transition period a lot of violent disruptions and pain can be avoided by encouraging social experimentation, by letting embryonic forms a chance to thrive, by allowing them to test new patterns which have already proven effective at dealing with structural change in other parts of the world. This is the way nature has been doing it successfully for five billion years. Can we afford not to learn from it?

What follows next is a description of the development of a four-level monetary system. One already exists – the conventional bank-debt national currency system. The development of the three new money systems is synthesized in three timetables, revealing that the emergence of these new systems is in fact an organic development of trends which have been prevailing for decades, each pushed by its own logic. In parallel to these three new levels, it is assumed that the conventional national currency systems will be able to operate roughly as they do today. The only significant difference is that they are not anymore perceived as the only game in town.

The monetary system of 2025: A multi-tiered gear box

Let us imagine that we are living in 2025. Almost all corporations and many individuals are dealing routinely in currencies at different levels. For a small transaction fee, it has become very simple to exchange any of these currencies somewhere on the Net or via mobile phones. Just like with today's frequent flyer miles, mixed payments are common (you can buy a ticket in national currency, and pay for an upgrade in frequent flyer miles).

The multi-tiered monetary system operational in 2025 would be the following:

- A global reference currency
- Three main multinational currencies
- Some national currencies
- Regional currencies
- Local complementary currencies
- A variety of functional currencies

A global reference currency

Several corporate scripts are competing on the Net, issued by the likes of Amex, Microsoft, and an alliance of European and Asian corporations. Some have created special subsidiaries – with strong and liquid balance sheets – to issue these currencies and provide them with stronger credibility. One such currency has taken the form of the Terra described earlier or some variation of it, and arose from a systematization of corporate barter.

Three multinational currencies

It has indeed become obvious that regional economic integration can reach maturity only when a single currency levels the playing field for all economic participants. A single currency is the only way to structurally guarantee a unified information field. Such multinational alliances have evolved in Europe around the Euro; but there are also multinational currency zones in Asia (triggered by a deal between Japan and China); and in the Americas (around an Amero, after a reform of the US$).

National currencies

In many countries, national currencies will still be used for a long time. They continue to play an important role within any country that has not joined a formal multinational currency integration system. Most exchanges continue to involve national currencies at least in partial payments, if nor no other reason that they remain the official 'legal tender' with which national taxes are being paid.

The main difference from the past is that national currencies do not maintain their totally monopolistic role as medium of exchange. Many payments are mixed – involving both national currencies, corporate scripts, or Internet currencies in a single transaction. The only places where the national currencies have kept intact their old monopoly are a few underdeveloped countries and backward dictatorships, where the priority given to political control over the Net has kept the cybereconomy completely out.

Regional currencies

Under pressures to reduce long-distance transport, a source of a significant part of carbon emissions, businesses have tended to re-organize their supply chains in regional networks. The C3 mechanism (described in Chapter 10) was one of the pioneers of this process. Supply chains around specific industrial sectors have also emerged, such as food production and processing, or automobile components.

Local complementary currencies

In reaction to economic globalization and running in parallel to it, self-organization at the local level has become very popular. The Information Revolution also meant a systematic reduction of production and service related 'jobs.' As jobs grew scarcer, communities created their own currencies to facilitate local exchanges among their members. Once critical mass was attained, complementary currency clearinghouses on the Net made it possible for members of these communities to participate in the cybereconomy as well.

Functional currencies

The field where most creativity has emerged is in special function currencies, which have barely been touched in this book. They include systems like reputation currencies (such as relationship satisfaction ratings on the model pioneered by e-Bay); learning currencies; environmental currencies, etc.

Conclusions

A monetary ecology would provide a lot more flexibility in the both choice and the nature of our exchanges. Although it may appear confusing at first sight, that complexity will only apply mainly to academics who are trying to track all the exchanges in our society. In practice, most citizens would deal with two or three different types of units: your national or multinational currency that is official legal tender in your country, a regional or local currency, and some of your favorite volunteer organizations. Just like today they manage to hold a job, while also belonging to different volunteer organizations and practice various sports, without confusing their roles and scores in each. In fact, for them it would be an extrapolation of the commercial loyalty currencies, like they do for their supermarket points or airline miles.

Together, these different systems would certainly ensure a lot more resilience to our economic and social networks. If one of those old or new systems fail, and some certainly will, others will pick up the resulting slack. Our societies would be in the process of learning to operate on a higher level of complexity. Just like when a disease hits a particular tree, or a specific flora or fauna species in a diversified ecosystem, some stress would still be the result, but the ecosystem as a whole adapts and continues to flourish in a slightly different way.

The technical argument for a single currency in a country is that it makes price formation and exchanges most efficient, which is a valid point. In 1953, Milton Friedman took the next step: he proposed to let on a global level an unfettered market of currencies freely optimize efficiencies (Friedman 1953). This approach was actually implemented by President Nixon in 1971. Giant banks and titanic financial markets emerged, very efficient in terms of the growth of their financial throughput capacity. They also reinforce themselves as powerful political lobbies. For instance, in the case of the US, a study by two nonpartisan groups, Public Citizen and the Center for Responsive Politics, found that in 2009 there was a 'small army' of 1,400 financial lobbyists officially registered in Washington, lobbying for the biggest financial institutions. They included at least 73 former lawmakers and 148 ex-staffers connected to the House or Senate banking committees. More than 40 former Treasury Department employees also now ply their trade as lobbyists for Wall Street firms. For every sitting member of Congress, the study shows, there are three former colleagues or government staffers lobbying for banks. David Arkush, director of Public Citizen's Congress Watch division, said 'Wall Street hires former members of Congress and their staff for a reason,' especially at a time when lawmakers are debating a historic overhaul of the way Wall Street does business. 'These people are influential because they have personal relationships with current members and staff,' Arkush said. 'It's hard to say no to your friends, but that's what Congress needs to do.'

Should it be surprising that financial institutions that are protected in this way become 'too big to fail'. In parallel, massive financial bubbles emerge, and when they burst, new bubbles are being generated as the best remedy to contain the collateral damage. All these processes are components of what our theoretical framework identified as 'autocatalytic forces', and are a logical symptom of an over-efficient Yang system.

With a genuine monetary ecology in place, with money systems operational at different scales, the 'good old days' when a systemic bank failure spelled the collapse of an entire economy and society would also be behind us.

Notes

1 Note that the commodity itself that is being sold (in this case, oil) may or may not have to move physically during the process. What matters it that the Terra Alliance becomes now the beneficial owner of the commodity. The legal framework for such transfers is already routinely used today. For instance, the commodity trading departments of an oil company can have a

shipment of oil in a tanker change owner several times before it arrives at its destination.

2 A futures market transaction is the purchase or sale today at a given price for delivery at some future date. A spot transaction is the direct purchase or sale of a commodity at the price of today, with delivery today.

3 Note that all exchanges in Terras would occur through high-level secure electronic exchanges, as these transactions would tend to be of high value.

4 The payment conditions would normally have been already determined when the oil rig was put up for bidding.

5 In order to produce the corresponding cash for the Terras that are handed in, the Terra Alliance sells an appropriate volume of commodities of the Terra basket in the commodity markets.

6 http://www.barternews.com/archive/06_27_06.htm

7 See for example in chronological order: W. S. Jevons, *Money and the Mechanism of Exchange* (1875); Ian Gondriaan, *How to Stop Deflation* (London, 1932); Benjamin Graham, *Storage and Stability* (New York: McGraw Hill, 1937) and *World Commodities and World Currency* (1944); Harmon, Elmer, *Commodity Reserve Currency* (New York: Columbia University Press, 1959); Grondona St. Clare *Economic Stability is Attainable* (London: Hutchison Benham Ltd, 1975); Albert Hart of Columbia University, Nicholas Kaldor of Cambridge University and Jan Tinbergen: 'The Case for an International Reserve Currency,' Document UNCTAD 64-03482 (Geneva: presented on 2/17/1964) (in this last case the purpose wasn't to replace the conventional money, but to stabilize the prices of Third World country commodities).

References

Friedman, M. (1953). 'The Case for Flexible Exchange Rates', in *Essays in Positive Economics*, pp.157–203. Chicago: University of Chicago Press

Stodder, J. (1998) 'Corporate Barter and Macroeconomic Stabilization', *International Journal of Community Currency Research*, 2(2). Online at: http://www.geog.le.ac.uk/ijccr/volume2/2js.htm.

Wray, R. (1998) *Understanding Modern Money: The Key to Full Employment and Price Stability*. Northampton, MA: Edward Elgar.

12
The State-Issue of Currency without Usury

Peter Challen, Simon Mouatt and Rodney Shakespeare

> The intrinsic values of real economy must be those that work for everyone and protect the earth...
>
> Canon Peter Challen

Introduction

We humans are in the midst of a potentially terminal economic, social and environmental crisis. In order to address that crisis this chapter outlines a proposal for the structural reform of a national monetary system, with practical and beneficial consequences. It is recognized, of course, that monetary reform *per se* is not a holistic panacea to all of our global ills. Yet, it is hoped that the incremental transition recommended, using the national bank to issue interest-free currency (credit-money), could promote the cause of social and economic justice through a more sustainable monetary system. In addition, interest-free currency could be used to finance other reform proposals such as the spread of capital ownership or the creation of a basic income. At the core of the reform is the insight that, *usury* (defined here as an interest-charge in excess of justifiable administration cost) *is not necessary*. Whilst it can be argued that administration charges, collateral and properly conceived repayment plans are imperative for the proper functioning of credit markets, usury is not so easily defended (especially for state expenditure) unless the motive is to profit the private financial sector and their investors.

These ideas, of course, resonate with the great religions of Islam, Christianity and Judaism that have a historical tradition of opposing usury on ethical grounds. Yet, in recent centuries, the faiths have compromised these values and therefore been complicit in the levying of usury as capitalist credit relations have evolved. Sadly, we appear to be stuck with debt and the interest it generates. We are presently informed by the economics profession that there is no alternative method of recycling monies from surplus to deficit agents that will practically provide the necessary liquidity for the efficient operation of a modern free-market economy. Yet, interest diminishes the consuming capacity of a borrower (and, when compounded, can eliminate it altogether) thereby breaching the basic market principle that producers *should* be able to spend the income emanating from their production. Indeed, as Magrit Kennedy has observed, interest also instigates an inflationary tendency and is generally responsible for the exacerbation of global income disparities (Kennedy 1995). Ironically, if a modern government were to seek to expand its income redistributive function, through the expansion of tax, this would be fiercely resisted. Yet, as El Diwany notes, the usurer extracts substantial tribute from the productive economy and this income stream, in contrast to wealth held in other forms, is not subject to the universal principle of entropy (El Diwany 2003). For money *rentiers* this means that there is an increasing accumulation dynamic through time that, in conjunction with bank consolidation, helps form what Lenin referred to as a 'financial oligarchy' which then wields an increasing amount of social power in world affairs (Lenin 1996). Meanwhile debt, and its associated suffering, reaches epidemic proportions. Is there a way out? The proposal outlined here suggests that there is but, first, let us consider the activities of creditors (and their extraction of usury) in closer detail.

Creditors and usury

The historical practice of usury has had serious practical consequences, which inevitably raised ethical debates. Marx (p.740) cites this passage from Martin Luther (Marx 1976).

> The heathen were able, by the light of reason, to conclude that a usurer is a double-dyed thief and murderer. We Christians, however, hold them in such honour, that we fairly worship them for the sake of their money...Whoever eats up, robs and steals the nourishment of another, that man commits as great a murder (so far as in him lies) as he who starves a man or utterly undoes him. Such does a usurer, and sits the while safe on his stool, when he ought rather to be hanging on the gallows, and be eaten by as many ravens as he has stolen guilders, if only there were so much flesh on him, that so

> many ravens could stick their beaks in and share it. Meanwhile, we hang the small thieves...Little thieves are put in the stocks, great thieves go flaunting in gold and silk...Therefore is there, on this earth, no greater enemy of man (after the devil) than a gripe-money, and usurer, for he wants to be God over all men. Turks, soldiers, and tyrants are also bad men, yet must they let the people live, and confess that they are bad, and enemies, and do, nay, must, now and then show pity to some. But a usurer and money-glutton, such a one would have the whole world perish of hunger and thirst, misery and want, so far as in him lies, so that he may have all to himself, and every one may receive from him as from a God, and be his serf for ever more. [This is what gladdens his heart, and also] to wear fine cloaks, golden chains, rings, to wipe his mouth, to be deemed and taken for a worthy, pious man...Usury is a great huge monster, like a were-wolf, who lays waste all, more than any Cacus, Gerion or Antaeus. And yet decks himself out, and would be thought pious, so that people may not see where the oxen have gone, that he drags backwards into his den. But Hercules shall hear the cry of the oxen and of his prisoners, and shall seek Cacus even in cliffs and among rocks, and shall set the oxen loose again from the villain. For Cacus means the villain that is a pious usurer, and steals, robs, eats everything. And will not own that he has done it, and thinks no one will find him out, because the oxen, drawn backwards into his den, make it seem, from their footprints, that they have been let out. So the usurer would deceive the world, as though he were of use and gave the world oxen, which he, however, rends, and eats all alone... And since we break on the wheel, and behead, highwaymen, murderers, and house-breakers, how much more ought we to break on the wheel and kill...hunt down, curse, and behead all usurers. *(Martin Luther, 1540, An die Pfarrherrn, wider den Wucher zu predigen).*

These are strong words from Luther but they contain several points worthy of discussion. Firstly, he suggests that the heathen is capable of identifying the crime of usury whilst, the religious person is not, suggesting that religion is in consort or denial with the lenders. This is consistent with Marx's own analysis whereby religious leaders, through acquiescence towards the ruling order, condone injustice by default and assist in the appeasement of the masses. Marx is perhaps misrepresented as opposing Christianity when, instead, he may be simply opposing religious hypocrisy. Secondly, Luther argues that usurers extract a surplus from the productive sector and likens this to theft on a grand scale. This view can be contrasted, of course, with the *bourgeois* notion of money-lenders as 'capital providers', who receive an income (interest) for their service to production. A small reward for *rentiers* would probably be uncontested but, as Lenin noted (p.53), the usurer's return on monies lent (combined with bank fees) often greatly exceeds the surpluses of productive capitalists and helps to form the 'financial oligarchy'(Lenin 1996). Another interesting detrimental consequence of usury, as Francis Bacon had long ago observed, is that, in order to receive income, the usurer does not need to extend energies and attributes towards the productive sector, and, therefore, society is denied the benefit of their unused resources (Roll 1973).

This image of a thief is continued with Luther's use of Greek mythology, where the popular hero Hercules frees society from the fire-breathing monster Cacus, who is stealing from everyone for his own consumption. Hercules had previously been given a task by Eurystheus to defeat the three-bodied Geryon who had a herd of oxen that, perhaps, could be considered to be analogous to the resources required by the productive economy. Whilst returning with the spoils, Hercules had some of the cattle stolen by Cacus. It is interesting that he tried to conceal the crime by dragging the oxen backwards into his cave, to give the impression that they had moved in the other direction. Hercules becomes wise to this and defeats Cacus (Linderman 1997). Perhaps the modern usurer manages to conceal their activity (crime) because the common understanding is that there is no alternative to credit (nowadays, of course, created *ex nihilo* by private bankers) and, consequently, debate rarely takes place. When Hercules comes to defeat the giant Antaeus (son of Gaia and Poseidon), who had been terrorizing society, he becomes wise to the secret of Antaeus's strength – 'mother earth'. Having unearthed the secret, Hercules is able to lift him off the ground and strangle him.

The history of monetary reform

There are various campaigning groups and individuals, who have studied the mechanics of credit and, to use the Lutheran analogy, 'unearthed' its secrets. These monetary reform groups have threatened to undermine the prevailing monetary vested interests and have therefore, unsurprisingly, been resisted. The reformers have generally proposed to replace the current fractional reserve system, where private banks issue credit-money *ex nihilo*, with either debt-free *fiat* money or interest-free credit-money (or some combination of the two) both of which could be issued by the state. Modern monetary reform has antecedents that can be traced back to the events leading to the 1776 American War of Independence. Ellen Brown explains how the American people, controlled by British colonialists, having to pay endless financial tribute to England and faced with shortages of money, had issued their own paper currency (Brown 2007). The paper currencies then lead to a sustained period of productive stability, poverty-alleviation and full-employment. Indeed, on a visit to England, Benjamin Franklin noticed the relative level of poverty and unemployment that existed in London and attributed this to a private debt-based (scarce) money system. When asked to explain the relative prosperity of the American colonies he stated that the issue of paper money by the authorities was the reason for economic success, providing that it was created:

> ...in proper proportions to the demands of trade and industry ...we also *[emphasis added]* issue it to pay the government's approved expenses and charities. We make sure it is issued in proper proportions to make the goods easily pass from the producers to the consumers...In this manner, creating for ourselves our own paper money, we control its purchasing power, and we have no interest to pay to no one. You see, a legitimate government can both spend and lend money into circulation, while banks can only lend significant amounts of their promissory bank notes, for they can neither give away nor spend but a tiny fraction of the money people need. Thus, there is always a debt principal to be returned and usury to be paid. The result is that you have always too little credit in circulation to give the workers full employment. You do not have too many workers, you have too little money in circulation, and that which circulates, all bears the endless burden of unpayable debt and usury...
>
> (Brown 2007)

Franklin's statement clearly posits the view that sensible state control, regulation *and issue* of money, with a restrained role for the private banking sector, were the preferable options. Under the 'Pennsylvania plan', for instance, the colonial authorities had issued *debt-free* money for government projects, in place of taxes, and also discovered that it was non-inflationary. In addition, credit monies were provided for the private sector at 5% interest rather than the more prohibitive 8% charged by the private bankers. The colonial financial system was heralded as a success in Pennsylvania (and other colonies) but, unfortunately, in New England, an over-issue of notes led to the currency's depreciation and this began to affect the investments of British merchants. The result was that, in dealing with the colonial issue in 1751 Britain, also being anxious to retain the colonies in their role as suppliers of raw materials, issued a decree banning the issue of new paper money in New England, forcing the local people to borrow from the English bankers abroad. Within a year, Franklin noted, beggars had returned to the streets and, soon, anger began to rise eventually resulting in sufficient revolutionary fervour to challenge the British in the 1776 War of Independence.

The benefit (and need) of sufficient circulating liquidity is a recurrent theme in history. Thus, during the Keynesian 'golden-age' era of the fifties and sixties, for instance, the availability of 'cheap money' (low interest rates) is often cited as a major contributing factor to the prevailing (favourable) macroeconomic climate (Pettifor 2006). Even the monetarist Friedman had cited the Federal Reserve credit squeeze, and subsequent lack of money, as the key contributory factor to the 1930s Depression (Friedman 1956). It appears that the lack of liquidity is often the prelude to economic strife, leading to political and social instability. The *debt-based* money system, controlled by the private banking infrastructure, is seen as the root cause of the lack of liquidity by contemporary monetary reformers. When interest-bearing credit-money is created, through the production of loans by the banks, there is enough circulating currency to repay the principal of the loan *but not to repay the interest.*[1] This results in the so-called 'impossible contract' and so, the economic system then relies upon the further expansion of credit in order to service existing debt and provide liquidity. If compounded interest is also taken into consideration the problem is far worse. The monetary reform campaigner, Ellen Brown, has likened this (impossible) credit process to a game of 'musical chairs' where the inevitability of default is intrinsic to the system as someone is expected to be left 'holding the chair' (Brown 2007). In short, as credit-money grows in relation to fiat money, the problem deepens. At the time of WWII, 'high-powered' money (mainly notes and coins) constituted approximately 50% of the money supply whereas it now only constitutes 3% in the UK, and less than 1% in the US (Shakespeare and Challen 2002). Firms, consumers and governments all need to find additional revenue in order to meet debt interest payments and this puts substantial pressure on prices, resources and the environment (Kennedy 1995).

The 'fractionally-backed' gold certificates of the goldsmiths, as an early form of credit money, have often been suggested as antecedents for modern (private) commercial banking. Yet, whilst the goldsmiths had to ensure that issued notes were an appropriate multiple of guarded specie deposits in the vaults, their modern private banker counterparts are *not* subject to *de facto* reserve restraints. Today, when commercial banks make loans they simply press computer buttons to make accounting entries on their assets and liabilities sheets and so the (subsequently circulating) deposit bank-monies are literally created *ex nihilo* i.e. out of nothing. The view that bank deposits are initially formed from pre-existing monies is completely fallacious. In short, today's money is created and issued by the banks in response to a request for its creation (Rochon 1999; Howells and Bain 2008).

In explaining how this began, United Kingdom monetary reformers further point to the Free Coinage Act of 1666 which enabled the issuance of money by the private banks, thereby starting to replace the English government 'tally-stick' system of accounting. Following the Glorious Revolution of 1688, which installed William of Orange as King, the development of the Bank of England in 1694 granted private investors license to produce legal tender (i.e. permission to create money *ex nihilo*) in order to lend to the government and business. Hitherto, the English monarchs (or their agents) had been responsible for their own currency issue, and so 1688 was really a 'glorious' revolution for the bankers who had succeeded in legitimizing their position as official creators of interest-bearing money. This new money, issued by private banks as interest-bearing debt, then began to serve as *legal tender* money, thereby establishing today's statutory and common-law currency practice that permits a *de facto* private banking cartel to be able to extract substantial tribute from the wealth and income of the productive economy. Whilst the state has experienced periods of stronger intervention in monetary matters, such as the period following the Great Depression, this has been short-lived. Soon after, as Helleiner noted, the private bankers (and sympathetic politicians) were vociferous in lobbying for an increased role for the commercial banks (relative to the state) in the financial system. The financiers particularly pushed for substantial market deregulation that has led to, arguably, potential (and actual) destabilizing effects to both the state and society's productive structure (Helleiner 1994).

The situation today is such that the levels of consumer, corporate and state debt have reached such alarming proportions that it will not be long before the interest cannot be paid and so the debt will quickly become unsustainable. The largest debtor in the world today, for instance, is the United States, with federal debt alone presently running at $7.713 trillion in 2007, and at current trends predicted to reach 'unsustainability' within the next few years as annual interest exceeds taxation receipts. Since the US dollar is used as the global reserve currency, with foreign central banks and institutional investors holding substantial amounts, the ramifications of a major debt default and subsequent dollar devaluation are colossal.

The current monetary reform movement

Monetary reformers generally agree on the nature of the perceived international problems but posit varying proposals for the transformation of domestic financial systems. Stephen Zarlenga for instance, from the American Monetary Institute based in Chicago, suggests that the state should create a legally sanctioned 'money of account' that gradually replaces credit-money to become 100% of the money supply. The money is provided interest *and* debt-free (Mouatt 2008). Joseph Huber and James Robertson in their 2000 book *Creating New Money* also propose a debt-free issuance for the purposes of government expenditure (Huber and Robertson 2000). Under these proposals the money is not backed by specie, only by the force of law. The private banks are also *only* permitted to conduct lending on a 100% fractionally backed system, which means they can only lend their own money (investor capital) and/or, with permission, that of depositors, but may not create new money as they do today. This necessitates, of course, much stronger state (financial) regulation.

Yet, there are critics of the Zarlenga type of proposal. The veteran Canadian reformer William Krehm, for instance, opposes the Zarlenga 100% fractional backing approach on the ground that this would lead to a centralization of financial power in the hands of the state that, at least potentially, may lead to state abuse. He favours instead a 50/50 system, where the currency issuance (before circulation) is shared between the state and private banks, that will deliver many of the benefits of reform yet maintain a (safer) plurality of social power through public *and* private involvement in the money-isssue (McConnachie 2006).

The Islamic world also has monetary reform proposals, where interest (riba) is forbidden by Koranic law. The literal translation of riba is *increase,* although it is usually understood as interest which can be extracted when credit is extended or derived from trade. This, of course, presents difficulties for today's Islamic economic policy-makers (and bankers) who are seeking to implement religious law as well as creating problems for Moslems living in non-Islamic financial systems.

This is because when monies are provided in the form of credit there needs to be incentives for parting with liquidity (whenever credit is derived from existing deposits) and the levying of administration costs, even without the extraction of profit for financial *rentiers*. In order to do this, and to be allegedly following Islamic injunction against riba, Islamic Banking has evolved over the last forty years and its general characteristic is that interest is not charged yet, by the use of different legal contracts, other charges are levied that compensate for this (El Gamal 2006).

Notwithstanding policy differences, most monetary reformers (including Islamic reformers) claim that their proposed measures will be anti-inflationary on the grounds that the principal cause of inflation (usury) would be removed. By implication, therefore, the reformers also challenge the mainstream conception of the *causes* of inflation, which presuppose 'quantity theory of money' explanations, and emphasize instead the substantive role of debt-driven inflation. This 'debt-driver' theory posits that the interest on debt reduces incomes and revenues, and subsequently creates pressures to raise prices and wages in order to compensate thereby inducing inflation. It is also considered, as Adams has noted, that debt puts pressure on the environment, since the need to repay interest as well as the principal necessitates a greater level of economic activity than would otherwise occur (Adams 1991).

The case for interest-free currency issue

The authors argue that interest-free monetary reform proposals are preferable to debt-free policies for several reasons. Firstly, debt-free issuance implies that there is no specific limit to the amount of currency that could be created, which increases the likelihood of *moral hazard* i.e. the lack of suitable sanctions to mitigate irresponsible spending or profligacy. There may, for instance, be a lack of adequate constitutional safeguards preventing an ambitious state from constructing luxurious state buildings or increasing the wealth of politicians. Governments do not, unfortunately, have a very good historical track record in this regard. Secondly, there is no incentive for state spending to be conducted in an efficient manner. In the practice of public procurement, monies that need to be *repaid* would tend to be allocated more carefully. Given the depletion of finite resources and environmental concerns today, this is of prime importance.

Thirdly, debt-free issuance can be considered *fiat* money, since it remains in circulation rather than being retired in the manner of credit-money. This means that there could be a tendency for economic agents to hoard part of the money-stock, thus creating circulation blockages to the detriment of an efficient *real* economy. The formation of monetary elites (or plutocracy) may follow, mitigating the citizen empowerment that is necessary for effective social justice. Fourthly, the interest-free issue of credit-money is, arguably, less likely to be inflationary. In contrast to the present system, it is posited that both of the monetary reform proposals are likely to mitigate inflationary pressure since there is no interest to pay. However, given that interest-free money is 'created for purpose' and then retired from circulation, there is *less* likely to be an excess of monies in circulation that could trigger aggregate demand (otherwise not occurring) and subsequently raise prices.

Finally, given the *realpolitik* of the political process, debt-free proposals are too revolutionary and threaten monetary vested interests with substantial curtailment. It is suggested here that interest-free issuance of currency is more likely to resonate with the *values* of diverse groups in society, ensure a future for the private banking sector and achieve a general political consensus for reform. In addition, the interest-free proposal outlined below is reasonably close to the proposals that Keynes, popular in many circles, put forward in the thirties.

A proposal for national bank-issued interest-free loans

In this plan, conventional interest-bearing loan money is gradually phased out (or reduced), as debt time-contracts are resolved, and is replaced by state issued interest-free currency produced to finance the government budget deficit or capital projects. State issued credit-money could then circulate as money in the same way that bank deposit currency does today (in conjunction with private credit monies) only without the interest. Interest-free loans (arguably) combine efficiency with social and economic justice. They are directly related to the real economy, made repayable and, when repaid, the monies are then cancelled thus ensuring that productive assets always provide tangible backing to a society's currency. Crucially, because interest is not necessary, the loans allow capital projects to be constructed for a fraction of the present cost. This is the key attraction. Moreover, the loans do not create an inflationary pressure. In the case of public capital projects (such as roads, bridges, hospitals, schools, waterworks) the national bank can lend interest-free money to the government, as stated, for the purposes of the government's own capital expenditure. However, the capital projects can still, if wished, be built by the private sector, managed by the private sector, even owned by the private sector. Interest-free loans for public capital projects have been used by the Channel Island of Guernsey over the years. Guernsey, perhaps as a direct consequence, has minimal public debt. Malaysia is also believed to be experimenting with such loans and, in recent times, has achieved some remarkable feats of construction. Over the period 1939–74 (a particularly prosperous period) Canada used interest-free loans and, even today, many Canadian municipalities are demanding their use again to upgrade poor infrastructure. In the United States, 3,400 governmental bodies (such as civic authorities), and six State governments, support the idea of interest-free money for infrastructure. A national legislative proposal, introduced in the late 1990s, managed to reach Congress but was defeated by powerful vested interests. After 1935, New Zealand also used such loans for, *inter alia*, hydro-electric power schemes, railways and state housing and enjoyed a remarkably prosperous period as a consequence (Ashford and Shakespeare 1999).

The state-issue of interest-free currency can also be used to transform the fractional reserve banking system, by making funds available to private banks, thus gradually increasing bank reserves to 100%. This is in contrast, of course, to the debt-free monetary reform proposals mentioned above. Commercial retail banks will, therefore, be left with the duties of lending their own capital, interest-free reserves and (with permission) the deposits of their customers. Credit could then be provided to consumers and businesses on market principles, such as the ability to repay and the existence of collateral.[2] Monies are repaid, firstly, to the commercial bank, which then repays the money to the central bank and the debt is retired. It is also assumed that these processes would involve much more state intervention (and regulation) of credit markets by monetary authorities, such as the imposition of lower interest rates, in the manner envisioned by Keynes (Keynes 1936). The threat of a bank-run would also be eliminated. The transition towards a 100% fractional reserve system, therefore, offers (arguably) a more stable and resilient currency-issue than at present. Yet, interest-free money can also be used to spread the social ownership of capital as suggested by binary economists.

Binary economics

Binary economics has been based upon the seminal work of Louis Kelso and, continues to be developed and promulgated by several adherents.[3]

Their notion of the *economic problem* is that, to varying degrees, states have under-utilized resources, concentrated capital ownership and widespread wants. Since it is assumed that incomes are derived from both capital and labour (hence the term binary), they further suggest that labour incomes are only capable of purchasing a *proportion* of total output. New capital investment and the state consume a further portion and the rest is hoarded, leaving credit expansion to aid the sustainability of the capitalist order. This is regarded as entirely unsatisfactory, since it perpetuates capitalist crises and uneven development (Kelso and Adler 1958). Their proposals therefore aim to use interest-free loans to create 'effective participation' by broadening the ownership base of existing productive capital, and encouraging the formation of new

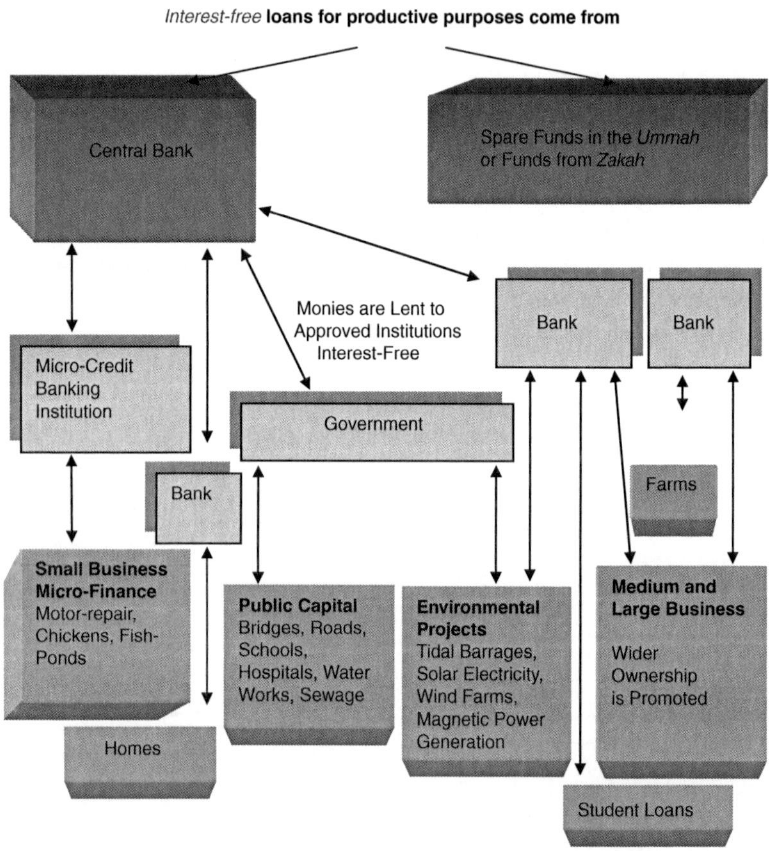

Figure 12.1 Binary Proposals for the Interest-Free Issue of Money

capital with a broader social ownership.[4] The measures are also expected to be implemented within the confines of the present functioning of the capitalist order, with minimal disruption (see Figure 12.1). The concentration of capital ownership is therefore discouraged, and the use of credit diminished. Debt principal is to be paid from incomes (in the form of dividends) derived from the capital acquisition and, when the monies are repaid they are cancelled thus leaving an ongoing income for the capital recipient. It is argued that this would also be counter-inflationary providing there is spare capacity and that money expansion is matched by new production. The national bank could then become the source of newly-created money for the purpose of spreading the income from the *real* economy to every person in society. In the case of private corporations, a key condition for the receipt of interest-free loans could be that the investment finance is associated with the creation of new shareholders, thereby distributing the ownership of new capital assets throughout society. In practice, this means that not only workers but people in the dependent population (such as women, carers, students or children) may be provided with a basic income, thus revolutionizing the current taxation system.[5]

It is not suggested, of course, that the proposals outlined in this chapter are a complete solution to the periodic financial crises that tend to occur in the present monetary order but, it is hoped, they should be able to make a significant contribution towards monetary resilience. The greater the proportion of interest-free credit money in circulation, for instance, the less likely it is for a default crisis to occur, with its associated ramifications.

Notes

1 It could be argued that the 'impossibility contract' does not actually exist since *a priori* any interest payment paid is then transformed into financial sector income and, if there is sufficient circulation before the next debt repayment, future principal and interest payments could be made from existing monies. However, this would still not cover the last repayment of a given time-based debt contract and, therefore, the 'impossibility contract' remains valid. In addition, it is unlikely that sufficient circulation from creditor to debtor will always occur.

2 At present, monetary discipline is maintained by the state by ensuring (through the audit process) that retail banks are liable for any default. It is envisaged that this practice would remain the same.

3 The Washington Centre for Economic and Social Justice is at the forefront of the present movement advocating spreading capital ownership from the work of Kelso. Professor Rodney Shakespeare, conversely, has developed the

binary ideas to include interest-free lending for public expenditure, micro-credit, social housing, student loans, environmental projects and basic income.
4 In the early 1950s, Taiwan used these basic binary mechanisms to spread the ownership of the farms.
5 It could be argued that it is very difficult to posit the existence of universal human rights when individuals do not have sufficient income to enjoy a minimal basic living standard.

References

Adams, P. (1991) *Odious Debts: Loose Lending, Corruption and the Third World's Environmental Legacy*. London: Earthscan.

Ashford, R. and Shakespeare, R. (1999) *Binary Economics: The New Paradigm*. Lanham, Maryland: University Press of America.

Brown, E. H. (2007) *The Web of Debt*. Baton Rouge: Third Millenium Press.

El Diwany, T. (2003) *The Problem with Interest 2nd Ed*. Birmingham: Kreatoc.

El Gamal, M. A. (2006) *Islamic Finance: Law, Economics and Practice*. USA: Cambridge University Press.

Friedman, M. (1956) *Studies in the Quantity Theory of Money*. Chicago: University of Chicago Press.

Helleiner, E. (1994) *States and the Re-emergence of Global Finance: From Bretton Woods to the 1990's*. USA: Cornell University Press.

Howells, P. and Bain, K. (2008) *Economics of Money, Banking and Finance: 4th Edition*. Gosport: Pearson.

Huber, J. and Robertson, J. (2000) *Creating New Money: A Monetary Reform for the Information Age*. London: New Economics Foundation.

Kelso, L. and Adler, M. (1958) *The Capitalist Manifesto*. New York: Random House.

Kennedy, M. (1995) *Inflation and Interest Free*. Canada: New Society Publisher.

Keynes, J. M. (1936) *The General Theory of Employment, Interest and Money*. London: Macmillan.

Lenin, V. (1996) *Imperialism: The Highest Stage of Capitalism*. Bristol: Pluto.

Linderman, M. (1997) *Encyclopaedia Mythica*. Sourced at: www.pantheon.org.

Marx, K. (1976) *Capital: Volume One*. St Ives: Penguin.

McConnachie, A. (2006) *Clarifying Our Money Reform Proposals: A Report for the Tenth Annual Bromsgrove Conference*. Bromsgrove Conference, Bromsgrove, England.

Mouatt, S. (2008) 'Evaluating Stephen Zarlenga's Treatment of Historical Monetary Thought', *International Journal of Social Economics*, 35(11).

Pettifor, A. (2006) *The Coming First World Debt Crisis*. Chippenham: Palgrave Macmillan.

Rochon, L.-P. (1999) 'Endogenous Money', *Journal of Economic Issues*, 33(1).

Roll, E. (1973) *A History of Economic Thought*. Oxford: Faber.

Shakespeare, R. and Challen, P. (2002). *Seven Steps to Justice*. Chippenham. New European Publications.

13
The Future: Competition from the Technology Arena

Carl Adams

This chapter will explore the practicalities of developing serious competition to the financial and banking sector. As covered in previous chapters, the theoretical arguments point to systemic weaknesses within a mono-financial system. Earlier chapters also show the growing importance of non-banks within the traditional banking activity:

a) non-banks have developed key capabilities to provide services covering the movement and exchange of money – helped considerably by banks outsourcing much of the development work (to non-banks),
b) banks do not have all the technological capability to develop low transaction cost-based systems that is called for in the information age,
c) banks' business models are not based on low or micro transactions and,
d) innovations within the electronic world are mostly coming from the non-banks.

The preceding earlier chapters also give further possible examples of competing and complementary systems. However, the examples are mostly theoretical or relatively small scale. The big question that emerges as we come to the concluding chapters of the book is: can monetary and financial competition emerge to a scale significant enough to provide a stabilizing effect on the economy? Realistically, can big scale money, finance or currency competition emerge? This chapter addresses that question and shows that not only can it emerge but we are at a conflux of events where it is set to emerge. Indeed, it is only now that major competition can arrive since all the ingredients are in place or rapidly moving to be in place. Further, the chapter shows that the emergence of a competing system, based on the needs and characteristics of the information economy, is likely to result in increased economic activity and an increase in tax revenues – key ingredients if competing systems are to have long term success. These are big claims, so let's see how we get there.

In the first chapter we argued we are in a 6th Kondratieff long wave cycle and that this surge of innovation is significantly different to previous innovation surges and rivalled that of the Industrial Revolution. The 5th Kondratieff cycle was based on computerization; the 6th is based on ubiquitous access to the internet, Web 2.0/Web 3.0 technologies, social media, social networking, mobile technologies and rapid input and collaboration from individuals around the globe. The information revolution is about unleashing the intellectual and creative capital of a global population. Going from the 5th to the 6th Kondratieff wave can be considered as going from connecting computer systems to connecting and empowering people. It is going from a technical computer network to a ubiquitous 'cloud' seamlessly connecting people to global information resources regardless of location. Global competition is being augmented with global coordination and collaboration of individuals. Global collaboration within the Information Revolution offers the capability of bringing together the potential of vast human resources – input from thousands, tens of thousands, hundreds of thousand or even million of people from around the globe – to address problems and come up with innovative solutions. The examples of utest, wikipedia and Galaxy Zoo (see Chapters 1 and 7) show the potential and speed of such collaboration.

The key structures in the existing banking sector emerged out of the Industrial Revolution, and they emerged to meet the needs of industry and the economy at the time. We are set to see new key structures emerge to the meet the needs of the Information Revolution. For new structures to emerge there must be some gaps in the existing provision and drivers for change. The next section will examine some of the problems and emerging 'gaps' that are the main driving force for change.

Problems with the existing system

Search engines: Inefficiencies in the market

The advertising model of Internet search engines has proved to be very successful for the larger search engines. Advertising revenues is the predominant business model for search engines, such as Google, Bing and Yahoo (which is now linked into Microsoft) who get of the order of 90% or more of their revenue from advertising. The advertising market place is very competitive with a variety of channels that are competing with the search engines, including TV, radio as well as other internet sources such as social networking sites. The long-term advertising revenue base of search engines could become increasingly fragile as time progresses. Within the electronic world new entrants into a market can be swift – as demonstrated by Google, Twitter etc. The competition from the social networking sites has been fairly minor to date because they have not generally gone for an advertising model (indeed, too much advertising would likely kill off much of the current social networking sites). However, some of the social networking sites, such as Facebook, Twitter, Myspace, Renren (the main social networking site in China), have tens and even hundreds of millions of regular users. The large numbers of users, with many of them spending upwards of an hour a day on the sites, show that they hold some risk as potential competing advertising channels for the search engine companies. The existing market leaders within search engines have to invest large sums of money just to remain competitive and key players. This has involved buying competing companies, particularly smaller start-up companies or companies with complementary expertise.

However, even if a major search engine company, say Google, invests large sums of money in developing new functionality the potential returns from the marketing revenue base is effectively capped: the revenue stream is limited by the amount of advertising budget that companies are willing to invest and not by how much users want to use any new services. There are further inefficiencies in having such a large proportion of revenue coming from advertising in that the final user is not paying directly for the services. Indeed, the final user is paying in a very indirect and convoluted way. Advertisers pay the search engines either by pay-per-click (i.e. pay per customer that clicks on the advertised website displayed prominently in a users search results list), or by paying a fixed price for a particular level of advertising or display prominence in search results. There is also a balance to be had in displaying sponsored or advertised links. If search engines display too many less relevant sponsored links instead of the specific information the users requested then users will go elsewhere for their internet searches. Search engine advertising is a very competitive market space and customer allegiances can change quickly.

There is continual interaction between advertisers and search engines as each try to minimize their costs and maximize their profits. The dynamics between search engines like Google and the advertisers is summarized by Cohen (2010) 'Google's profit-per-page view is determined by how many pages they can fill with ads and how much they can charge per click. They [*Advertisers*] want to get as many profitable clicks as possible at the least possible price.'

Of course the main search engines have a considerable amount of influence and control over the Internet since they strongly influence (or even dictate) where people are directed to after a search. Anything not included in the first page of advertising results is not likely to be looked at by people searching for information. Having a prominent position, at least on the first page of any loosely relevant search requests is important for advertisers, and consequently they pay considerable fees to be placed prominently on search results. The dominant advertising model then is acting as a barrier to people finding information since the search results are directing people away from the *most suitable* information they seek towards the *best advertised loosely relevant* information. This *information access barrier* resulting from the dominant advertising model of search engines is likely to be one of the main driving forces towards change and innovation. Not everyone notices the sponsored advertised sites in the Internet search listing, however for some people it can be an annoyance.

There is very little mechanism for people to pay for the relevant information even if they wanted to. A user-pay-for-search (U-PFS) model could work but not within the current dominant model of payment systems. The challenges would be to find the right level of payment and provide a suitable payment infrastructure, and of course change the mindset of users to accept a pay-for-search model.

Changing the mindset of Internet searchers is a significant challenge. However there are precedents elsewhere of different models been successful, especially for the younger 'digital natives' comfortable with the new technology. The monthly contract common in the mobile phone industry revolves around customers having a monthly quota of 'free' telephone calls and texts. A similar approach could be applied to searching where customers can purchase a monthly quota of searches. Given the billions of searches performed each week a U-PFS model could be an attractive option for search engine providers. The model would then not be limited to the amount of advertising budget 3rd party companies have available. Also for individuals it would be attractive since it would provide more relevant information, without the 'less relevant' advertised items cluttering up the search results.

One could argue for a public information utility model within the digital information society based so heavily on access to information. Information finding/searching resources could be classed as a needed utility in much the same way that electricity or the road infrastructure is. Indeed, having access to digital information resources is a pre-requisite for future economic activity. Different funding models exist for public utilities from paying through taxes, paying through a private utility company, either based on a pay-per-use model or a flat rate, or a mix of both. A convenient subscription utility could operate via broadband service providers, or directly through search engines, or possibly through any of the existing utility providers (e.g. getting an information search utility quota or subscription via an electricity utility company).

Getting the right price for searches will be critical. Most search requests would be very small value items. Some might be more sophisticated or involved and more valuable to the customer. Some of the challenges would be to have a variable charging model, along with a simple standard of change. Either way there is a need for micropayments to pay for searches. The smaller the micropayments then the more utility there will be in the system. Fees at sub penny/cent level will bring the U-PFS model to be viewed as virtually free for many people. When search traffic is at the hundreds of millions and billions level per week for the main search engines then the business model looks attractive. Further, the revenue is tied to the volume and relevance or quality of searches and not on the advertising budgets of 3rd party advertising companies alone.

A pay-for-search model could bring in innovation and new entrants, such as more focused and specialized search provision. For instance, there could be search support focussed on people with regular specific interests or with a variety of disabilities (say displaying results of web sources that are suitable for people with a specific kind of colour blindness).

Duel or multiple systems could operate where 'free' searching could be provided based on the advertising model, alongside other models – such as pay-per-search or utility models. One might assume that if there is enough critical mass moving towards the pay per-search-model then the 'free' advertising space would become even more crowded with advertisement sponsored searches – and so hasten a move towards a pay-per-search model. Also if there is enough critical mass in a pay-per-search model then businesses would change how they advertise and what services they provide. There may even be more of an efficient market space emerge as companies focus on providing services the market space requires rather than on advertising. In addition, by keeping the existing advertising model of search engines it would provide a safe transition route towards a U-PFS model for search engine provision. By offering both customers can see which is the best for their search requirements.

As with the rest of the discussion in this book, a mono-system whether it be a financial system or a search engine system, has embedded systemic weaknesses. Diversity and competition is needed for long-term market stability. From a user-pay-for-search (U-PFS) model it is only a small step towards a user-pay-for-information/content (U-PFI/C) model.

Paying for information: New business models and opportunities

There is a lot of free[1] information and content available on the Internet. Some of this is of questionable quality, however, there is a lot which is useful or of value to people. The amount of freely available information and content on the Internet represents a huge amount of human capital and time. Much of this is provided freely from a philanthropist perspective – people want to make a contribution to knowledge, want to be recognized or participate in a worthwhile community spirited activity (such as wikipedia or GalaxyZoo) – all of which is to be commended and encouraged. However, there is certainly opportunity for many information and content providers to make some financial gain for their hard work, innovation or intellectual property.

For instance, there are many items that are freely available on Youtube, the online video community, that reach millions and hundreds of millions of plays/downloads (such as 'Charlie bit my finger' or the 'Sneezing Baby Panda'). There are many, many more items that have tens of thousands of downloads/plays. These are created by a whole range of people of all ages from all walks of life. In most areas of society when people provide entertainment to large numbers of people it is usually paid for. The main challenge is finding the right level of payments for the content provided, along with the right payment mechanism. The more expensive the content is then fewer people will pay for it. Given the potential large numbers of people accessing content then a micro payment for such content becomes attractive.

Consider Youtube type websites. The success of sites like Youtube has been that it is free to users to play short videos from the general public or companies that want to provide the content. The content provision is moderated to ensure that it is legal and non-offensive. Youtube, like any other business needs to make a profit to survive and they do this by operating an advertising model, like the search engines. A user-pay-for-information/content (U-PFI/C) model could be very attractive to Youtube and similar providers by sharing some of the U-PFI/C fees. It would certainly be attractive to content providers as they have access to a potential revenue stream. It would be attractive to users if it increases the range and quality of entertainment provision. The smaller the fees then the more people will want to play the items.

A ten thousand play/download clip from Youtube, for instance, a 0.1 to 0.5 pence/cent per play would provide an income of £10/$10 to £50/$50. For a million plays this would be a respectable £1,000/$1,000 to £5,000/$5,000. Regular contributors could make a living from providing entertainment over the Internet. The most popular played items could provide a comfortable living for their contributors. One could consider getting the pricing to match performances at say at live gigs, concerts or events, based on similar returns for the amount of minutes per person watched.

Charging for downloads/plays on sites like Youtube is likely to have some impact on the willingness for people to download/play entertainment items. However, sub penny/cent levels for downloads/plays may be viewed as 'virtually free' by most users and so may not significantly decrease the volume of downloads/plays. In addition as with the searching example, it is possible to accommodate multiple models – a 'free' advertising model, a U-PFC model and a utility model.

A U-PFI/C model for Youtube type organizations could stimulate innovation and creativity in the contributions as well as increasing the quality of the contributions. Budding filmmakers, musicians, performing artists, comedians etc. could hone their skills and at the same time generate an income stream. Indeed, successful artists and entertainers could make a successful living just by providing material via Youtube type organizations within a U-PFI/C model. There may be opportunity to develop new genre based on short-medium length entertainment provision over the Internet. New technology helped film and television emerge from the music hall and theatre. They similarly went through issues of finding the right funding models in the early years. Similarly the introduction of videos and DVDs, as well as the introduction of digital TV (such as through Sky), changed the market space for entertainment. Also note that the cinema did not kill off theatre, that television did not kill off film, and that videos did not kill off cinemas or TV. Competition has been healthy for the entertainment industry. All varieties of entertainment (theatre, TV, cinema, video/DVDs, Digital TV) flourish together. Indeed, video/DVD film releases are orchestrated to fit in with cinema releases – as too are plays/replays of prequels on TV; TV stars are used in theatre and pantomime to bring in audiences.

Other industries could make use of this infrastructure, such as education, current news and entertainment items or providing specialist information or advice.

Account-based systems offer the opportunity for very low transaction costs since it is just 'moving data items within a database'. Youtube already operates an account-based system where users can login and get their personalized Youtube presence – and also a login is needed for access to the more adult content. Most of the infrastructure is in place to move towards a U-PFI/C model. True micropayment mechanisms, of say less than a penny/cent, or even less than a 10th of a cent/penny, would be needed to pay for some of the more micro-value content in order for it to be viewed as virtually free for customers.

A further challenge of moving towards a U-PFI model would be how to keep the philanthropist contributions from people who want to make a worthwhile to the wider community. A U-PFI model may commercialize voluntary activity which may have a negative effect on society. Conversely, it may encourage people to provide free information and content as samplers for paid for content.

Within the current information revolution, commodities are based on information, but much of the information provision (in its wider form from search information, specialist information and entertainment) are not well met by the existing financial and payment mechanisms. The current information revolution is characterized by very large numbers of people accessing very small value items of information. Some form of micropayment system is called for to appreciate the full economic potential of the information revolution. This is an area calling for innovation.

The wrong 'virtual' business model for information commodities

Banks have been *virtualizing* their traditional business space, particularly with new financial services, commodities and exchange systems (such as currencies, stocks, bonds). There has also been an increased level of abstraction of financial products with items such as derivatives (in the form of futures/forwards, options and swaps), commodity futures markets and short-selling (where credit monies are leveraged for speculative purposes). Other examples include the collating together of virtual financial components to form new financial securities – possibly the most prominent example of this was the manner US sub-prime mortgages were combined with AAA-rated approval that heralded the financial upheaval in 2008/2009. Financial components can be interlinked between different types of products and different banks. A loan for a mortgage could have input from several banks and the different collateralized parts of the mortgage may be traded between different banks.

The financial sector has seen much innovation. It is a competitive environment with the potential for very high returns. However, their focus has been on the large-scale transactions, the big money flows and the quick returns. There has been innovation with the retail banking sector covering electronic payment mechanisms, as covered in previous chapters, but again the focus has been on the small- to medium-sized transactions, and accommodating relatively high transaction costs. In addition, most of the innovation in the electronic payment activity has come from the non-bank entities, or when it has come from banks it has often involved non-bank, usually technology based, partners. There has been little interest in micropayment systems and activity from the traditional banking and financial sector.

In addition, the banks do not have the technical capabilities to fully develop and innovate into micropayment activity. Their existing infrastructure – which is big, expensive and secure – is aimed at interaction between defined banking and financial sector entities and a well structured and effectively vetted customer base. It is an expensive infrastructure tied into many physical entities such as ATM machines and the credit and debit card machines operating in retail outlets. The banking infrastructure is not aimed at the mass market of millions, even hundreds of millions of users – users that can be transient.

Banks really do not have the expertise or mindset to fully move into the business space of micropayment systems required of the information economy. However, technology companies do. Many of the large international technology companies already operate 'micro-value' account based systems. Companies such as Microsoft, Google, Youtube, Yahoo, Facebook, Bebo, RenRen, Twitter and ebay, all deal with many millions of users and handle a variety of interactions with the users that can be classed as micro-value interactions. Similarly the telecommunications companies also handle micro-transactions and interactions with their large user base.

Several of these technology companies already successfully operate some form of payment mechanism, for instance Apple, Google, Amazon, Paypal and the telecommunications companies such as Vodafone. A lot of the success is related to the existing provision of services offered by the company or related partner. For instance Apple's micropayment system is successful because of the very successful iTunes, Paypal is very successful because of the peer-to-peer auction market of ebay. This symbiotic relationship and support is important because it means that the technology company payment mechanisms have a solid foundation; the payment mechanism is backed by the solidity of the technology companies and the critical mass of the user base.

However, as seen in previous chapters with the example of Simpay from the European telecommunication companies, electronic payment systems (even with big backers) are not guaranteed success. What is missing in the array of existing offerings is some further coordination and collaboration. In short, there need to be more standardization between the various offerings from the technology companies. However, *technically* that is not really a problem: Technology companies are good at developing and using standards, indeed the whole complex workings of the Internet is based on many interlocking standards. The big challenge is getting collaboration from the technology companies – a significant challenge where many of the technology companies are fierce competitors of each other. This, of course, is a common problem in the capitalist mode of production.

However, the prize of collaboration is access to a market space that will rival and potentially exceed their existing business space. Moving into financial activity-based on micropayment systems, particularly where there is standardizations and inter-operability between the different providers, is set to be a very lucrative and growing market. The critical mass effect of inter operable systems is a really key ingredient in order for companies and persons to reach their full potential: The more people involved in the system then the more useful the system will be, and consequently the more people will want to be involved in the system. Monetary collaboration is beginning to happen. Social networking organizations, for instance, are adopting a standard micropayment system – SpareChange (see sparechangeinc.com). However, there are many hurdles to overcome in developing the standards (such as which standard to use, Microsoft or Google or someone else's?) and getting buy-in from relevant partners.

Increased tax, different tax

One important influence on success for a competing financial system is the impact on tax revenues. Any system must not detract from the tax revenues collected and preferably should increase tax revenues. If not then there will be considerable problems to get support and buy-in from governments. If the new system(s) has a negative impact on tax collection then governments will seek to eliminate them. Though no one likes paying taxes they are important to keep governments functioning and providing a full range of services to their citizens. Legal infrastructures, police, fire services, transport and healthcare all require the financial support of governments (as well as private investment for some of the services).

The argument given above is based on capturing mostly new and untapped (from a tax perspective) economic activity. The existing financial sector does not really address these, so effectively the information economy is not been taxed as it should. In addition, there is clearly potential for the new electronic payment systems to stimulate economic activity – this increased economic activity will, in turn, result in increases in tax revenues and (therefore) public welfare.

Much of the existing activity discussed above is based on payment mechanisms tied into the existing financial and banking systems – they ultimately translate to the existing 'real' currency (such as pounds or dollars). Even some of the new forms of money have some nominal relationship with existing 'real' money: Second Life's *Lindens*, for instance, are nominally attached to the US dollar (or other currency through an exchange intermediary), as well as Farmville's *Farm Coins* and *Farm Cash*. However, they do not have to be. Some independent token or voucher-based system could equally work as well, or even improve the functioning of the traditional currency based system. It is only a small step away from the current practice in the virtual world for the token/voucher system to become a currency in its own right. There are some further examples of voucher systems that are effectively independent of the traditional currency systems, The airmiles and voucher point schemes, for instance, which are usually associated with some of the main retailers, enable vouchers or points to be exchanged for a variety of goods and services. It is true that these have a traditional financial equivalent, yet often it is at a different rate of exchange than the appropriate one-to-one equivalence (Tesco vouchers can be converted to access hotels and entertainment theme parks at less than the full price in traditional currency). This enhances their attractiveness and, therefore, usage.

There is a clear potential for the rewards of collaboration between technology companies, in conjunction with other business sectors such as retail, to result in significant increases in economic activity. This also does not have to be based on the traditional currency system of the financial sector. As with the retail voucher systems, they become more attractive with the more people that use them and the more services that can be purchased with them. The capabilities, market space, operating practices and user base and practices of the technologies companies are strong indications of a clear route to achieve critical mass in any new financial or token-based system.

If collaboration is solely based on the existing financial systems of the traditional banks (using existing traditional currencies) then the banks will have a big stake in the new system. They will be provided with new revenue streams and be able to extract profit from the system. They will also be directing activity closer to the banks own business models – which are predominantly based on traditional (non micropayment) systems and, will consequently slow down or hinder the development of such systems. If the technology companies take ownership of the development of new collaborative technology token-based systems then they will have ownership of the systems and the full profits from the systems. There is a strong business case for collaboration from the technology companies (along with other non-banks, such as retailers) and for these to develop their own token or currency. There will, of course, be an opportunity for the development of exchange transactions (and converting systems) between any technology token monies and other currencies.

The discussion so far has focussed on micropayment activity and micro value transaction of information commodities. However, transactions and the new token-based systems do not have to be limited to micro-value items. Indeed, many information commodities may be quite large. By designing the system to accommodate micro-exchanges then it encompasses more transaction activity (activity that is not captured by the traditional banking system), but it also does not limit use for small, medium or large transactions. Such a system has greater utility than the traditional banking currency and payment systems and is also likely to be cheaper. Different checking activity or processes, of course, may be needed for the different sizes of transactions.

From a tax perspective, there is clearly the opportunity to collect taxes in the new technology token money – indeed, by doing so it would add legitimacy to the new token money. However, the challenges will be in being able to use those token money taxes to keep government working and provide appropriate services to citizens. At one level it matters little if any taxes collected can be used to directly pay for the provision of government services (such as buying materials or paying for wages) as long as there are exchange intermediaries that can convert collected technology tokens into national currency. There may be some loss in value in this route due to exchange expenses (some profit will go to the exchange companies). There may also be some areas of government that would be particularly appropriate to use any technology tokens. For instance, in a utility model discussed earlier, people would have some quotas for accessing information and searching – in which case these can be provided as technology token-based money. Such a system can collect traditional bank-based currency in exchange for (information/search) token quotas. For the members of the population that receive government benefits (such as pensioners or unemployed) then they can be provided token quotas directly as part of their support package. Indeed, a vibrant digital in-formation based economy, with a separate revenue stream based on technology tokens, may bring employment to people that would not be net tax contributors within the existing economy. Further, the increase in economic activity based on technology token systems is likely to increase the overall economic activity spilling over to that covered by the traditional banking systems.

Perhaps one of the biggest motivations for governments to support a technology token-based money system is that it provides real competition to the mono-system of the existing banking sector. This is desperately needed to provide a stabilizing effect on the banking sector. Society and governments still need to have a strong traditional banking sector, after all this is the mainstay of the mainstream economy. The introduction of technology-based competition will not replace the sector, but it will both complement it and provide competition to it. It would complement it by covering aspects of the economy not well covered by the traditional banking sector – and not able to be covered since they lack expertise and it is outside their business models. It would provide competition by having an overlap where customers will have a choice in using a technology-based token or traditional currency. The development of intermediaries to handle exchanges between the traditional currency and the technology token will provide further moderating effects on the overall system.

Conclusion: It is already happening!

As shown in the discussion above, much of what is needed for a competing technology-based token system to operate successfully is already happening. There are examples of collaborations and innovations moving towards technology token-based systems – offering true competition to the traditional currencies and banking system. The multinational technology companies already handle micro-interactions between many millions of people. There is clearly a need for recognizing the huge amount of human creativity and innovation that is already taking place within the information economy. Significant numbers of people are not being rewarded for their contributions to entertainment, their innovative and creative ideas, or their endeavours in generating useful information. By providing the mechanism (such as a technology-based token payment system) these contributions can be recognized within the formal economy. Further, such an information-based economy will likely stimulate further innovation and contributions, as well as increase the quality of contributions. New formal economic activity can be generated, which can be tied into a tax-based system.

Banks really don't have the expertise, motivation or mindset to provide adequate support to enable the information economy to reach its full potential. Innovation will need to come from the technology sectors – and indeed some already has arrived. However, achieving critical mass is essential in order for the new information economy to reach its full potential, and this will need the involvement of some of the key players and the development of standards. For critical mass to happen it requires the ability to exchange token items between different systems. Also, there needs to be some standardization and exchange mechanisms (between different technology token systems and between the technology token systems and the traditional currencies).

Moving into financial activity based on micropayment systems, particularly where there is standardizations and interoperability between the different providers, is set to be a very lucrative and growing market. The more people involved in the system then the more useful the system will be, and consequently the more people will want to be involved in the system. Collaboration is happening, for instance social networking organizations are adopting a standard micropayment system – SpareChange (see sparechangeinc.com). However, there are many hurdles to overcome in developing the standards (for instance which standard should be used, Microsoft or Google or something else?) and getting buy-in from relevant partners.

The technology sectors are fiercely competitive places with technology companies encroaching upon each other core markets (such as search engines, social networking, operating systems, software applications). Achieving any significant collaboration and cooperation is likely to be a mammoth task. However, the prize of being able to grow virtually virgin economic space, that could be as lucrative as their existing businesses, is likely to be enough to bring competitors together – at least to develop a common standard. We may yet see the likes of a Micro-Google (Micro-oogle?), or Googo-Soft tokens emerge as a significant currency in the digital economy.

The real economy is evolving to incorporate more of the information-based activity. The existing traditional banking sector is not well placed to provide support for this new economic space. Lessons from the Industrial Revolution show that new structures emerge to fill the needs of the economy. Everything seems to be in place for such a change in the current information revolution.

Note

1 Here we are referring to legally free content and information. There are of course examples of people accessing material without paying the due fees.

References

Cohen, A. (2010) *Google Wants Your Profit Margin, Should You Give It To Them?* Search Engine Watch, April 14, 2010, available from http://searchenginewatch.com/3640076, accessed 18/4/2010.

14
A Complementary and Competitive Monetary System for the Future?

Carl Adams and Simon Mouatt

This book has explored the transformations taking place within the wider economy at a very interesting time when systemic weaknesses are starting to be very visible. We have looked at the past, examples from the present and explored some possible future directions to address these weaknesses. The book has tried to show that systemic weakness within the banking sector is due, in a considerable part, to the characteristic of having a dominant mono-financial system. Any system that lacks competition will have systemic weaknesses affecting long-term stability. The book has also tried to show that the current financial systems are and always have been dynamic and changing. From a longer perspective it is normal and healthy for systems to change and evolve.

In this book we have looked at the past along with examples from the present and possibilities for the future. The past provides insight on how systems evolve and the driving forces for change. It provides a cognitive lens to examine the role of innovation, technology and capital in shaping an economy and the longer-term cycles within an economy. Examples from the present provide insight on what is currently possible and do-able. It also provides a measure of where further support is needed and which entities are able to provide that support. The examples demonstrate that there are alternatives to the current dominant mono-financial system way of doing things. Examining possibilities for the future helps think through different alternatives identifying the potential benefits, challenges and the support structures needed.

The preceding chapters have highlighted the growing influence that the banking sector has had on the economy. The extremely high levels of personal and government debt certainly feel like we are in an age of financial serfdom to the banking sector. There are clear parallels with Hayek's work, 'The Road to serfdom', which covers the need for individual freedom and the dangers of the far left and right. Hayek's answer was more individual freedom and competition to develop a stable society. The current high levels of indebtedness by citizens and governments indicate that societies are facing a different type of serfdom in which the balance of power has shifted towards the unconstrained financial markets. Competition is one route towards more stability. The book has argued that we are embedded in the throes of an Information Revolution that is bringing about significant changes. The corporate, technological and social aspects of the Information Revolution provide the base for new thinking on how to break the serfdom to the traditional banking sector.

Big problems often require some radical new thinking or out-of-the-box thinking. Continuing on in the same mindset is likely not to come up with long-term workable solutions they will just address the symptoms and not the underlying problems. As Einstein famously stated 'we can't solve problems by using the same kind of thinking we used when we created them.' A range of new concepts have been presented in this book. Key themes within the book include:

- The book identifies systemic weaknesses in the traditional financial infrastructure, namely that it is a mono-financial system and consequently suffers the weaknesses of existing mono system (e.g. lack of resilience and sustainability). This is the big underlying problem, and for answers we have to go outside the mono-system.
- The book proposes some radical rethinking – new forms of money, complementary money systems and interest-free money issue. The examples in the book hopefully demonstrate that these systems can actually work.
- This book also provides complementary theoretical bases for changes and cycles in the financial system and wider economy. The theoretical foundations provide the cognitive lenses to view and describe the instabilities, the crashes, as well as identifying how to achieve stability.
- The Marx perspective on the macro economy illustrates that the capitalist mode of production has an endogenous propensity towards recurring crises as pre-requisites for the restoration of the profit rate (in abstract labour terms). In addition we have noted the natural tendency for surplus capital to gravitate towards the financial markets in search of profit. In addition, it is noted that the 'fictitious' nature of

financial market activity illustrates the fragility of the capitalist financial order.

- The book has also pointed out that the financial capabilities of the state, as an extension of the interests of capital, have been eroded in the modern era. It was further suggested that, whilst it certainly appears that the private banking infrastructure has been the main beneficiary of social (financial) power, emerging *corporafinance* is showing signs of subjugating traditional banking over the longer term.
- The book has suggested that we are in a 6th Kondratieff cycle or Information Revolution, based on the information superhighway where commodities and services are information-based. Also the dominant model for business and social activity is that of large numbers of people and small value interactions: Millions of people interacting, collaborating and disseminating, entertainment, innovations and information.
- The book shows how banks are not well placed to deal with this changing technological and economic environment and that technology-based companies have both better skills and matching business models to provide the needed support.
- The book shows how that there has been considerable innovation in the Banking sector, based on the capabilities of ICT, but it has a different focus, a focus towards the large and abstract transactions. There has been unprecedented level of virtual wealth created within the financial sector. However, the real economy has been moving in a different virtual direction. The mono-financial system of the traditional banking sector has become increasing 'divorced' from the real economy, but equally the real economy has moved to a different place.
- The book has argued that there is a conflux of events, innovations and changes in the economy leading to a moment in history where further significant change is imminent. Things are set in place for change to happen. Indeed, the financial crash may have provide both the impetus for change and, by weakening the very strong banking sector, the capability for international collaboration and oversight to drive through changes.

A further underlying theme to the book is the pursuit of social and economic justice. Indeed, a long-term stable economy requires social justice. Many of the examples and discussion in the book have been about complementary systems. Systems that recognize there is more to money than just a store of value and means of exchange. Exchanges also have social interaction and can have a net social benefit. Complementary money systems can tap into the vast reserves of social capital within society and break the modern debt slavery that has proven to be so pervasive in our debt-based (mono) monetary system.

However, the book also argues that we need a strong banking sector. The competition suggested in this book is not meant to replace the banking sector it is meant to complement and compete with it. The argument is that the systemic weaknesses within the banking sector need to be addressed by appropriate competition. Serious competition will exert pressure on banks to both innovate and to operate with less risk. With a mono-system based banking sector it is difficult for governments to allow poor performing banks to fail since the economy is so intricately entwined with the banks – as demonstrated by current banking crisis with governments around the globe having to pump many billions of dollars/pounds into the economy to keep their banking sector afloat. Serious competition will also make it more likely that banks will be allowed to fail if they are too risky in their business activities or over stretch themselves. Competition provides a strong stabilizing force – the market will punish excessive risk-taking or bad business models. Competition allows for the economy to keep operating and even flourish when elements of the system fail. It is ironic, however, that the Washington Consensus, whilst supporting an unfettered role for the (real economy) market has never fully embraced this notion for the financial (mono) sector. Maybe, now is the time for thinking 'outside of the box'.

One of the main challenges is how to achieve a significant competing system where it can provide a stabilizing effect. The book has shown a few possible future scenarios and systems to achieve critical mass. The systems are quite complementary to each other as well as the existing mono-financial system. However, they each provide significant overlap to provide stabilizing competition. They also have enough uniqueness to provide long-term stability as systems in their own right.

There are still, of course, challenges ahead for introducing complementary and competing financial systems. The questions that need to be asked, for instance, could include: 'what items can be covered by competing currency and money systems?', 'how do we regulate the non-banking money/currency sector?' or 'How do we collect and spend tax generated by the competing currency and money systems?' But first let's break free of the financial serfdom.

Appendix A
Mathematical Demonstration for Quantifying Sustainability of a Complex Flow Network: Evidence for *Yin-Yang* in Nature?[1]

Contemporary science is preoccupied with that which exists; it rarely accounts for what is missing. But often the key to a system's persistence lies with information concerning lacunae. Such unutilized reserve capacity is complementary to the effective performance of the system, and too little of this attribute can render a system brittle to the point of collapse. We can now measure with a single metric a system's sustainability in terms of the tradeoff allotment of each. This approach provides heretofore missing theoretical justification for efforts to preserve biodiversity whenever systems have become too streamlined and efficient.

It is critically important to understand that the findings described below arise from *structural* variables of a network. This means that they apply to any other complex flow network with a similar structure. This makes them directly applicable to economic processes and particularly to the flow of money in a financial network or an economy.

The starting point is Boltzmann's classical equation of surprisal,

$$s = -k \log(p), \tag{1}$$

where s is one's surprisal at seeing an event that occurs with probability p, and k is an appropriate (positive) scalar constant. One can read this equation as defining s to gauge what p is not. That is, if p is the weight we give to the presence of something, then s becomes a measure of its absence. If p is very small, then the ensuing large magnitude of s reflects the circumstance that most of the time we *don't* see the event in question.

We will show that the interplay between presence and absence plays a crucial role in whether a system survives or disappears. It is the very absence of order (in the form of a diversity of processes) that makes it possible for a system to persist (sustain itself) over the long run.

The product of the measure of the presence of an event, *i*, (p_i) by a magnitude of its absence (s_i) yields a quantity that represents the *indeterminacy* (h_i) of that event,

$$h_i = -kp_i \log(p_i), \tag{2}$$

When $p_i \approx 1$, the event is almost certain, and $h_i \approx 0$; then when $p_i \approx 0$, the event is almost surely absent, so that again $h_i \approx 0$. It is only for intermediate, less determinate values of p_i that h_i remains appreciable, achieving its maximum at $p_i = (1/e)$.

It is helpful to reinterpret (2) in terms germane to evolutionary change and sustainability. When $p_i \approx 1$, the event in question is a virtual constant in its context and unlikely to change ($h_i \approx 0$.) Conversely, whenever $p_i \approx 0$, the event exhibits great potential to change matters ($s_i >> 1$), but it hardly ever appears as a player in the system dynamics (so that, again, $h_i \approx 0$.) It is only when p_i is intermediate that the event is both present frequently enough and has sufficient potential for change. In this way, h_i represents the capacity for event *i* to be a significant player in system change or evolution.

Seeking a perspective on the entire ensemble of events affecting a system motivates us to calculate the aggregate systems indeterminacy, H, as

$$H = \sum_i h_i = -k \sum_i p_i \log(p_i), \tag{3}$$

which we can now regard as a metric of the total capacity of the ensemble to undergo change. Whether such change will be coordinated or wholly stochastic depends upon whether or not the various events *i* are related to each other and by how much. In order better to treat relationships between events, it is helpful to consider bilateral combinations of events, which for clarity requires two indices. Accordingly, we will define p_{ij} as the joint probability that events *i* and *j* co-occur. Boltzmann's measure of the non-occurrence of this particular combination of events (1) thus becomes,

$$s_{ij} = -k \log(p_{ij}). \tag{4}$$

If events *i* and *j* are entirely independent of each other, the joint probability, p_{ij}, that they co-occur becomes the product of the marginal probabilities that *i* and *j* each occur independently anywhere. Now, the marginal probability that *i* occurs for any possible *j* is $p_i = \sum_i p_{ij}$, while the likelihood that *j* occurs regardless of *i* is $p_j = \sum_i p_{ij}$.[2] Hence, whenever *i* and *j* are totally independent, $p_{ij} = p_{i.}p_{.j}$. Here the assumption is made that the indeterminacy s_{ij} is maximal when *i* and *j* are totally independent. We call that maximum s_{ij}*. The difference by which s_{ij}* exceeds s_{ij} in any instance then becomes a measure of the constraint that *i* exerts on *j*, call it $x_{i|j}$, where,

$$x_{i|j} = s_{ij}^* - s_{ij} = -k \log(p_{i.}p_{.j}) - [-k \log(p_{ij})] = k \log\left(\frac{p_{ij}}{p_{i.}p_{.j}}\right) = x_{j|i}. \tag{4}$$

The symmetry in (4) implies that the measure also describes the constraint that *j* exerts upon *i*. In order to calculate the average mutual constraint (X) extant in the whole system, one weights each $x_{i|j}$ by the joint probability that *i* and *j* co-occur and sums over all combinations of *i* and *j*:

$$X = \sum_{i,j} p_{ij}\, x_{i|j} = k \sum_{i,j} p_{ij} \log\left(\frac{p_{ij}}{p_{i.}p_{.j}}\right) \tag{5}$$

The convexity of the logarithmic function guarantees that:

$$H \geq X \geq 0, \tag{6}$$

In words, (6) says that the aggregate indeterminacy is an upper bound on how much constraint (order) can appear in a system. Most of the time, H > X, so that the difference

$$\Psi = (H - X) = -k \sum_{i,j} p_{ij} \log \left(\frac{p^2_{ij}}{p_{i.}p_{.j}} \right) \geq 0 \tag{7}$$

as well. In the jargon of information theory Ψ is called the 'conditional entropy'.

Relationship (7) can be rewritten as:

$$H = X + \Psi, \tag{8}$$

and it makes a very valuable statement. It says that the capacity for evolution or self- organization (H) can be decomposed into two components. The first (X) quantifies all that *is* regular, orderly, coherent and efficient. It encompasses all the concerns of conventional science. By contrast, Ψ represent the *lack* of those same attributes, or the irregular, disorderly, incoherent and inefficient behaviors, which conventional science tends to overlook.

Up to this point we have spoken only vaguely about events *i* and *j*. Without loss of generality, we now narrow our discussion to consider only transfers or transformations. That is, event *i* will signify that some quantum of medium leaves or disappears from component *i*. Correspondingly, event j will signify that a quantum enters or appears in component j. We now identify the aggregation of all quanta both leaving *i* and entering *j* during a unit of time – or, alternatively, the flow from *i* to *j* (or the transformation of *i* into *j*) – as T_{ij}. Thus, T_{ij} might represent the flow of electrons from point *i* to point *j* in an electrical circuit; the flow of biomass from prey *i* to predator *j* in an ecosystem; the transfer of money on a microeconomic scale from economic actor *i* to actor *j* in an economic community; or the transfer of money or from sector *i* to sector *j* at the macroeconomic scale.

We introduce the convention that a dot in the place of a subscript indicates summation over that index. Thus $T_{i.}$ $(= \sum_j T_{ij})$ will represent everything leaving *i* during the unit time interval, and $T_{.j}$ will gauge everything entering *j* during the same duration. In particular, $T_{..}$ $(= \sum_{i,j} T_{ij})$ represents the total activity of the system and is given the name 'total system throughput' (which corresponds roughly to the concept of GDP in economic theory).

These definitions allow us to estimate all the probabilities defined above in terms of their measured frequencies of occurrence. That is,

$$p_{ij} \sim \frac{T_{ij}}{T_{..}}, \; p_{i.} \sim \frac{T_{i.}}{T_{..}}, \qquad \text{and } p_{.j} \sim \frac{T_{.j}}{T_{..}}. \tag{9}$$

Substituting these estimators in equations (3), (5) and (7), yields

$$H = -k\sum_{i,j}\frac{T_{ij}}{T_{..}}\log\left(\frac{T_{ij}}{T_{..}}\right);\; X = k\sum_{i,j}\frac{T_{ij}}{T_{..}}\log\left(\frac{T_{ij}T_{..}}{T_{i.}T_{.j}}\right);\text{ and }\Psi = -k\sum_{i,j}\frac{T_{ij}}{T_{..}}\log\left(\frac{T^2_{ij}}{T_{i.}T_{.j}}\right), \quad (10)$$

respectively.

The dimensions in the definitions (10) remain problematic, however. All of the ratios that occur there are dimensionless (as required of probabilities). To change that into a useable metric, we will scale each index by the total system throughput, T.. , which conveys the overall activity of the system. In order to emphasize the new nature of the results, we give them all new identities. We call

$$C = T_{..}\cdot H = -\sum_{i,j}T_{ij}\log\left(\frac{T_{ij}}{T_{..}}\right) \quad (11)$$

the 'capacity' for system development (Ulanowicz and Norden 1990).

The scaled mutual constraint,

$$A = T_{..}\cdot X = -\sum_{i,j}T_{ij}\log\left(\frac{T_{ij}T_{..}}{T_{i.}T_{.j}}\right), \quad (12)$$

converts into the measure of a system's 'throughput efficiency',[3] so-called because it measures the capacity of a system to process volumes of whatever that particular system deals with (e.g. biomass in an ecosystem, electrons in an electrical distribution system, or money in an economy).

The scaled conditional entropy,

$$\Phi = T_{..}\cdot \Psi = -\sum_{i,j}T_{ij}\log\left(\frac{T^2_{ij}}{T_{i.}T_{j.}}\right),, \quad (13)$$

we rename the system 'reserve',[4] for reasons that soon should become apparent.

Of course, this uniform scaling does not affect the decomposition (8), which now appears as

$$C = A + \Phi. \quad (14)$$

In other words, (14) says that the capacity for a system to undergo evolutionary change or self-organization consists of two aspects: It must be capable of exercising sufficient directed power, enough throughput efficiency A, to maintain its integrity over time. Simultaneously, it must possess a reserve of flexible actions that can be used to meet the exigencies of novel disturbances. According to (14) these two aspects are literally complementary.

A system lacking throughput efficiency has neither the extent of activity nor the internal organization needed to survive. By contrast, systems that are so tightly constrained and honed to a particular environment appear 'brittle' and are prone to collapse in the face of even minor novel disturbances. Systems that endure – that is, are sustainable – lie somewhere between these extremes. But where?

In order to be able to answer that question, we define a = A/C and notice that 1> a >0. Here a is a relative measure of the organized power flowing within the system. Using Bolzman's formulation, –klog(a),we shall call an ecosystem's 'fitness for evolution',

$$F = -k\, a \log(a), \tag{15}$$

our measure of the system's potential to evolve or self-organize. F = 0 for a = 1 and approaches the limit of 0 as $a \to 0$. One can normalize this function by choosing k = e log(e) (where 'e' is the base of natural logarithms), such that 1 > F > 0.

One way to permit the maximum to occur at an arbitrary value of a is to introduce an adjustable parameter, call it β, and to allow available empirical data to indicate the most likely value of β. Accordingly, we set $F = -k\, a^{\beta}\log(a^{\beta})$. This function can be normalized by choosing k = e/log(e), so that $F_{max} = 1$ at $a = e^{-\frac{1}{\beta}}$, where β can be any positive real number. Whence, our measure for Sustainability of a complex network – its 'fitness for evolution' in natural ecosystems systems – becomes:

$$F = -\,[e/\log(e)]\,a^{\beta}\log(a^{\beta}) \tag{16}$$

The function F varies between 0 and 1 and is entirely without dimensions. It describes the fraction of activity that is effective in creating a sustainable balance between A and Φ. That is, the total activity (e.g., the GDP in economics, or T.. here) will no longer be an accurate assessment of the robustness of the system. Our measure, T.. , must be discounted by the fraction (1–F).

Equivalently, the robustness, R, of the system becomes

$$R = T_{..} \cdot F\,. \tag{17}$$

This measure of robustness, R, can be employed to indicate which features of a given configuration deserve most remediation to attain sustainability.

In terms of graphic representations of the relationships between all these variables, it has proven useful to plot the networks, not on the axes A vs. Φ, but rather on the transformed axes $n = 2^{A}$. and $c = 2^{\frac{\Phi}{2}}$

The reasons for this choice of this particular exponential scaling are fully explained in Zorach and Ulanowicz (2003). The variable n gauges diversity, in a natural ecosystem it represents technically the effective number of trophic levels in the system; or how many transfers, on (logarithmic) average, a typical quantum of medium makes before leaving the network. The variable c measures the effective connectivity of the system in links per node, or how many nodes on (logarithmic) average enter or leave each compartment.

These two variables n and c have revealed themselves the two most important *structural* variables of any complex network. They will become the common reference variables for all our graphic analyses, because they best capture the structural issues that emerge in complex flow networks.

What can we tell *a priori*, mathematically, about the shapes we should expect of the variable C, A and Φ in terms of these two structural variables?

The functions C, A and Φ all happen to be homogeneous Euler functions of the first order. This means that the derivatives with respect to their independent variables are relatively easy to calculate.

Starting from our definition of robustness (17), we seek to establish the direction in which this attribute responds to a unit change in any constituent flow. That is we wish to calculate ($\partial R/\partial T_{ij}$.) Employing the chain rule of differentiation, we see that

$$\frac{\partial R}{\partial T_{ij}} = F + T_{..}\frac{\partial F}{\partial T_{ij}}$$

$$\frac{\partial R}{\partial T_{ij}} = F + T_{..}F'\frac{\partial a}{\partial T_{ij}} \tag{18}$$

$$\frac{\partial R}{\partial T_{ij}} = F + \frac{T_{..}F'}{C}\left\{\log\left[\frac{T_{ij}T_{..}}{T_{i.}T_{.j}}\right] + a\log\left[\frac{T^2_{ij}}{T_{i.}T_{.j}}\right]\right\}$$

Where F' is the derivative of F with respect to a, i.e.,

$$F' = -e\beta a^{\beta-1}\left[\frac{\log(a^{\beta})}{\log(e)} + 1\right] \tag{19}$$

In particular, when the system is at its optimum (F = 1 and $F' = 0$) we see from (18) that a unit increment in each and every flow in the system would contribute exactly one unit to system robustness. Once away from the optimum, however, contributions at the margin will depend on which side of the optimum the system lies, and where in the network any particular contribution is situated.

When $a < a_{opt}$, then F' will be positive, so that those flows that dominate the inputs to or output from any compartment will result in a positive sum within the braces, and the contribution of that transfer at the margin will be >1. For the relatively smaller flows, the negative second term in braces will dominate, and the contribution of those links at the margin will be <1.

As we have seen, the notions of *both* presence and absence, respectively what the Chinese tradition called the Yang and the Yin energies, are explicitly built into this framework. Such architecture accounts for relationships like (8) and (14) wherein complementary terms of 'what is' and 'what is not,' share the same dimensions and almost the same structure. That is, one is comparing apples with apples. Furthermore, the effects of lacunae no longer remain external to the statement of the dynamics; they become central to it.

The model just discussed highlights the necessary role of underused capacities in sustaining ecosystems or any other complex flow system. It contrasts with Darwinian theory, which unfortunately is espoused by many simply as the maximization of efficiency (e.g., the survival of the fitt*est*.) Such emphasis on efficiency is evident as well in some mistaken approaches to ecology, such as optimal foraging theory; and is practically universally assumed in economic theory. Our results alert us to the need to exhibit caution when it comes to maximizing efficiencies. Systems can become too efficient for their own good. Autocatalytic configurations can expand to suck away resources from non-participating or marginally participating actors, leaving them to wither and possibly to disappear.

It is exactly what we claim has happened in the monetary domain.

The technical argument for a single currency in a country is that it makes price formation and exchanges most efficient, which is a valid point. In 1953, Milton Friedman took the next step: he proposed to let on a global level an unfettered market of currencies freely optimize efficiencies (Friedman 1953). This approach was actually implemented by President Nixon in 1971. Giant banks and titanic financial markets emerged, very efficient in terms of the growth of their financial throughput capacity. They also reinforce themselves as powerful political lobbies. For instance, in the case of the US, a study by two nonpartisan groups, Public Citizen and the Center for Responsive Politics, found that in 2009 there was a 'small army' of 1,400 financial lobbyists officially registered in Washington, lobbying for the biggest financial institutions. They included at least 73 former lawmakers and 148 ex-staffers connected to the House or Senate banking committees. More than 40 former Treasury Department employees also now ply their trade as lobbyists for Wall Street firms. For every sitting member of Congress, the study shows, there are three former colleagues or government staffers lobbying for banks. David Arkush, director of Public Citizen's Congress Watch division, said 'Wall Street hires former members of Congress and their staff for a reason,' especially at a time when lawmakers are debating a historic overhaul of the way Wall Street does business. 'These people are influential because they have personal relationships with current members and staff,' Arkush said. 'It's hard to say no to your friends, but that's what Congress needs to do.'

Should it be surprising that financial institutions that are protected in this way become 'too big to fail'. In parallel, massive financial bubbles emerge, and when they burst, new bubbles are being generated as the best remedy to contain the collateral damage. All these processes are components of what our theoretical framework identified as 'autocatalytic forces', and are a logical symptom of an over-efficient Yang system.

Notes

1 This appendix is summarizing parts of the paper by Ulanowicz, Goerner, Lietaer and Gomez 'Quantifying Sustainability: Resilience, Efficiency and the Return of Information Theory' in the *Journal of Ecological Complexity* Vol. 8 #1 (March 2009). In this appendix only the bare mathematical bones of the argument are extracted from this paper. The reader who wants a step by step justification for the logic, its implications and concrete examples of this process should consult the original paper.

2 For the remainder of this essay a dot in the place of an index will represent summation over that index.

3 We will abbreviate this variable simply as efficiency. The original ecological literature refers to this variable as 'ascendency', hence the choice of the letter A for this variable (Ulanowicz 1980).

4 From here on 'reserve' will apply to what heretofore has been called 'reserve capacity'.

References

Friedman, M. (1953) 'The Case for Flexible Exchange Rates', *Essays in Positive Economics*, pp.157–203. Chicago: University of Chicago Press.

Zorach, A. C. and Ulanowicz, R. E. (2003) 'Quantifying the Complexity of Flow Networks: How Many Roles Are There?', *Complexity*, 8(3), pp.68–76.

Index